Sedition and Alchemy

Sedition

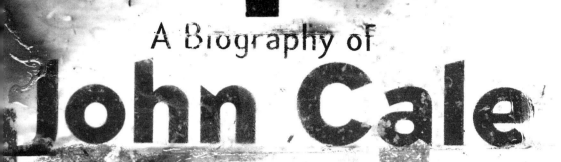

A Biography of

John Cale

Alchemy

By Tim Mitchell

Peter Owen
London and Chester Springs

PETER OWEN PUBLISHERS
73 Kenway Road, London SW5 0RE

Peter Owen books are distributed in the USA by
Dufour Editions, Inc., Chester Springs, PA 19425-0007

First published in Great Britain 2003
© Tim Mitchell 2003

Lyrics to 'Guts' reproduced by kind permission of
John Cale Music, Inc., BMI

ISBN 0 7206 1132 6 (pb)
0 7206 1207 1 (limited edition)

A catalogue record for this book is available from the British Library.

Cover and publication design by Dave McKean @ Hourglass

Printed in Croatia
by Zrinski SA

For Claire

Sedition and Alchemy

ACKNOWLEDGEMENTS

I would like to offer thanks, first of all, to John himself for all the help he has given throughout the course of the book's writing and for supplying his own photographs of the aftermath of the World Trade Center attacks. Second, I must acknowledge the invaluable contribution of Gary Fox, who has provided large amounts of background material and a host of other information; I cannot thank him enough for his efforts and support. Many thanks, too, should go to Nita Scott for all her hard work; to Margaret Moser, who helped with illustrations and research materials as well as her own memories; to Sturgis Nikides,* who contributed beyond the call of duty; to Mark Vernon of Firebrand Management, who provided assistance from start to finish; and to Gruff Rhys of the Super Furry Animals for his foreword. I am also very grateful to all the people who willingly gave up their time to be interviewed: Al Aronowitz, Zoe Beloff, Joe Bidewell,† Joe Boyd, Chris Carr, Tony Conrad, Berian Evans, John Fryer, Claudia Gould, Denzil Jones, Harry Kraut, Phil Manzanera, John McClure, Billy Name, Roy Noble, Judy Nylon, Gareth Simmonds, Joan Simmonds, Chris Spedding, Joe Stefko, Chris Thomas, Mike Thorne, Lynne Tillman, Moe Tucker, Richard Williams, Mary Woronov and David Young. My gratitude as well to everyone who kindly provided photographs†† and to John Knight at Table of the Elements, Tony Chidell, Mark Webber, Bill Allerton, Chris Whent, Will Matthews, Will Robards, Marko Stamenkovic, Joe Foster, Jon Leach, Claire Singers and Toshiaki Nomura.

I must mention two superb websites: 'Fear Is A Man's Best Friend' (http://huizen.dds.nl/johanm/cale/index.html) by Hans Werksman, which is the ultimate John Cale resource, and Olivier Landemaine's encyclopaedic and stylish 'The Velvet Underground Web Page' (http://members.aol.com/olandem/vu.html).

Finally, a big thank you to all at Peter Owen Publishers.

*Freelance producer Sturgis Nikides can be contacted at envoid@mail.com
†Musician/photographer Joe Bidewell can be contacted at www.joebidewell.com
††Some of the photographers who provided images can be contacted as follows: Patty Heffley (New York): patty@inch.com; Paul Jonason: www.pauljonason.com; Gin Satoh: gin-photo-studio@mug.biglobe.ne.jp

Qui creavit Coelum

Conductor : Mr. J. Sellers

FIRST YEAR WOMEN'S CHORAL GROUP

4.   QUINTET IN A FOR PIANO AND STRINGS (first movement) *Schubert*

Violin : Miss B. J. Gower   Viola : Mr. J. Cale
Cello : Mr. Q. Williams   Bass : Mr. J. R. Denham
Piano : Mr. J. A. Clamp

5.   PART SONGS   Hymn to the Virgin   *Benjamin Britten*

Cradle Song   *B. J. Dale*

Soprano solos : Miss W. E. Moxon   Miss R. Garson

Terly, Terlow   *Holst*

Oboe : Mr. N. D. Blow   Cello : Mr. Q. Williams

THE ASSEMBLY CHOIR

SHORT INTERVAL

FOREWORD BY GRUFF RHYS

YEAR: 1984
LOCATION: Bethesda, Wales

At the age of thirteen I was sifting through the pile of records that had accumulated at the side of the family record-player when a mysterious new LP caught my attention. My brother's friend had forgotten to take his copy of the Velvet Underground's *White Light/White Heat* home with him. I stuck it on the deck and, on hearing the Garnant 'Lower East Side' accent on the John Cale-narrated 'The Gift', I initially concluded that this must be a contemporary South Wales post-punk act. Finding the Velvet Underground opened up a whole new world of East Coast junkie music to me, which I adopted as my own.

The implausibility of such an important figure in contemporary music as John Cale coming from the modest industrial village of Garnant, apart from giving me great encouragement, confirms to me that often the places that are regarded as peripheral are actually bang in the middle. Likewise, while Cale's contribution to music has often been unacknowledged while it is being made, time has consistently been kind to his output as a musician and producer. Today, records by the likes of the Velvet Underground, the Stooges, Nick Drake, Patti Smith, Nico and the Happy Mondays, which hardly set the world alight when they were released, are considered era-defining and have become hugely influential. Meanwhile, the trajectory of Cale's solo career observed today seems like a road map of current musical territory where the Beach Boys, Punk Rock and the avant-garde live side by side in perfect harmony. Time and crystal-clear production values have given his solo recordings an incredible timeless quality.

Working with him during the filming of 2000's *Beautiful Mistake*, as he was composing his song 'Things', I noticed that he seemed to have an iron vision that would not bend. This is a quality that may explain his volatile relationship with another tough guy, Lou Reed. Working on our own Furry Animal song 'Presidential Suite', however, he was determined to take the back seat and make sure that all decisions came from us — or at least making them seem to. In this context he dubbed himself 'musical janitor', a stance that may explain his skills in coaxing individual musical interpretations out of a variety people.

Somewhere within this musical duality lies the key to unravelling the life and purpose of this most unorthodox, uncompromising and enigmatic individual, who has been travelling into what seems to be a parallel musical future to the rest of us over the past half-century, and who has, in the process, become a quiet giant of our time.

Gruff Rhys (Super Furry Animals)
Cardiff, 2003

PART II

6. **Two Dances from the Ballet** *Love the Magician*   *Falla*

   THE MUSIC SOCIETY ORCHESTRA

7. **Part Songs**   The Lover's Ghost   *arr. Vaughan Williams*
   Wassail Song   *arr. Holst*
   Ronde   *Ravel*

   THIRD YEAR MUSIC GROUP

8. **Madrigals**   Matona, Lovely Maiden   *Orlando Lasso*
   The Lute Book Lullaby   *George Oldroyd*
   Hodie Christus natus est   *Sweelinck*

   THE MADRIGAL GROUP
   Conductor : Mr. A. L. Cyphus

9. **Two Poems by Laurie Lee** set for unaccompanied voice
   John Cale (Present Student)

   Bird

   Black Edge
   Counter-tenor : Mr. G. J. Dibbens

10. **Cantata**   The Country beyond the stars   *Daniel Jones*
    (words by Henry Vaughan)
    1. A Hymn to Peace
    2. The Bird
    3. Symphony : Joyful Visitors
    4. The Morning Watch
    5. The Evening Watch
    6. Cheerfulness

    THE MUSIC SOCIETY CHOIR AND ORCHESTRA

(The Orchestra is assisted by members of the Goldsmiths' Symphony Orchestra
and others)

GOD SAVE THE QUEEN

CONTENTS

Illustrations Between Pages 128 and 129

'The music business is a cruel and shallow money trench, a long plastic hallway where thieves and pimps run free and good men die like dogs. There's also a negative side.'

— HUNTER S. THOMPSON

'My fingers emit sparks of fire with Expectation of my future labours.'

— WILLIAM BLAKE

tzarabretonduchampcagelamonteyoungcale

In Paris, 1919, the avant-garde artistic community mourned the deaths of Jacques Vaché, the embodiment of Surrealism, and, still, that of Guillaume Apollinaire the previous year, its namer and arguably most important antecedent. The group, however, was also ready to move forward with their ideas and anxiously awaited the arrival from Zurich of Tristan Tzara, author of the *Dada Manifesto 1918* with its revolutionary message of destruction and rebuilding.

Paris in 1919 also saw the publication of the first issue of the Surrealist magazine *Littérature* and the first example of automatic writing, *Les Champs Magnétiques*, both co-produced by Surrealism's leader and standard-bearer André Breton. In Paris in 1919 Jean Cocteau was arguing, Pablo Picasso impressing more than ever and Marcel Duchamp had returned home from New York for the first time in four years. Between August and December Duchamp produced some of his most important work: *L.H.O.O.Q.*, *Paris Air* and *Tzanck Cheque*. Duchamp would return with his *Paris Air* to New York, where it would oxygenate the artistic community for years to come.

Tzara was not the only one on the outside looking in. Francis Picabia wrote to him of the necessity of moving to Paris, as it was the centre of avant-garde activity, while at home in Zurich he was dismantling a clock piece by piece and using the parts to make a new work of art. At the end of the year, from his sanatorium in Neuchâtel, Switzerland, Antonin Artaud made plans to begin his real artistic life in Paris, and thoughts of the city were also in the mind of James Joyce, who would move there in 1920, followed by Ezra Pound. By the early 1920s Igor Stravinsky, Maurice Ravel and Virgil Thomson were all in the French capital and would soon be joined by Aaron Copland.

In Paris, 1919, the Versailles Peace Treaty, signed in the Hall of Mirrors, decided the shape that the Western world would take after the Great War.

UNIVERSITY OF LONDON

LDSMITHS' COLLEGE

NEW CROSS

1962

ISTMAS CONCERT

URDAY, 8th DECEMBER

At 7 p.m.

**Part I
Calends
(a beginning)**

Ammanford Grammar School was a mixed school of about 650 pupils and geared to turning out potential young professionals with a maximum of O- and A-level qualifications — the cream of South Wales's Amman Valley. Individuality was outside the school's remit, but it was a word that might almost have defined John Cale. His appearance — black hair, tanned, almost olive complexion, dark eyes — and an immedi-

a little
festival

of new

music

ately apparent personal intensity gave him a brooding presence that separated him from his schoolmates. Most of them thought of him as someone near the edge, occupying a position they did not understand. Set apart, he was a loner, a story-writer, with music both a passion and an exceptional talent. Music would eventually bring him closer to his peers, once he had begun to join a succession of orchestras as a viola player.

Progressing from school to county level, at the age of thirteen he became a member of the National Youth Orchestra of Wales. Having started piano lessons at the age of seven, he went on, while still at Ammanford Grammar, to become church organist and to appear on BBC Radio, playing one of his own compositions. Sport, and rugby in particular, was a mainstay of the school, but Cale bucked the trend here, too, ignoring tradition in favour of the solitary character building of long-distance running. Not keen on joining societies or clubs, Cale made an exception for the Drama Society and would make a brief appearance at the age of sixteen in 1958's Christmas *Strife*.

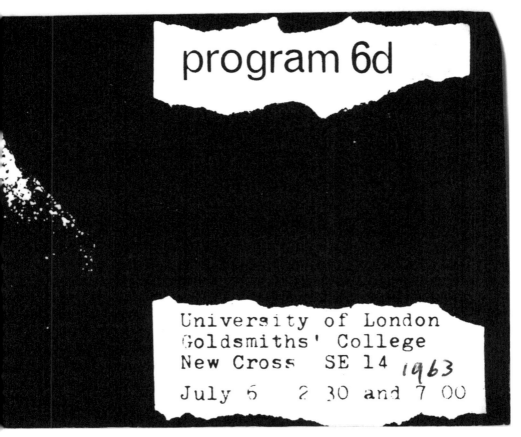

A colleague of Cale's, Berian Evans, followed the same progression through orchestras as he did, from school and county level on to the national stage. In their limited spare time at school the two would play sonatas together, Cale on piano and Evans on violin. Evans remembers Cale always searching for something new in both his listening and what he played. He explored Berg, Schoenberg and Stravinsky and introduced his friend to a notoriously difficult piece by Webern, which they attempted to play together.

Part of their studies involved attending courses at Trinity College in Carmarthen, and in the evenings they would frequent the local public houses, with Cale developing a fondness for cider and Worthington E beer. In this environment he would loosen up and become amusing company, displaying an irreverent sense of humour and quick-wittedness. Once they were in the sixth form Cale and Evans used to venture into the town of Ammanford for dances and other social events. The two lived in small villages near by, with the dullness of daily home life usually brightened only by the occasional visit to a neighbour's house. Cars were scarce (neither the Cales nor the Evans family owned one), and any travelling would usually be done by public transport. Evans remembers Cale's village, Garnant, as 'a road on the way to somewhere'.

```
La Monte Young
For Henry Flynt
First British Performance
John Cale        piano
Fluxus copyright
```

Although his teachers were as mystified by what made Cale tick as his fellow pupils, they recognized his musical talents, which eclipsed his still more than acceptable academic accomplishments. The school had a much-prized grand piano about which the staff were very protective. Only three people were allowed to play the piano: the headmaster O.J. Evans, the music teacher Mr Jenkins and Cale.

In 1957 Cale and Berian Evans made their first tour abroad with the National Youth Orchestra of Wales to Holland. On the voyage over, Cale was badly seasick. Once they had docked and reached the Burgomaster's reception that had been arranged for them, however, he recovered and partook freely of the Stella Artois beer, champagne and cigars provided.

Cale's interest in the new did not stop at the boundaries of modern classical music; it also ventured into jazz and rock 'n' roll. Radio Luxemburg allowed him to listen to Elvis Presley, but jazz was something that Cale actually got the chance to play — upsetting the school staff in the process. Another schoolmate, Denzil Jones, formed a band to play at the school dance in 1959 — the big 'boy meets girl' event of the school calendar — and here, with Cale on piano, they played three dixieland tunes in the style of Chris Barber. The teachers present, for whom jazz was not acceptable music for a school function, even one as informal as this, were shocked by the performance — not just by the form of the music but by what they grudgingly had to admit was the competence of the musicians. When the band had finished, O.J. Evans, as regimented and conservative in his musical tastes as he was in most other things, came up on stage and said, 'Well, that was nice, boys, but make sure you keep the beat.'

```
La Monte Young
Piano Piece for David Tudor   no. 2
First British Performance
Cornelius Cardew    soloist
Fluxus copyright
```

Towards the end of the final sixth-form year, Cale, together with the many of his classmates, began applying to colleges and universities. Even in this he was contrary. One day he came in to school with two large parcels under his arm. Denzil Jones asked him what they were and was told that they were Yale and Harvard prospectuses. America would have to wait, however, with Cale eventually accepting an invitation to study at London's Goldsmiths' College.

On the final day of term at grammar school, assembly, which was a sacrosanct occasion for O.J. Evans, took place as usual. As was the rule, the whole school, with the exception of the sixth form, stood as the music teacher played the introduction to the first hymn on the piano. He then hit the bottom 'G' that was the cue for the sixth form to rise as well, but no sound emerged from the instrument. Cale had stuck a plastic comb underneath the strings.

On the day John Cale was born, 9 March 1942, work began on construction of the Alaska Highway. It was pioneering work in a hostile environment, and lives were risked and sometimes lost. Passage was gouged, tunnelled and carved, frontiers were pushed back, landscapes transformed, maps changed, the modern world redrawn. New ground was broken.

```
John Cage
Music of Changes   Book IV
First British Performance
Fred Turner         piano
```

Will Cale, a non-Welsh speaker, married Margaret Davies in 1939 and moved into her home in Garnant, South Wales, where her mother lived. The house was double-fronted and detached but not large. Old-fashioned and filled with ageing furniture, it was homely and comfortable, with a big coal fire stacked with the cheap coal to which Will, a miner, was entitled. Although Will's dangerous and exhausting job provided its fuel, Margaret's mother would only have Welsh spoken 'at the hearth' — and in Wales any rules regarding the hearth covered the rest of the house as well. Will was stranded as a result, cut off from the rest of the family. Margaret was a teacher, and her mother probably believed that she had married beneath her, an impression that would only have added to Will's feeling of separation. When their son, John, was born in 1942 it was into a Welsh-speaking home — this was the only language that he spoke until the age of seven, when he began to learn English at the primary school where his mother had taught. To Will, it must have seemed that his son had been born and was destined to be raised on the other side of the divide that had been created in his home.

As Will listened to the conversations in Welsh going on around him, he did began to pick up the language but would never use it in the house. Although he understood what was said, he would not contribute to conversations — and in this way he made a silent rebellion against his mother-in-law's edict. Communication did take place between him and his growing son, but its natural expression was artificially restricted, and the relationship, as a result, was unable to develop normally.

The house in Garnant was dominated by Margaret's side of the family, and the young Cale was surrounded by her relatives, hardly ever seeing any of his father's. Christmas was a time when the balance shifted, however, and Cale would be taken by his father to see Will's brother Charles, sister Edith and nephew Derek to exchange presents. On these visits Will showed that he was proud of his son, who behaved politely and seemed well brought up. The two gave the impression of getting on very well.

La Monte Young
For Henry Flynt
First British Performance
John Cale   piano
Fluxus copyright

As Cale grew up, however, his father remained a distant figure. Margaret was the controlling influence in the house, particularly after her mother died when Cale was fourteen. Towards the end of Will's mother-in-law's life, and particularly when she succumbed to her final illness, it was Will who did most for her, a fact acknowledged by his wife. Indeed, not long before she died Margaret's mother informed her daughter that her husband was a good man.

Although Margaret was the dominant parent, she asked her husband to administer the corporal punishment she felt necessary for her son, a regime that eventually resulted in Cale turning on him and threatening to hit him back if he ever did it again. Cale's family life continued to revolve around his mother. Her mastectomy and prolonged hospital stay shortly before his grandmother's death constituted a defining episode that, he says, propelled him into adolescence. By now his father was working nights, which meant that he saw even less of his son.

Cale suffered for a large part of his childhood with bronchial problems. The opium mixture administered to help him sleep brought strange dreams and a psychological unsteadiness. Having to depend on drugs in order to sleep was a formative experience.

Cale's uncle Evan was a vicar, with a vicarage near the Taff Estuary at Laugharne, and Cale was sometimes sent there in his holidays in an effort to alleviate the affliction. In fact, the problems may actually have resulted from the damp earth underneath the unsealed slate slabs that made up the living-room floor in his parents' house; after the floor was cemented over his health gradually improved.

At the age of sixteen, however, Cale collapsed at home, seemingly suffering from meningitis. His next memory was of waking up in the ambulance with 'a ferocious headache and no motor responses'. Once hospitalized, he was found to have had a nervous breakdown. This was Cale's first desperate, unconscious attempt at escape from the narrowness of small-town Wales and the pressures of home life.

```
John Cage
Concert for piano and orchestra    with Aria
First British Performance
Michael Garrett    piano        Enid Hartle    voice        R(
John Cale    conductor
```

Although his musical studies were going well, he had begun to suffer academically as he spent less and less time on schoolwork. As a result, he felt that his mother, who had wanted him to become a doctor or lawyer and now saw such hopes disappearing, was showing less affection towards him. Meanwhile, communication with his father was still difficult; Cale had been unable to reveal to his family that he had been sexually molested on several occasions by a music teacher and, separately, by another man. The effect had been a confusion of feelings over the impossibility of reconciling his father's distance from him with his abusers' closeness. The reduction in his mother's warmth and his father's continuing coldness also resulted in a lack of self-worth — so much so that he says that he hated himself at this point. Cale was convinced that the hospital to which he had been taken was for the mentally ill, but it turned out to be a hospital for communicable diseases. He remembers the staff being preoccupied by the dangers of 'parakeet access and animal contacts'. He also remembers recovering rapidly once his doctor mentioned the prospect of a spinal tap. He soon left the ward with its peaceful view over Swansea Bay.

Cale returned home to his uneasy adolescence during which he retreated into a world of his own, where he wrote stories and listened to jazz and rock 'n' roll. Having made one unsuccessful escape attempt, he knew that next time he had to succeed.

```
    John Cale
    Piano Piece (unsequel music 212b)
assistant First British Performance
    Michael Garrott    piano
```

At Goldsmiths' College in London, between 1961 and 1963, Cale was meant to be studying music in order to become a teacher. He cut a dashing but smart figure, hair flopping down over his forehead, a brown and green cardigan with suede shoulder pads the stand-out item of a largely conventional wardrobe. His musical concerns mirrored his appearance, with the conventional pieces that made up his study vying for attention with the classical avant-garde works that captured his imagination. Enthusiasms ran wild in him, and he could communicate them to those around him; sociable with the other students, his antisocial instincts were reserved for the music he wanted to make. Accommodation during his time at Goldsmiths' was shared between the college's halls of residence and lodgings at a Mrs Budgen's in Chamberlain Street, near Regent's Park. Cale's girlfriend of the time, Eileen Simpson, was a constant and devoted companion, even if she did not share his more obscure musical interests, and her devotion was reciprocated. The music that Cale was given to perform in the college orchestras, where he played in the viola section, never seemed to present problems to him, and sight-reading in the choirs came similarly easily. This was not all down to innate ability, however; he worked hard at the viola and spent hours perfecting his performance of the notoriously arduous Hindemith Viola Sonata, which he had chosen, precisely because it was so difficult, to play for his final examination. Cale took composition lessons from Humphrey Searle, whose musical austerity may have had something to do with his wartime experiences as an instructor in the Special Operations Executive; here he had taught members of the French Resistance, among other things, the art of 'silent killing'.

```
La Monte Young
Composition 1960  no. 3
First British Performance
George Maciunus   soloist
Fluxus copyright
```

Each Christmas the students at Goldsmiths', under the direction of their teachers, would put on a concert, designed to showcase their talent. In the 1961 performance 'Mr J. Cale' played the viola in the first movement of Schubert's 'Trout' Quintet and 'John Cale' had composed settings of two poems by Laurie Lee for unaccompanied voice. Cale was also part of the orchestra for the evening's finale, a new cantata by Welsh composer Daniel Jones. The Laurie Lee poems were set for counter-tenor, and the exceptionally high vocal range of this voice gave the two pieces an otherworldly quality. Mrs Spaul, who was in charge of the Women's Dormitory (the perimeter of which was often breached by Cale in order to visit Eileen), pronounced that she quite liked it but that in future he should write for a more conventional voice. The cantata by Daniel Jones was so new that the music had not yet been published and the orchestra had to play from handwritten parts; Cale had had to persuade the Head of the Music Department to depart from convention in performing such a new work and also had to track down the score himself.

Every Thursday at Goldsmiths' the Symphony Orchestra rehearsed, and Cale would be in attendance. The orchestra gave concerts at the college, and Cale contributed to works by Beethoven, Tchaikovsky, Brahms, Rimsky-Korsakov, Debussy and Sibelius. He was made leader of the viola section but was displaced around the autumn of 1962 after the arrival of a new member of staff. The teacher was given Cale's position, despite being an inferior player, and Cale was not best pleased.

By Christmas 1962 Cale was in his last year at Goldsmiths' and assuming an even more prominent role. The concert of 8 December featured him (as 'Mr J.D. Cale'), playing a fairly conventional solo piece, *Elegy for Solo Viola, String Quartet and String Orchestra* by Herbert Howells, as well as a difficult and obscure work by Holst, *Terzet*, which involves each of the three performers playing in a different key.

Festival Piece

The audience is invited to bring with them any inaudible (not public) sound or combination of sounds to which they may refer during the proceedings

When we separate music from life what we get is art (a compendium of masterpieces). With contemporary music, when it is actually contemporary, we have no time to make that separation . . . and so contemporary music is not so much art as it is life.

Modern art has no need for technique. (We are in the glory of not knowing what we are doing.)

I remember loving sound before I ever took a music lesson.
(Excerpts from Silence by John Cage)

By now, Cale had begun a musical association and friendship with Cornelius Cardew. Cardew was an avant-garde composer well acquainted with the revolutionary work of John Cage, together with that of La Monte Young, who was also taking up some of Cage's thinking. Cale had begun to correspond with Cage and also with another proponent of Cageian ideas, George Macunias, figurehead of the Fluxus group of neo-Dadaists.

Towards the end of his time at Goldsmiths', Cale was growing more and more frustrated with its classicism and increasingly desperate to release that frustration in an expression of revolutionary energy.

Cale had bumped into his old school friend Denzil Jones, now a dental student, in central London. Walking up Charing Cross Road, Jones had been startled by a shout from a bus queue. Standing there was Cale, and Jones went over to say hello. Once pleasantries had been exchanged, Cale asked where he got his 'Dr Kildare tops'. Jones, who had to wear the white jackets during his training, told Cale where to find a supply and asked why he wanted to know. Cale replied that he wanted to wear them for 'parties and gigs I'm doing'. Esoteric items of clothing such as this would continue to fascinate him well into his performing career.

At the end of the summer term of 1963 Cale arranged 'a little festival of new music' to be performed at Goldsmiths' on 6 July. Surprisingly, the Warden of the College, Lord Chesterman, had agreed to help publicize the event, and part of his contribution was to fund a small advertisement in the *Observer* newspaper. It included the following sentence, which also appeared on the first page of the programme printed for the event: 'The audience is invited to bring with them any inaudible (not public) sound or combination of sounds to which they may refer during the proceedings.' The idea was to recruit an unconventional audience, and in that it was to succeed. The programme's cover, designed by the Art Department at Goldsmiths', featured the title of the festival within a clenched fist.

On a hot July afternoon, after most of the students had left for the summer, the love of traditional classical music seemed to disappear with them, and the college began to fill instead with a very different kind of musical appreciation. Cornelius Cardew, who had played a major part in organizing the performance, was in attendance; also present were associates of Cale and/or of Fluxus, such as Fred Turner, Robin Page, Edwin Mason, Tomas Schmitt and Emmett Williams.

The concert was divided into two halves, the first to begin at two thirty in the afternoon, the second at seven in the evening. Examples of Cage's 'prepared pianos' were used for some of the performances — objects such as nails and drawing-pins had been placed on the strings inside the frames of the instruments — together with violins bowed on their bodies rather than on their strings.

The afternoon featured the first British performances of works by John Cage — *Music of Changes Book IV* and *Concerto for Piano and Orchestra* (the latter conducted by Cale) — and of Cornelius Cardew's *Autumn '60 for Orchestra*.

The Cardew piece involved the individual musicians writing or planning their own part beforehand — each had been given a piece of paper, blank except for a stave, on which to do this. Cale and Cardew were disappointed that many of the participants had not put in the necessary preparation and consequently played anything that came to mind. Cardew, inspired by Cage, had come up with a series of symbols that instructed the musicians in *how*, rather than *what* to play, and they would have to look up from their scores at intervals to read these.

Although the afternoon concert presented music that was challenging and unconventional, it was the evening event that was most extreme in terms of content, performance and reaction. *Two Pieces for String Quartet* by George Brecht consisted of the musicians (including Cale) coming on to the platform and polishing their instruments with dusters, thereby producing a variety of rubbing and screeching noises. There was also the British première of Cale's *Piano Piece (unsequel music 212b)* and Robin Page's performance of Cale's *Plant Piece*. For the latter a potted plant had been put on the stage; up on the balcony Page began shouting at this plant that it would die. Rushing from the balcony down towards it, he continued screaming his threat, ending up by verbally abusing it, at point-blank range, on the stage itself. The plant did not die, the real threat having been to the sensibilities of the audience, and the same could be said of Cale's first British performance of La Monte Young's *X for Henry Flynt*, an exercise in closely observed repetition. For this Cale knelt on the floor in front of a grand piano and, with his hands linked, spread his arms wide so that, elbow to elbow, they extended to about four feet. He brought his arms crashing down on the keys, over and over, sending wave after wave of noise into the ears and nervous systems of the audience. After about five minutes of this sonic bombardment some of the listeners, part of the group attracted by the offer in the programme notes, mounted a counter-attack on the stage and attempted to drag the piano away. Cale followed on his knees, assisted by Cornelius Cardew, but the invaders would have had to push the instrument off the stage completely to achieve victory, and it was Cale who was to emerge triumphant from the battle. Not only had he vanquished the forces of barbarism he had also succeeded in nothing less than the overthrow of the reactionary forces of Western classical musical tradition — by pounding atonal, disharmonic, primitive, anarchic chaos into its symbol: the well-tuned grand piano.

"JOHN DAVIES CALE = I'D CANE-LASH JOVE"

Bundled like an immigrant in a shapeless rough woollen parka, his hair as tangled as a nest from which the bird has flown, his eyes wide, scared, as if they sought the whole dreadful truth of America at once, he came into the zero cold of a frosty bright morning at Idlewild Airport.
(From Dylan Thomas in America by John Malcolm Brinnin,)

Effervescing with vim, bile, hunger and spleen, Cale leaped across the Atlantic Ocean in the summer of 1963. Having aimed for New York, the new centre of avant-garde artistic activity, he stopped to refuel in Tanglewood, Massachusetts, from where he would ready himself for the final push.

Looking to escape from the classicism of his youth and of Goldsmiths' College, Cale had been interviewed by Aaron Copland for possible acceptance at the summer school held at the Berkshire Music Center, Tanglewood.

Upon his return to the USA after interviewing Cale, Aaron Copland called Harry Kraut, who ran the summer school at Tanglewood, telling him that Cale was possibly a musical genius, was certainly full of energy and original ideas and the kind of person they should have on the course. It was decided that he should be given a Leonard Bernstein Scholarship, as he was the kind of artist likely to appeal to the man who had founded the academy for the purpose of encouraging talented young musicians and composers. Cale was to study composition under Iannis Xenakis, guest teacher for that course in the summer of 1963. Xenakis used mathematical logic and probability as a way of expressing the patterns of natural forces, such as weather, and also translated his engineering training into music by using the figures calculated for architectural plans to construct 'buildings of sound'. Xenakis was not only a fiercely independent and revolutionary composer, his bravery had also been more physically evident as a hero in the Greek Resistance during the Second World War. Having fought against the Germans, he found himself having to defend his country again, this time against the British, who were trying to secure it from the communist leadership of the Resistance fighters. Badly wounded in a street battle (an incident that would leave a long, deep, bottle-shaped scar around his eye), he was later forced to flee Greece under sentence of death.

At one point during the summer at Tanglewood, Harry Kraut held a party at the small house where he lived, situated on a private lake a few miles from the academy. The composers were all invited, along with some members of staff. Xenakis and Cale both attended and went swimming in the lake, discovering an old rowing boat buried in weeds at its edge. Dragging the boat into the middle of the lake, they allowed people to swim over and climb in, after which each took turns to launch submarine attacks on it, sinking it and ejecting the occupants into the water.

Fuelled by alcohol, the party went well, and Cale, struck by the idea of leading a procession of fire around the house, grabbed one of the kerosene-fuelled garden torches that lit the surrounds and kept off mosquitoes. The movement of the torch through the air resulted in the burning liquid spilling on to his clothes, setting them alight. Covered in flames, he leaped into the lake. Unharmed but slightly singed, he emerged from the water in good humour to receive the praise of the onlookers for his spectacular performance.

Socially, Cale got on well at Tanglewood, and academically Xenakis was an inspirational figure. In terms of the music Cale was writing and wanted to perform, however, he found that it could be restricting. On arriving at the academy, Cale had been struck by the huge number of pianos available there — eighty-eight. He soon became obsessed with the idea of writing a piece to be performed upon all of them and asked Harry Kraut to arrange it. Kraut explained that logistically it would be impossible to move all the pianos from all corners of the centre into a place large enough to house them, even assuming that enough pianists could be found to play them. The performance of the piece would have necessitated the temporary suspension of almost everything else that was going on there. Cale was unimpressed by this argument and considered that his artistic vision had force enough to move the necessary mountains. This would not have been a traditional concert performance. What Cale intended was to place the pianos in boats on Tanglewood Lake — one piano per boat per note played. As he recalls, the performance would consist of the 'group of pianos playing each note as a cluster spaced in hearing distance from the other while the plugs were pulled from the bottom of each boat, sending the upright pianos in their boats to the bottom'.

At the end of August, with the term drawing to a close and many of the students preparing to use what they had learned in order to find the more highly prized jobs in their field, Cale was finally allowed to perform one of his compositions — the climax of which involved pulling an axe from a piano and smashing it down on a table.

In early September Cale reached New York. No longer on the outside looking in, he was now in the centre of radical artistic exploration – the contemporary equivalent of Paris in 1919. He wasted no time in contacting by phone and then visiting La Monte Young, the central figure in New York's musical avant-garde. Cale had performed Young's *X for Henry Flynt* while at Goldsmiths' College, and Young invited him to rehearse with what would soon become known as the Theater of Eternal Music.

Another phone call that he made was to John Cage. This took the form of an urgent request for help in finding a way to earn enough money to stay alive. Within a day a call came from Nick Cernovitch, a lighting designer with Merce Cunningham, the choreographer who had been working with Cage since 1943. Cernovitch ran the Orientalia bookshop and offered Cale a job there. Cernovitch was a friend, too, of Billy Linich (later Billy Name), who had worked as his lighting assistant and whom he had also introduced to La Monte Young. After this introduction Name became a member of La Monte Young's group from the summer of 1962 until June 1963.

Cage soon helped out again. He had arranged a performance, to take place over the course of 9 and 10 September, of Erik Satie's *Vexations*, a 180-note piece to be played 840 times at the Pocket Theater on Third Avenue. This was to last for eighteen hours and forty minutes and was played by a relay of a dozen pianists, one of whom was a bespectacled, suited Cale. Others included David Tudor, Joshua Rifkin and Cage himself. The event was featured in the *New York Times*, in which Cale commented on the problems prompted by the process of the piece, 'The head goes first.' Cage, talking about the performance years later, would say: 'I wasn't the same afterwards.' In the audience was up-and-coming artist Andy Warhol, who loved the experience and claimed to have sat through the whole thing.

I felt the need to purge myself . . . you're not as empty as you think.
(Marcel Duchamp)

By the end of the month Cale's rehearsals with La Monte Young were being recorded, and he was an acknowledged member of his group. Discipline ruled these sessions, but it was not a discipline that restricted the musicians within the musical bars of a cage; it was a path that, followed assiduously, led to the domain of an undiscovered country, whose wide-open landscape dazzled and entranced with the colours of a new spectrum.

In August Young, together with his wife and collaborator Marian Zazeela, had moved to a permanent new home at 275 Church Street, and it was here that Cale would rehearse intensely with them and violinist Tony Conrad over the next eighteen months. Drugs were an accepted part of the group's lifestyle, the 'dominant hobby', as Billy Name remembers: 'La Monte always had the best stuff, i.e. grass, hash, LSD, opium. None of us really talked a lot. Talking was like a special gig and for taking care of practical things. Grooving was the way.'

john, lou and i are all pisces sun, tropically, and aquarius sidereally.
(Billy Name)

Cale lived initially in a loft in Lispenard Street, below Canal Street, which he shared for a while with Terry Jennings, who had been introduced to him by La Monte Young. Jennings had been a child prodigy, arranging Stravinsky's *Rite of Spring* for his high-school orchestra. He had met Young at school and, playing saxophone, was a long-term collaborator. The loft was a 'dark, cavernous, silent, sepulchral place', as Tony Conrad remembers it, shared with 'the largest cat in New York City', called Marcus. Jennings was a contemplative conversationalist, whose speech was characterized by long pauses and hugely protracted reaction times. At this point he was following an extreme diet that sometimes involved abstention from protein. At a time when a good meal in a loft on the Lower East Side might consist of chicken hearts and oatmeal, this was not an easy regime to maintain. With Jennings almost definedly taciturn and Cale not given to unnecessary small talk, it was a quiet loft. As Conrad remembers: 'They seemed to potter backwards and forwards in this space, occupied with strange undertakings.'

Occasionally Cale would visit Conrad at his own place, an unheated three-room apartment on the top floor of a slum building at 56 Ludlow Street. There was no electricity either, lights being powered via an extension cable to another apartment. The bathroom was in the hall and the rent, paid to a gun-toting landlord with a hardware store on the ground floor, was $25 a month, which Conrad was usually able to share with a room-mate. A railroad apartment, furnished 'from the street', it was basic and just about functional. When Jennings left Lispenard Street it seemed the obvious thing for Cale to move in with Conrad.

This apartment was far livelier. At the end of the hall lived Theater of Eternal Music percussionist Angus MacLise and underground-film actor Mario Montez; next door was film-maker Piero Heliczer. Montez's director, Jack Smith, would often come over. All were part of the thriving artistic community on the Lower East Side.

While Cale worked as a clerk at the Orientalia bookshop (also for a while bizarrely combining the activities of dealing drugs and, according to Young, 'Hoovering, polishing'), Conrad survived on part-time work such as opening envelopes or delivering inter-office mail. Even on minimum wage, which at the time was $1.35 an hour, it was possible for two weeks' 'regular' work such as this to fund a subsequent month of the kind of work he and Cale really wanted to do — creating a new music.

The Lower East Side was teeming with artistic life — poets, painters, musicians, sculptors and film-makers, many attracted by the cheapness of accommodation — and cross-fertilization across a multitude of disciplines was a natural expression of this varied community. There was cultural diversity, too, with Chinese and Latin music a part of the musical landscape along with the classical music already familiar to Cale and Conrad, as well as the rock 'n' roll that was constantly pumping out of radios. On the streets of the Lower East Side Cale and Conrad reached up into the air and pulled classical music down from its elevated position to fight its way through the sidewalks and alleyways with all the other varieties.

This iconoclasm fed on and expressed the revolutionary work of John Cage and his own relationship with the theory and practice of Marcel Duchamp. Duchamp, with his 'readymades', had created new worlds where objects had lives far removed from those they lived in the old world. Cage had created another new world where sounds were able to express themselves free from the constraints of the composers whose work enslaved them. Cage was and would remain a hugely creative force. Duchamp, even in his eighties, was still both very much alive and visible — and living in New York. (In his private hours he continued secretly to construct his final work, *Étants donnés . . .* , which, after nearly twenty years, was nearing completion.) Here was a real embodiment, across more than forty years and two thousand miles, of the essence of the artistic avant-garde of Paris, 1919.

La Monte Young had taken the musical freedom discovered by Cage's work and, in the Theater of Eternal Music, laid out specific ways of exploring it. Cale and Conrad brought bowed string instruments into the ensemble and created new musical dimensions there, building on the conceptualism of Young's earlier pieces such as *Composition 1960 #7*, with its instruction: 'Play a B and an F# for a long time.'

Young was playing sopranino saxophone, but the new harmonic possibilities conjured up by Conrad's violin and Cale's viola and the saxophone's incompatibility with them led him, by the summer of 1964, to change to voice. Months of concentration on the mathematical basis for the perfect intervals they were pursuing, on tuning and on combining the drones of Conrad's and Cale's strings so that they became an integrated whole, and combined again with the vocal drones of Young and Zazeela, would come to fruition with the creation of a minimalism that was truly a new music.

Cale tried various different viola techniques in the Theater of Eternal Music, including playing in Young's saxophone style and using upper harmonics on the strings. The sound that was really to define the group at this time, however, came about with the combination of filing down the instrument's bridge, allowing him to bow three strings at the same time (Conrad played 'double stops' on two), using heavier guitar strings — and amplifying it.

Conrad bought some cheap contact microphones, the kind of pick-ups that John Cage used and which were available from any street corner electronics store. They were primitive, but they gave the kind of shrill, penetrative sound that suited the music the group were trying to make. Conrad fixed these first to an acoustic guitar, which he would bow, and then to his violin. Without any specialized amplification equipment at first, however, the pick-ups were wired up to Young's home hi-fi system, which, unaccustomed to such use, blew its speakers.

When Cale had first joined the Theater of Eternal Music it had been a completely acoustic affair, but once amplification had been introduced all the members employed it. Conrad's initial motivation for using a pick-up was to try to bring the tiny 'difference tones' that only he, so close to his violin, could hear while playing to the ears of the other members of the group and to the audience. When Cale bowed the viola with a flat bridge, this would overdrive the pick-ups, which would start to rattle, and the sound would resemble that from an overdriven electric guitar amplifier.

Once amplification became an organic part of the group's music the drones with which they had been experimenting took over completely, creating revolutionary music, one that, seemingly forced into a tiny space, actually inhabited an alternative universe.

Angus MacLise had been a member of the Theater of Eternal Music since 1962, employing a distinctive Indian-influenced drumming technique, which he said was influenced by the sound of falling rain, on a variety of percussion instruments. Still part of the group when Cale joined, he continued as such until leaving for an extensive trip to the East in February 1964, although on his return he did still occasionally drum with them.

While living on Ludlow Street, MacLise collaborated with Cale and Conrad (and a varying cast of other performers) on a series of musical explorations. Conrad recorded these, and they would eventually build up into a huge archive documenting the kaleidoscopic panorama of the musical activity that took place within the artistic community of the Lower East Side in the early and mid-1960s.

This was what Conrad describes as the 'downtown documentary' style of performance, casual musical conversations between people with different influences and different ways of playing who had come together to communicate with each other — and for the sheer pleasure of sharing and developing their love of music. Some of the flavour of this can be discerned from the collaborations, particularly those with

Angus MacLise and Terry Jennings, on Cale's *Sun Blindness Music, Dream Interpretation* and *Stainless Steel Gamelan* CDs, and also on the recordings made by Cale, Conrad and film-maker Jack Smith.

Smith would come round to the Ludlow Street apartment and, against his spoken improvisations, Cale and Conrad would invent musical backdrops. These would take shape through the use of a variety of instruments (Cale had now begun occasionally using a sarinda, a bowed, Eastern instrument with a skin top, a hollowed-out body and a very resonant sound) but also tape recorders, excerpts from records, other voices and 'found' percussion. One of the pieces they recorded together, on 5 September, can be heard on the title track of the CD *Silent Shadows on Cinemaroc Island*. The soundtrack to Jack Smith's film *Flaming Creatures* was created by Tony Conrad, and the film featured Mario Montez, Marian Zazeela and appearances from La Monte Young and Angus MacLise. A sequel, *Normal Love*, which was never properly completed, was to have featured a soundtrack by Conrad with contributions by Cale.

Boundaries were removed in these and the other collaborations that took place on the Lower East Side during this time, and its prevailing ethos was most apparent in the Fluxus movement. Taking its lead from the Dadaists, Fluxus was both playful and revolutionary. Its manifesto, written by its deviser and chief practitioner George Macunias, echoed the *Dada Manifesto 1918* in its instructions to 'Purge the world of dead art . . . promote a revolutionary flood and tide in art'. Like La Monte Young (who, in Macunias's 'Fluxiosity' was identified as a Fluxus artist), the movement had absorbed the conceptualism and the libertarianism of John Cage, with their roots in Duchamp, employing them in 'performance art' pieces such as Nam June Paik's *Danger Music #39*, with its instructions to 'climb into the vagina of a live female whale'. While at Goldsmiths' College in London Cale had met up with some of the Fluxus artists and felt a common cause with them. In *Fluxus Review* in 1963 a contribution from 'John D. Cale' was included. From his *Outdoor Pieces for Robin Page, Summer 62* were printed:

2. Make love to a piano without arms . . .
8. Follow the wind and listen to it.

At Goldsmiths', the historic 'little festival of new music' that Cale and Cornelius Cardew had produced had introduced both Fluxus music and Cage's *Concerto for Piano and Orchestra* to a British audience. (Cardew himself would later rehearse but not perform with the Theater of Eternal Music.)

Within months of arriving in New York Cale had worked alongside John Cage, struck up a long-term working relationship with La Monte Young and had opened himself up both to the mass of influences swirling around the Lower East Side and the artistic audacity of Fluxus. Before attending Goldsmiths' he had listened to rock 'n' roll, which had hit him with something of the force of an epiphany, and this, too, soon became part of his musical equation.

When Cale moved into the Ludlow Street apartment he had been surprised to find that Tony Conrad, his companion in the ascetic experimentation of the Theater of Eternal Music, was avidly collecting rock 'n' roll records. Conrad had never liked rock 'n' roll until hearing Cage's call for new ways of listening. He had begun to listen more closely to it and found elements there that he enjoyed. As a result, Cale and Conrad would spend many hours listening to rock, pop and country music and found a wealth of interest on a variety of levels. This music, too, would begin to feed into that which they were making in the apartment.

Cage's work had taught Conrad and Cale to question assumptions — both their own and received wisdom — regarding music and, more generally, sound. One method he taught for doing this was either the customizing of musical instruments (as they had done with the introduction of pick-ups and the flattening of the viola's bridge) or the creation of new ones. To this end, they built and modified a series of mainly string and brass instruments and used objects as simple as a conch shell. Conrad had an acquaintance, Dave, with connections in the recording business, who gave him a reverb unit that he had built himself. Conrad, in his straitened financial situation, would never have been able to afford one on his own, and this was a dream come true. The unit consisted of a huge metal mesh, approximately one yard by two, suspended on strings in a box lined with fibreglass. The pick-up built into it was a phonograph tone arm, and this rested on the edge of the mesh. Also attached to the mesh was an amateur disc-cutting head for cutting vinyl records, with a needle sticking out. When a signal was applied to the cutting head it would vibrate the needle; this would vibrate the mesh, which in turn would cause the phonograph needle to vibrate, and in this way the sound would be picked up. With a transducer in and a transducer out the result was a reverb unit. The theory behind the device made it possible to build something similar out of almost anything, and Cale and Conrad would undertake a variety of experiments on this principle.

In early 1964 the Theater of Eternal Music recorded a series of tapes with the idea of presenting their music to Harry Kraut from the Berkshire Music Center in Tanglewood, in the hope that he might be able to find a commercial outlet for it. Kraut agreed to attend a performance by the group in La Monte Young's apartment. In town for a concert by the Boston Symphony Orchestra, and therefore in black tie and suit, he emerged into the Lower West Side loft to a very different musical culture from that of the concert hall. Intrigued, none the less, by the thought of what he was to hear, Kraut sat in the large chair that had been provided for him in front of a table on which were placed a single glass and a bottle of Scotch. The musicians sat on the floor: Cale playing viola, Young sopranino saxophone and Conrad bowing tuned metal discs that made a gong-like sound. Occasionally varying the depth of intonation but without changing the basic harmonic structure, they set out on a three-and-a-half-hour exploration of a single chord.

During the course of the performance Kraut went through a series of mental states: curiosity, anxiety, boredom, anger, defiance and then, almost miraculously, a Zen-like experience of transcendence and peace, as if emerging on to an open plateau of empty space upon which the smallest movement away from the pervasive stillness had huge significance, a new white landscape against which the tiniest dash of colour lit up the whole vista.

Musically the experience may have opened up a new world, but the path had been a long and arduous one, and Kraut could not see how the necessary numbers of people could travel there to make the journey commercially viable. Cale was disappointed but still determined to continue with his experiments.

When their own contributions started to have a real impact on the direction of the group's music, Cale and Conrad begin to believe that they should receive due credit for it. In flyers for live performances now each of the four musicians would receive equal billing around the title of the piece to be performed. These titles would change from performance to performance and would be concocted by the group sitting around smoking grass and coming up with 'words that hung together in a provocative way', as Conrad recalls. They would play at small theatres such as the Pocket, which they had to rent themselves and where Cale had performed in *Vexations*, store fronts, the odd private occasion organized by an art-world luminary and occasionally out of town, where appearances included a gig at an art school in Pennsylvania and a festival on Long Island.

Spring also saw Cale narrowly avoiding a potentially lethal turn of events. When he had been given his Green Card, enabling him to work in the USA, he had been told that it was his duty to serve in the armed forces; now he received papers summoning him to a physical examination at a Marine recruitment centre on Wall Street. Fortunately for him, he failed the test, having had hepatitis, and the trip to Vietnam that would probably have resulted from passing it was averted.

In October, November and December the first performances officially to come under the banner of 'The Tortoise, His Dreams and Journeys', which would become an ongoing project for the Theater of Eternal Music, took place. Shows over three days in October/November and another three later in November were entitled 'The Tortoise Droning Selected Pitches from the Holy Numbers for the Two Black Tigers, the Green Tiger and the Hermit'; the two black tigers were Young and Zazeela, the Green Tiger Conra, and the Hermit Cale.

At the beginning of 1965 Cale met Lou Reed. Piero Heliczer had sublet his apartment and some female friends of the subtenant, David Gelber, had spotted the long-haired Cale and Conrad, pegged them for rock 'n' roll types and got Gelber to ask them along to a party midtown on New York's East Side. There they were introduced to Terry Phillips of Pickwick Records. He happened to be looking for a band to promote a single he had released ostensibly by a band called the Primitives but in fact cobbled together by the Pickwick staff, which included Lou Reed. Pickwick put out sound-alike records in currently popular styles and put names of non-existent groups on them. When they decided that they might have a hit single on their hands with a song called 'The Ostrich' they decided they needed a real band to promote it. Cale and Conrad looked the type and, when they revealed that their 'band' had a drummer, they were invited to come over to the Pickwick studio and listen to 'their' single. Here they met Reed and, over a cup of coffee he made them from a hot tap, the deal was done. Pickwick now had a manufactured band to promote its manufactured record.

The drummer Cale and Conrad had earmarked to join them in this venture was Walter de Maria, who lived in Walker Street near Cale's old loft in Lispenard Street. De Maria and Cale saw each other weekly. One snowy evening they sat around decorating with ink and paint a consignment of white ties they had found in an abandoned haberdasher's stockroom above Young's studio. This was for a legitimate art dealer — and he was doing it on behalf of Marcel Duchamp. Cale accidentally spilled wonton soup on one of his ties; with the addition of the title 'Soup Tie' on the bottom it was bought by sculptor Robert Morris.

De Maria actually *was* a drummer, but his interest was in jazz and conceptual drumming, and he would make a series of recordings in this vein, some of which have recently been released while others remain unheard. His main interest was in sculpture (some of his wooden sculptures could be played), and his later work would include the highly acclaimed *Lightning Field* from 1977. He had about as much connection, then, with playing rock 'n' roll as Cale and Conrad did and so seemed the perfect ally. For all of them this would be a chance to subvert not just their own artistic backgrounds but also, in their own small way, the world of pop music — and to have some fun.

The band was to plug the single at a series of promotional appearances. For these, they would be driven to a high school or a supermarket, where they would be met by screaming kids anxious to see this hot new group from New York City. On the way to the gig they would be handed the instruments to be played, and the members would choose whether to play guitar or bass on each occasion. They had only to remember two songs — 'The Ostrich' and its B-side, 'Sneaky Pete' — as these were all they were ever asked to play. Both were simple enough constructions for slumming avant-gardists, particularly when they found out that all the guitars were tuned to the same note — exactly the technique they had been using on the other side of the musical world with La Monte Young. On stage their bizarre combination of musical skills never added up to commercial-pop competence: de Maria's jazz drumming helping to inspire a lifelong resentment in Cale of the use of ride cymbals, Conrad's violin playing proving to be poor training for the bass guitar and Cale's guitar playing untutored. However, the star-struck kids in the front row, to whom Cale would make 'constipated faces', he remembers, did not care — they would wait for autographs afterwards anyway. Occasionally the band would even rehearse briefly before shows, Reed sometimes surprising the others with the dexterity of his folk-picking, and it was on these occasions that Cale and Conrad began to appreciate that the talent in these particular records was all his. Not knowing anything about him or where the songs came from, once they began playing them with him they realized that rock 'n' roll was deep within him, that, as Conrad puts it, it 'came out of him like sweat'. In 'rehearsal' someone would start a riff, and they would begin to jam together. Immediately Reed would start generating songs, improvising whole lyrics — rambling stories of how the band had travelled to the gig, the charm of which, as Cale remembers, was their incorporation of 'our tales of woe into a humorous and enchanting relief'. Living rock 'n' roll, just like the stuff they had been listening to at one remove in Ludlow Street, would be conjured out of nothing right in front of them. It was an inspirational experience, particularly for Cale.

After performances over half-a-dozen weekends and a small amount of media coverage it became apparent that the single was not going to make it, and the Primitives were disbanded. Although the experience had been exciting and eye opening for all of them, Conrad had by now made the decision to concentrate on film-making and De Maria was set on a future in conceptual art; neither was interested, therefore, in continuing what they had begun. For Cale, however, another new world had opened up.

At the end of eighteen months of hard, disciplined work in the Theater of Eternal Music he had begun to feel the need to escape — not least because he felt that his own musical contribution was not being acknowledged. Now he saw an opportunity to head in a very different direction but one that held out the promise of a whole new field of exploration. Lou Reed was not just improvising narratives in the way that Jack Smith was doing in Ludlow Street; he was, in a way, practising his own form of the Surrealists' automatic writing — creating art with words from nothing, giving voice to his subconscious.

Finding out that 'The Ostrich' had been played by guitars whose strings were all tuned to the same note tied in with something that Cale and Conrad had already picked up on: the unusually close harmonies sung by the Everly Brothers on 'All I Have to Do Is Dream'. That their own experiments in the world of the avant-garde could be mirrored in the world of rock 'n' roll in this way caught Cale's imagination — here were whole new possibilities for widening his artistic vision. While continuing to play with the Theater of Eternal Music throughout 1965 he also kept in touch with Lou Reed, and before long the relationship would catch fire.

Early on in 1965 Reed played Cale some of the songs that he had been writing and which had been rejected by Pickwick. Although he had recognized Reed's talent for spontaneous performance, Cale initially rejected these songs as identikit folk. Badgered by Reed to examine the lyrics, he found on second glance that there was much more to them than that.

Cale and Reed began to improvise on Reed's songs and found that their opposing musical experiences collided beautifully. Theirs had been the kind of chance meeting that André Breton regarded as full of meaning, creating, in the tradition of Surrealist encounters, a new art. For Cale, the opportunity to rediscover the power of words after so long in the borderless terrain of musical minimalism brought a surge of relief but also the knowledge that what he had learned in that landscape could now be uniquely applied elsewhere.

In February, a chance re-encounter on the subway D-Train around Seventh Avenue between Reed, who was with Cale at the time, and Sterling Morrison, with whom he had previously attended Syracuse University, brought another element into the burgeoning artistic collaboration. At this stage the music they made was played mainly for the same sort of reasons that Cale had jammed with Tony Conrad, Terry Jennings, Jack Smith and others. There was little talk — particularly in the light of the recent failure of the Primitives and the domination of the New York music business at the time by production-line pop — of turning what they were doing into something long term. In this spirit of unpressured creativity it was natural for Angus MacLise to join in, and the four soon began to play together. Reed had taught Cale bar-chording on the guitar for his performances with the Primitives, and Cale would sometimes play this instrument as well as the viola and the bass guitar. 'Hot Scoria', for example, later to be released on the *Dream Interpretation* CD, was recorded on 2 March, Cale hammering out one chord on an acoustic guitar against MacLise's cimbalom runs and then against spare picking from his collaborator, lurching into a series of manic strummings like those of a demented flamenco guitarist. One thing Cale failed to do at this time, and it was a failure that had a profound effect on his work during the whole of his time in New York, was to play any kind of keyboard. The well-tempered tuning of the piano and its associated instruments held in its restrictive frame the whole structure of classical music that Cale was trying to fight against. One way out had been to take an axe to the piano, and other 'hands-on' ways of dealing with it would present themselves before long, but for now Cale was to oppose its seductive dictatorship by ignoring it.

For Cale there was plenty of potential in his new collaboration, but it would require work to turn that potential into achievement. In the meantime he continued his involvement with the Theater of Eternal Music, which included a performance on 4 March at the East End Theater.

One of the invitations that La Monte Young had received from the art world had come from Henry Geldzahler, then Curator of Twentieth-Century Art at New York's Metropolitan Museum. The group played at his 79th Street home on 7 March 1965, and among the audience were Jackie Kennedy and Andy Warhol. On 25 April Henry Geldzahler was invited to a dinner party at La Monte Young's home, and on this occasion the music that would later be released as *Day of Niagara* was recorded. By now Warhol had developed a friendship and working relationship with Billy Name. Name had met Warhol in 1960 through Ray Johnson, collage artist, Mail Art pioneer and employee of the Orientalia bookshop. When Warhol moved his studio into a new loft at 231 East 47th Street towards the end of 1963 Name was asked to decorate it and proceeded to turn it silver, transforming it into what became the first and most important of Warhol's Factories.

By 1965 Warhol was in the middle of his most creative period and was one of the most famous people in New York. Already behind him were the Campbell's Soup Cans, the Marilyns, Electric Chairs and the Most Wanted Men. His silkscreens used repetition in a way analogous to that of the Theater of Eternal Music. As a Pop Art icon, he was seen as someone who was hammering in one of the last nails into the coffin of Abstract Expressionism and was also acclaimed as a neo-Dadaist. As well as this, however, he was acquainted with and an admirer of the painters — and associates of John Cage — Robert Rauschenberg and Jasper Johns, whose work was neither in one camp nor the other. In 1963 he had met Marcel Duchamp, had later bought his 'Box in a Valise' and would go on to film him in 1966. He had also already filmed *Jack Smith Filming 'Normal Love'* (just visible himself in part of the actual film by Smith) and had also featured Smith in the title role of his film *Batman Dracula* in 1964.

By now Sterling Morrison had become a regular member of the jam sessions in Ludlow Street, and he, Cale, Reed and MacLise had something almost recognizable as a band. Piero Heliczer had moved out of the building into one on Grand Street, and Cale and Morrison, bumping into MacLise on the corner of Essex and Delancey one day, were asked if they felt like going along to see him.

It turned out that Heliczer and MacLise, under the auspices of their own Aquarian Productions, were organizing *Launching the Dream Weapon*, to be performed at Jonas Mekas's Film-Makers' Co-op, also known as the Cinematheque, at 434 Lafayette Street. Heliczer by now had already completed several films, one of which, *Soap Opera*, had featured Conrad and Cale, and some of these were to be projected against sheets, together with slides, all of which would collide with coloured lights. There would be dancers, too — and musicians. Cale, Morrison and MacLise enrolled themselves immediately.

Together with Reed, over the course of the summer and into the winter, they would perform anonymously at several screenings of underground films, first of all by Heliczer and then by people such as Barbara Rubin and Kenneth Anger. Another regular presence at these screenings was Jack Smith. Warhol was later to say that the whole of the downtown scene at this time numbered no more than five hundred people – and that included the audiences. Everyone knew everyone else and the worlds of art, music, film-making, theatre and ballet were in a state of constant collision.

Tony Conrad had also moved out of Ludlow Street, initially to try to make films full-time with Jack Smith and then to pursue film-making on his own. Cale asked Reed to move in, which he, then living with his parents in Freeport, Long Island, was glad to do. It was now that the band began to take on real life, initially named the Falling Spikes and then the Warlocks. On a return visit to Ludlow Street, where he had left some of his things, Conrad brought them a book he had found discarded in the Bowery, entitled *The Velvet Underground*, which finally gave them what they all agreed was the perfect name. Shortly after this, one of the first two photos of the band would be taken, on the roof of Piero Heliczer's building on Grand Street.

Money was still in very short supply, and Cale and Reed resorted to making it both by donating blood and by allowing photographs of themselves to be used in exploitative photo-stories, as Cale recalls. 'We saw an ad in the *Village Voice* saying "$5 for a pint" and another which would be for *National Enquirer* where we were paid $15 apiece with the signing of a release that stated we would not sue if our pictures were used to depict murderers, thieves, rapists, etc. I was a gay junkie in a story, and Lou was a serial murderer who got caught because he tape-recorded the screams of his victims.'

By July they had enough material to record a demo tape. Now lost, it featured 'Heroin', 'Venus in Furs', 'Black Angel's Death Song', 'Wrap Your Troubles in Dreams' and another piece, possibly called 'Never Get Emotionally Involved with a Man, Woman, Beast or Child'. Vocals were courtesy of a reluctant Cale, Reed's soon-to-be distinctive style of delivery not yet ready. Cale took the tape over to Britain where he tried unsuccessfully to arouse some interest from record companies. One copy was pressed, via Kate Heliczer, wife of Piero, into the hands of Marianne Faithfull, in the vain hope that it might find the ears of the Rolling Stones. Another went to Miles Copeland, who would later play a significant part in Cale's solo career.

From slightly later comes the tape released as Disc One of the Velvet Underground's *Peel Slowly and See* boxed set. Here, Reed's songs – most now sung by himself – are caught halfway between the folk and urban blues styles in which they had begun and the menace and magic of the new soundscapes Cale was devising for them.

In August Cale recorded 'Summer Heat' on a solo acoustic guitar. Here a single chord is given the sternest of workings-over. Different strings are emphasized, bass strings opened and closed, and all the time the same rhythm is relentlessly beaten out. More an exploration of rhythm than anything else, the examination takes more than eleven minutes; something similar would later be used for the piano part on 'All Tomorrow's Parties'.

Drop everything . . .
Drop your hopes and your fears . . .
Set out on the road.
(André Breton)

On 21 October Cale performed with the Theater of Eternal Music at the Theater Upstairs, the Playhouse, Pittsburgh, although by September Terry Riley — soon to be a successful minimalist composer in his own right and who had recently moved to New York — had already started to replace him at rehearsals. In December Cale gave his last performance as an official member of the band. In September, too, Reed had finally given up his day job at Pickwick. Both were in the process of burning their bridges.

By now substantial work had gone into the songs. Arrangements had been developed over what had become concerted practice sessions (for everyone except MacLise, who kept to his own private schedule). Cale had become an arranger, and he had also found a way to continue to use the way of playing he had devised in the Theater of Eternal Music but to develop it in a different way, one that would revolutionize another form of music altogether, effectively constructing a new art form.

One visitor to Ludlow Street that autumn was journalist and scene-maker Al Aronowitz. Aronowitz was managing a band called the Myddle Class and had caught the nascent Velvet Underground playing at one of their underground film performances in the summer. Robbie Robertson of the Band had accompanied him and had been singularly unimpressed — so much so that he had walked out — but Aronowitz had been intrigued, and Barbara Rubin, the underground film-maker, had recommended that he sign them.

By the time of his next contact with the band it was winter. Unable to stand the cold any more in the unheated building in Ludlow Street, they had taken Piero Heliczer's recently vacated apartment on the fifth floor of 450 Grand Street. Heliczer had decorated a whole wall of one of the rooms of the apartment with photographs of single eyes cut from *Vogue*, and there were telephones in every room — whenever one line was cut off by the phone company, another was put in under a different name. With four bedrooms, a bathroom, kitchen and minimal rent courtesy of the art-loving landlord, this was just about the perfect environment. Here Aronowitz offered the band the chance of their first proper gig, supporting the Myddle Class at Summit High School in New Jersey on 11 December.

This was to be the first occasion on which they would be payed to play, which meant they would have to start at a certain prescribed time and finish at another — too much for Angus MacLise. A man who had devised a whole calendar of his own, redefining the very passage of time, could not possibly fit himself into such a construct, and he told the rest of the band he would not be able to play. (Al Aronowitz also remembers MacLise not wanting the gig because he was unwilling to carry his drums up and down from the fifth-floor Grand Street walk-up.)

A friend of Lou Reed's, Jim Tucker, had a sister, Moe, who drummed and had already played in a three-piece in Long Island. The Velvet Underground asked her to join them for the Summit gig and played her some of their songs. She liked what she heard and agreed. Tucker was almost as unorthodox a percussionist as MacLise, but influenced by African rather than Eastern rhythms. Her appointment proved an inspired one, and she went on to become the perfect replacement for MacLise. And she had a car: the band now had transport.

Soon after Moe Tucker joined the band the *Walter Cronkite Show* on CBS wanted to do a piece on underground film. They had come with Piero Heliczer's name and filmed him shooting his own film, *Venus in Furs*, in the Grand Street apartment. (The lyrics to Reed's song of the same name were also first published around this time in an artist's portfolio printed by Angus MacLise.) The Velvet Underground appeared playing 'Heroin', and for the occasion Margaret Boyce-Cam, who also featured in the film, painted the band's faces. Cale had his stomach painted, too, and his hair sprayed into position. When Heliczer had moved out of the apartment, he had left some costumes behind, and the band decided to make use of them: Moe Tucker wore a bridal gown and Bobby Ritchkin, who played bass, wore a bishop's regalia. By the time the band began to play the party was in full swing, and there was enough madness for the CBS crew to be more than satisfied. Heliczer, dressed in black like the non-costumed members of the band, was shown filming until he suddenly downed his camera, grabbed a saxophone and added its sound to the musical mayhem.

After the two performances on 5 and 6 December at the Cinematheque's new home, the Wurlitzer Building Auditorium at 125 West 41st Street, Cale effectively ended his career with the Theater of Eternal Music (although he would make the occasional appearance with them in later years). For these concerts they were joined by a projectionist, David Hayes, who helped to show slides that Marian Zazeela had created to be superimposed on the band's specially designed silken robes — another example of the kind of light-show that Andy Warhol would soon draw on for his 'Exploding Plastic Inevitable' presentations.

The day before the Summit gig, Piero Heliczer's *The Last Rites*, part of the New Cinema Festival, took place at the Cinematheque with Heliczer taking the part of a bishop and using the New Testament for his text. Jonas Mekas, who had organized the festival, described it as 'a ceremony, a ritual' involving actors in front of a tiny eight-millimetre image projected on to a large screen. 'First cimbalom' was Angus MacLise, 'First viola' Cale, 'First violin' Tony Conrad, 'First tambourine' Jack Smith and 'First recorder' Terry Jennings. Also featured was Heliczer's film *Dirt*, with a cast list including Edie Sedgwick, Andy Warhol, Cale, Marian Zazeela, La Monte Young, Jonas Mekas and the New York City Police Department.

At Summit High School there were parents with their children, there was a curtain that went up, just like on 'proper' performances, there was Cale dressed in black with silver jewellery and sunglasses, and there was the terrifying noise that the band hurled at the audience. The set consisted of just three songs, but that was enough to make the necessary impact. Many of those watching left before even these had been completed, but no one who attended, no matter how briefly, was likely to forget what they had seen. Al Aronowitz particularly remembers laughing at the uptight suburban audience's reaction to the first public performance of 'Heroin'. The show was sufficiently successful for him to invite the band to his house for an after-show party — and to book them into a residency at the Café Bizarre in Greenwich Village.

The Café Bizarre was on West 3rd Street, just east of MacDougal Street. The Velvet Underground's residency turned out to be very short-lived. The band had written new songs, including 'Run Run Run', in order to have enough material for a whole set, but the tension between these and the kind of material that the tourists who patronized the Café and the management who ran it wanted to hear was at breaking point from the time they first took the stage. Playing, as they did, with two and sometimes three instruments coming out of a single burnt-out amplifier certainly produced interesting sonic interactions, but the overall sound was too crushed and distorted to be used in the long term. Although they refused to change their set in order to maximize their money-making potential, it was obvious that they were going to need funds from somewhere in order to buy new equipment.

Andy Warhol was already familiar with the Café Bizarre, had seen Cale play with Cage and with Young and had been to some of the underground film showings at which the Velvet Underground had played. He was looking to expand his interests, having already covered art and film. Media interest in his 'superstars' had taken care of the fashion angle, and literature was pretty much under control, too, now that he had bought a tape recorder with which he would record the conversations that would make up his *a, a novel*. Next up, therefore, was rock 'n' roll. (He had earlier been part of a short-lived band in which he had sung backing vocals, La Monte Young had played saxophone and Walter de Maria — who had gone on to play in the Primitives with Cale and Lou Reed — had played drums. The lyrics had been written by Jasper Johns.)

Asked to open a discothèque to run under his own name, Warhol agreed with

Factory film director and manager Paul Morrissey that he would need to follow current practice by having a live band perform in addition to a disk-jockey playing records. Warhol's screen-printing assistant and right-hand man Gerard Malanga, meanwhile, was invited by film-maker Barbara Rubin to go to see the Velvet Underground at the Café Bizarre. (Rubin was already well acquainted with the band, having seen them play at screenings of underground films, which had included her own.)

Malanga went along and was immediately taken by what he saw and heard. Rubin encouraged him to get up and dance and after about twenty minutes he did, brandishing his trademark leather whip. The next night, Malanga returned, this time bringing Morrissey along as well. Morrissey also approved of the Velvet Underground and, in turn, he invited Warhol the following evening, informing him that they might just have found the band they were looking for. On this third occasion what was now a Warhol entourage also included Nico, a German singer whom Malanga had met in England and who was now pursuing fame and fortune in New York. Nico had appeared on the British television show *Ready, Steady, Go* singing her first single, 'I'm Not Saying', and Morrissey, immediately earmarking her as the person able to give the Velvet Underground what he regarded as some much-needed glamour, made plans to introduce her into the band.

Warhol, too, was impressed with the Velvet Underground, pronouncing them 'fabulous and demented', and invited them over to the Factory.

When they turned up the following day Warhol outlined plans he had for a mixed-media spectacle which would showcase their music, and they were intrigued. There was one problem, though. Warhol had agreed with Malanga that Nico should sing with them, and this was to be part of the deal. The band resented what they regarded as an intrusion into what was already a fully formed concept of sound and vision. However, weighing up this one negative against the many positives — which included money for equipment, a place to rehearse and the backing of the Warhol name — they found they had to accept his terms.

They soon managed to get themselves sacked from the Café Bizarre, after being forced to play on Christmas Day, by ignoring an instruction never to play 'Black Angel's Death Song' again.

By New Year's Eve they were travelling up to Harlem with Warhol and Malanga to see James Brown play, before returning in actress Edie Sedgwick's limousine to scene-maker Danny Fields's apartment. Here they watched themselves appear on television on the *Walter Cronkite Show*. Things were definitely looking up.

Part 2
Calefactory
(a container providing heat)

On 9 March 1934 Yuri Gagarin, the first man in space, was born.

It was during 1966 that Cale's art and life achieved a new dimension, courtesy of Andy Warhol. Warhol would bring money for equipment and instruments, media exposure, a record contract, rehearsal space and an orbit that included Bob Dylan and the Rolling Stones, even Salvador Dalí and Marcel Duchamp. He would also bring him into contact with his 'superstars', such as Edie Sedgwick, Susan Bottomley and Nico, with all of whom Cale had affairs. All of these things Warhol would bring because he and the Velvet Underground would create together the 'Exploding Plastic Inevitable', an outright assault on the senses on a scale previously not experienced in the entertainment world.

When Cale had first seen Gerard Malanga 'weaving like grass in the wind to the music' at the Café Bizarre, his first reaction had been one of antagonism. Malanga, as he saw it, was trying to get in on the act. Similarly, to arrive at Warhol's Factory and find the pop artist engaged in the kind of exercises in repetition that Cale and La Monte Young had been working on — and to see him so critically lauded and financially successful because of it — engendered more hostility. Neither of these feelings were to last, however. What Warhol offered was huge scope for the development of the Velvet Underground's art through mutual interest.

'Picabia could not live without being surrounded morning and night by a troop of uprooted, floating, bizarre people whom he supported more or less.'
(Juliette Gleizes)

For the band, Warhol's Factory, with its cutting-edge social swirl and fascinating, freaky crew, looked like heaven. Warhol himself was a godlike figure, omnipotent in a silver world of his own creation, and he ruled a paradise where creating art brought money, fame, celebrity and glamour. What he had to offer might even lead to artistic immortality. For Cale himself, there was 'a feeling of outrageous expectation in the air; we could say anything we wanted to anyone, no matter how famous . . . There was this magical empathy for the future and what it brought to us, albeit wrapped in a scathing indifference to the possibility of it's being a mirage.'

On 9 March 1959 Venus was contacted by radio for the first time.

Things started to happen quickly for Cale at the Factory. By his second day he had been introduced to Nico and been seduced ('kidnapped', as he recalls it) by Edie Sedgwick.

As Nico's pendulum swung towards Warhol, Edie's was swinging away. Each would appear on stage with the Velvet Underground at an appearance on 10 January at Delmonico's Hotel on Park Avenue, but this would be one of Edie's last appearances with Warhol, whereas it was Nico's first with his newly signed band. Cale's six-week affair with Edie, during which time he moved in with her at her exclusive apartment on East 63rd Street at Madison Avenue, came at a time when she was in the process of leaving Warhol for what she hoped would be a new career with Bob Dylan in Woodstock. Nico, on the other hand, had done her stint with Dylan and had effectively left Woodstock for Warhol.

'There is in every living psychiatrist a repulsive and sordid atavism that makes him see in every artist, every genius he comes across, an enemy.'
(Antonin Artaud)

Warhol had been asked to speak at the forty-third annual dinner of the New York Society for Clinical Psychiatry at Delmonico's but had decided instead to show a couple of films and to present the Velvet Underground. The entertainment was billed as 'The Chic Mystique of Andy Warhol'. As the psychiatrists began their roast beef, string beans and potatoes, the Velvet Underground began their assault on those responsible for the thoughts and behaviour of a nation. While Warhol filmed, Edie Sedgwick in a red dress and Gerard Malanga in a tuxedo danced. Long, deep Expressionist shadows created by camera lights loomed and lurched behind jewelled candelabra.

Cale was described by the *New York Times* afterwards as the 'leader of the Velvet Underground', and its review quoted one of the guests describing the evening as 'decadent Dada'. Lou Reed, who had previously been subjected by psychiatrists to electro-convulsive treatment, was 'seething almost the whole night', remembers Cale, who was 'delighted to hear that the comments elicited were of universal distaste, including the one suggesting we needed a long recuperative stay in a home'.

Nico had effectively been foisted on the Velvets as part of the deal with Warhol and, although they were not happy about having the music on which they had worked so hard 'hijacked', they decided to make the best of the arrangement. This was an inauspicious start to what would actually become a long and creative working relationship between Cale and Nico — one that would last, on and off, until shortly before her death in 1988. Nico had brought some songs with her that she wanted to sing. One that the band did design to perform live with her was Bob Dylan's 'I'll Keep

It With Mine', supposedly written for her, but they turned it into something more akin to their own 'I'm Waiting for the Man', with a heavy beat and loud electric guitar chords. Nico had come from another world, a world of high fashion, European cinema and the company of rock stars such as Dylan and Brian Jones; it was a world, however, with which Warhol felt more than comfortable and one that would help to bring the Lower East Side base of the Velvet Underground right uptown.

For Cale women and the Velvet Underground was a thorny issue. Significant new relationships with women for him had invariably been sexual ones, and when these involved music they seemed not to work. So far in life his musical world had been very male-dominated, and the band's involvement with women as collaborators had been unpromising. When they had been known as the Falling Spikes he and Reed had briefly included a woman called Electra in their band. Although she had had no song-writing role, she had wanted to make her mark. Her desire to become an actress of the 'method' school had affected her attitude to the music she made, and her keep-ing of the beat on an Afghani instrument, the sarinda, during a rendition of 'Wrap Your Troubles in Dreams' had led, literally, to bleeding knuckles. She had believed that the drawing of blood in this way was part of her initiation into membership of the band. When the blood had flowed again while she was playing guitar during a live performance and she had not even noticed, Cale and Reed had decided that she did not have the necessary stability for a long-term musical relationship with them.

Another volatile partnership between them and a woman called Daryl also failed to last the course, and a brief try-out as singer for Tally Brown, one of Warhol's actresses — at his behest — also came to nothing. For the Velvet Underground there-fore to begin 1966 with two female members was unexpected.

Moe Tucker looked to many people like a boy, and some were stunned to find out that she was a girl; in a sense she was an 'honorary guy' within the Velvet Underground. Her femininity removed her from some of the male competitiveness of the other members of the band, and her equable personality and lack of sexual involvement with them meant that her gender never became an issue. As a drummer she combined sta-bility with a sound that was at the same time primitive and exotic — the ideal rhythmi-cal conduit for Cale's and Reed's expressions and explorations of the subconscious. She remembers the relationship between Cale and Reed as one of 'mutual respect and admiration, with a musical goal — to introduce something new to rock 'n' roll'. Her first impressions of Cale were of someone 'very intense, very pensive, very smart'. After his initial misgivings — she recalls him being 'not too thrilled with the idea of a chick in the band' — it soon became obvious that she was the kind of girl with whom he could work.

With Nico the misgivings would not be misplaced. Independent, career-oriented, glamorous and used to the company of celebrities, she had also entranced Paul Morrissey, who was effectively managing the band with Warhol and who was keen to maximize her role in it. For Cale and Reed her independence, which might have interfered with the music on which they had worked so hard, had to be reined in, her glamour used as a way of promoting the band and her career aspirations, along with those of Morrissey, restricted by defining the role she was to play. Just as Moe Tucker gave the band an edge with her boyish appearance and African-inspired drumming, so, too, did Nico; not only was she blonde and beautiful, she had a German-accented and unusually deep voice. Her Europeanism, allied to Cale's own, would be an important contributory factor to what would emerge as the sound of the 'Velvet Underground and Nico' on their first album.

The Velvet Underground's music acquired a new dimension with the songs that Reed wrote for Nico to sing, but, apart from 'All Tomorrow's Parties', these were not ones on which Cale had much impact.

The hard-edged material, such as 'Heroin', 'I'm Waiting for the Man', 'Venus in Furs' and 'Black Angel's Death Song', was the heart of the Velvet Underground for Cale. When he and Reed had started writing together he had wanted to combine Reed's ability to sink into the subconscious through the spontaneous creation of lyrics with his own ability to reach under the skin of reality, which he had perfected through the long months of rehearsal and performance with the Theater of Eternal Music. From the days with La Monte Young drugs had played a part in the creation of Cale's new music. Marijuana had helped to provide the meditative approach necessary for the Theater of Eternal Music's experiments, but Cale had also experimented with LSD at this time. On visits to Harvard with Tony Conrad the two used to take cannabis with them; this they would trade for acid, which they would then take back to New York. Cale had a contact at Harvard, and this person's father worked at the CIA headquarters in Langley. The CIA in the early 1960s was effectively subsidizing the drug use of the Lower East Side by recruiting 'subjects' from the streets for its own experiments into LSD. Decidedly non-academic psychotropic experiments would follow Cale's return to New York after these expeditions, with the risks taken during them considered worth while in order to access further unexplored ground. Cale also applied to take part in sensory deprivation experiments at Columbia University but recalls being met with 'stunned silence', concluding that those running the programme probably thought that he was 'another nut looking for drug kicks'. The combination of risk and 'immersion' that would have defined his planned drug-laced sessions in the isolation tank actually did characterize his time with La Monte Young and with the Velvet Underground: create a new soundscape, climb in and explore.

With the Velvet Underground came Cale's exposure to heroin. Exploratory use soon became a shared habit with Lou Reed, which tied them closer together, increased their desires to take risks and influenced the band's sound. It also increased their own belief in themselves and hostility to pretty much everything else.

The Beatles and the Rolling Stones may have held sway in most of the rock world but not anywhere the Velvet Underground might gather together. With 'Venus in Furs', in particular, Cale felt that they had achieved something without equal, something uniquely theirs. After trying many different approaches they had finally come up with a musical 'tapestry' that wove different threads into a pattern — climbing guitar, arcing bass, ceremonially pounding drums and a viola that slid and slit its way against its own ritualistic drone.

The Velvet Underground began rehearsing at the Factory in January. One early practice session found their sound already unmistakably their own — in between the blues work-outs. A shrieking guitar from Reed was supported by rumbles and repetitious, thunderous booms from Cale's bass that concentrated on tone, volume and vibration rather than rhythm or the heart of chords. He would push his repetition to extremes of distortion and monotony. The drone of Cale's viola on 'Heroin' was rich and pure, before it began to slip off the edge of its own control into another musical world of feedback and distortion to match the plunging descent of the narrative.

Another rehearsal was filmed by Warhol as *The Velvet Underground and Nico* and famously interrupted on camera by the arrival of the New York police, who were following up a complaint about the noise level. Nico, centre stage, 'plays' an electric guitar on her lap, while her son by Alain Delon, Ari, shakes some maracas. The rest of the band all wear dark glasses; Moe Tucker and Sterling Morrison maintain a solid presence at the back, while Reed, leather-jacketed, remains aware of everything that is going on around him as he plays guitar. Cale, thin, with long, centre-parted hair and a slight beard, half sits on a chair at the start of the performance, hunched in front of an amplifier and a tall, thin piece of wood which is miked up to it. He plays with the controls on the amplifier and occasionally stands to make the piece of wood reverberate. Immersed in the music, he fails to notice when the police appear. When his plug is pulled he moves away off camera but, undaunted, returns shortly afterwards with his viola and resumes his place at the heart of the improvisation.

MUSICIANS, SMASH YOUR BLIND INSTRUMENTS
on the stage.
(Tristan Tzara, 'Unpretentious Proclamation')

The tall, thin piece of wood was actually part of the frame of an old piano that had been left in the loft of the apartment Cale and Reed were staying in, above the fire station on West 3rd Street. The piano had been abandoned, and Cale tore it apart, ripping off its skin and exposing its innards. Here was the proud symbol of Western classical music naked, its secrets revealed. Its hidden construction was exposed like the clockwork mechanism laid bare in Francis Picabia's *Réveil Matin*. Just as Picabia found new artistic life in his new arrangement of the timepiece's cogs, so Cale was able to do the same with the insides of the piano: 'It was the way then', he remembers, 'to take any materials you had and make music with them.' In his piece *Untitled (for Piano)*, recorded around this time on this instrument, Cale almost hauls himself inside the piano, exploring its guts from inside its ribcage, 'crawling inside the sound' (which is how he describes the purpose of the La Monte Young collaboration). 'Inside' the piano he bangs, scrapes and strokes the instrument's strings, hammering its sides, constructing machine-sounds and deadened arpeggios, building echoing storms of alien sound, creating the sounds of a hell's harp, rolling thunder, waves of sea-spray static. The piano is expressed in terms of its construction and mechanics but remains resolutely 'unplayed'.

Cale had hoped that the Velvet Underground would be able to take the deconstructed piano around with them and use it for their live shows, but this was to prove logistically impossible. At the Factory, however, part of its wooden frame would take its place alongside the 'autoharp, maracas, kazoo, car horn and pieces of glass' that Andy Warhol remembered the band using there. Throughout his time with the Velvet Underground Cale maintained an interest in using exotic and unconventional instruments, exploiting the new musical freedoms of John Cage, which allowed anything to be used for the purpose of making music — and any way of playing. For a piece entitled 'Stainless Steel Gamelan', later released on the *Stainless Steel Gamelan* CD, Cale and Sterling Morrison would even play the same guitar simultaneously, Morrison working the conventional parts of the strings (although in a highly unconventional way), while Cale attacked the 'dead' parts below the instrument's bridge. The result is almost like the soundtrack to a railway journey, with bell-like tolling, ripples and surges of movement, punctuations like the passing of bridges, as the two players move in and out of 'synch' with each other, suggesting changes of perspective through the piece.

Untitled (for Piano) was a dance suite that Andy Warhol had suggested Cale submit as part of a proposal to the Harkness Ballet Foundation shortly after the Velvet Underground had arrived at the Factory. Another part of the unfinished ballet was *Big Apple Express*, which is strongly reminiscent of the improvised music that the Velvet Underground were producing as a band at this time, with sawing viola against shaking, shifting mechanical rhythms occasionally exploding into feedback, shrieks and monstrous roars. The performance is abruptly curtailed by the entrance of another member of the emergency services — this time an incandescent fireman from the station below the apartment, complaining about the torrent of noise flooding through his ceiling.

Improvisation was a regular exercise for the Velvet Underground. Away from the hard work of arranging song structures, it was a chance to relax together, regroup and practise. It was a situation, too, that could create musical surprises capable of inspiring each member of the band to new heights. In this way it could also arouse a collective musical inspiration that re-emphasized the harmony between them. Each was forced to pay attention to what each of the others was doing and to try to guide the development of what was being played. For Cale, some of what he had learned from John Cage was again useful in this environment. He could 'compose' what was happening by recognizing the time slot they had in terms of 'packets of activity' and planning certain events to happen along the way. If inspiration was flagging he could instigate one of these events to get things moving again. When Reed and Cale first started working together, their collaboration had been coloured by Reed's mental state, which was to a substantial extent dictated by the electroshock 'therapy' that had been administered to him on the instigation of his parents. Cale recalls how this was dealt with: 'I feel convinced that when I first met him I did the right thing in focusing intensely on the role that music and art played in his psyche, a kind of mental therapy to bring him out of the misery he was living, under doctors' care, with drugs.' While this seemed to contribute towards providing him with a 'key' to the subconscious, it had set him apart from the world around him and given him a combination of arrogance and defensiveness about his abilities. Cale had a similar configuration within him (although conjured by different factors), and his own experiments into different mental states, when added to the mixture, meant that he and Reed were very much in tune with each other. When improvising together Cale would always be listening hard to what his partner was playing, responding to it and bearing in mind the whole of the piece that was being created; this ability to play in sympathy with and then take forward Reed's music 'eventually got him out of the gloom of his medical state'.

Andy Warhol had been handed the Cinematheque by Jonas Mekas for a week from 8 to 13 February 1966. The original idea had been to put on an Edie Sedgwick 'retrospective', but with Edie now estranged from the Warhol camp he had decided to showcase the Velvet Underground instead. What was basically a try-out for the 'Exploding Plastic Inevitable' shows of that spring, combining live music, lighting and film projections, took place over the course of the week, under the title 'Andy Warhol, Up-Tight'.

The day before the start of the run at the Cinematheque Warhol had been interviewed on television about his new band, and pieces of their music had been heard; 'Venus in Furs' and 'Heroin' were fully formed — already mesmerising and merciless.

Also in February stills were shot for Warhol's film *Hedy*, and the film itself started shooting. Having been filmed by Warhol twice already, Cale and Reed would now work as soundtrack writers and performers. Once the shooting of the film was finished they would overdub music to accompany the footage: a mixture of piano, reverbed guitar, feedback, unconventional percussion and Cale's 'thunder machine' – the head of a Vox Super Beatle amplifier dropped on the floor. There would be similar work later in the year for Warhol's *Chelsea Girls*; this was the beginning of what, for Cale, would be a career-long involvement in film soundtracks.

A languid, clean-shaven and long-haired Cale had already featured in Warhol's series of 'Screen Tests', which involved being 'interrogated' alone by his silent sixteen-millimetre camera for three minutes. Salvador Dalí blew his own 'Screen Test' by striking a pose and being unable to hold it. As well as *The Velvet Underground and Nico*, another film was shot around this time, simply entitled *The Velvet Underground*. This piece opens with Moe Tucker tied to a chair. Morrison and Reed approach her and offer her food and drink. Later Reed plays with a whip, and the scene ends in a kind of demented picnic with milk, orange juice and rubbish on the floor. Cale is the last to enter the action and the first to leave. He stands side on to the camera, black-suited with an ornate white collar, drinks, tries to catch grapes in his mouth, periodically tosses the hair out of his eyes, taps out a rhythm on his knees, drinks again from Morrison's bottle, talks to Reed, leaves; then, back on set and now seated, he taps his foot, takes another drink from Morrison, plays with his fingers, crosses his legs, drinks again, gets up and leaves once more.

Cale's uneasiness and apparent lack of interest in the film, paying it only brief attention, was an expression of his lack of patience with the way in which life at the Factory was sometimes conducted. Much of the time there was spent hanging around waiting, and some people were better at it than others. For Cale this was time that could be better used, and the waste, as he saw it, would sometimes make him short-tempered. On occasion he could scream, too.

In March, 'Up-Tight' went on the road, the series of performances a successful dry run for what was to come the following month: the 'Exploding Plastic Inevitable'. At Rutgers University, a fight before the show had attracted a large audience, and the element of confrontation was heightened by the band playing all in white, reflecting the brilliance of the stage lights back on to their audience.

Also in March, back in New York, Paraphernalia, the Pilgrim Clothing flagship store, threw a party. Fashion designer Betsey Johnson had been hired to put together their new line, and she asked Andy Warhol to organize the celebrations. He brought along the Velvet Underground to play against a background of his silver pillows. When Cale met Betsey she struck him immediately, he recalls, as a 'wonderful person'. Two years later she would become his wife.

Warhol's silver pillows were showcased officially in April at Leo Castelli's gallery in an exhibition that was described as the artist's farewell to fine art. Warhol's attention had turned to the mixed-media opportunities offered by the Velvet

Underground, and the opening coincided with the first week of the 'Exploding Plastic Inevitable', an unrehearsed, constantly evolving mixed-media offensive at the Lower East Side dance hall, the Dom.

The 'Exploding Plastic Inevitable' was a visual and aural assault that had the Velvet Underground as its centrepiece, casting them as cultural revolutionaries. In an organic setting of strobe lights, hugely magnified slide projections and Warhol films, with dancers giving movement to their music in contrast with their own fixed stage presence, the band found the perfect means of self-expression in the chaos. Their own thoughts about presentation had always been primitive and pure, limited, as Cale says, to a desire to play 'only in the dark with tremendous levels'. Here, though, new complementary visual dimensions were found which, for a while, formed the perfect complement to their music. Props, too, were brought in to combine with appropriate songs. One night Salvador Dalí turned up, on another Robert Rauschenberg skated through a screen. The first week of shows made the band so much money that, legend has it, they had to take it away in bags. For the first time Cale could see real acceptance and financial reward for the implementation of his musical ideas.

'We're waiting for th emoment when [André Breton]
Will reach a point of compression at which, like
dynamite, he explodes.'
(Georges Ribemont-Dessaignes, 391, No. 11)

Mary Woronov, who danced with Gerard Malanga at the Dom, remembers Cale's stage presence at the time as dark and threatening, with a rage quotient that was largely hidden but still tangible. Sombre and intense, he would pick up the viola in a sullen, morose manner and play from deep within himself, giving the impression of 'a stick of dynamite that was going to go off'. Often playing with his back to the audience, he concentrated solely on the music, a 'genius in the raw' with a strange, high intelligence to counterpoint Lou Reed's street-smartness, attitude and embodiment of rock 'n' roll's mythology. While hanging around waiting to go on, Cale would belie his on-stage seriousness by cracking jokes. The members of the band, often – with the exception of Moe Tucker – medicated to the hilt, would stumble on stage, knock into things and fall over.

By the end of April and the end of the run at the Dom the 'Exploding Plastic Inevitable' was already past its peak and, although those involved would have found it hard to believe, an era was already at an end.

In April, too, recording sessions began at Sceptre Studios on Broadway for the album that would become *The Velvet Underground and Nico*.

In the period around the recording of the album, Cale began seeing Lynne Tillman, then a college student, now a successful novelist. Lynne had watched him perform in the 'Exploding Plastic Inevitable' at the Dom and, having set herself on her future career, saw him as a fellow artist, devoted to his music and pursuing it single-mindedly. Her initial impressions of him were that he was 'dramatic, sharp-featured, lean, nervous, usually wearing shades and in black'. He sometimes wore turtlenecks, giving him a Bohemian air and, although projecting the impression that he was worldlywise, it was obvious that he was not completely at ease in New York. Cale was 'serious and exacting about his music and his performance, always self-critical'. Sometimes the two would listen to tapes he was working on, which he would bring over to her apartment. Often they would go to movie at one in the morning on 42nd Street and walk around the streets together afterwards. Cale would talk only a little about Lou Reed, but it would emerge from these conversations that 'they were incredibly and deeply involved in a complicated relationship'. In some ways, Cale was protective of his girlfriend; the Factory was not a place generally considered a good environment for a college girl, and he never took her there.

One night, together with Reed, they visited a rock club in the West Village. Part of a small audience, they sat close to the stage and watched the Byrds play; one of the highlights of the evening was seeing Roger McGuinn singing 'Eight Miles High'. On another occasion when the three went out together Saturday night turned into Sunday morning, and by around 5 or 6 a.m. they were in an apartment building on East 15th Street, where a friend of Reed's lived. Cale sat at a small pedal pump organ and began to play. Words were spoken and then sung and repeated. A song began to take shape out of the time and the circumstances, its 'tone and melody . . . completely right for the plaintiveness of Sunday mornings' — and so was born the song that would become the opening track on *The Velvet Underground and Nico*.

"JOHN'S ACE L.A. DIVE"

At the end of its run at the Dom the 'Exploding Plastic Inevitable' barely paused before travelling to Los Angeles for a residency of what should have been more than two weeks at The Trip. This stay, however, was to be prematurely curtailed when the club was closed down by the Sheriff's Office after only three nights, on the grounds that the performances were 'pornographic'. For the visitors from New York, Los Angeles during the 'flower power' era was enough to make them curl their lips in contempt, while the citizens of Los Angeles in turn winced with disgust at the East Coast 'degenerates'.

Most of the Warhol crew stayed at the Castle, a mock-medieval rock-star mansion complete with dungeons co-owned by Tom Law, whose wife Lisa photographed the band there. During their stay, as Cale relates, 'Gerard Malanga found and claimed as a piece of "found poetry" a sheaf of papers tacked to the noticeboard in the kitchen. It was the Dylan world tour itinerary, left there by his entourage before leaving for Sydney. We pored over it in awe trying to understand what the times and numbers meant.'

Two nights at Bill Graham's Fillmore Auditorium in San Francisco at the end of the month did little more than cement the mutual antipathy between the two polarized cultural groups, but the West Coast venture was not entirely without success, as the band managed to spend some time with Tom Wilson in TTG Studios, nearly finishing the recording of their first album.

Tom Wilson had been responsible for introducing electric guitars into folk music with his production of Simon and Garfunkel's *Sounds of Silence* and had also produced the groundbreaking 'Like A Rolling Stone' for Bob Dylan. Dylan was a constant presence for the Velvet Underground, both as a rival and, in a rare exception to their low estimation of other rock artists, a benchmark for what could be achieved when rock 'n' roll transcended its supposed limitations. As Cale recalls, 'in or around '65 . . . every word that [Dylan] wrote was burning its way deep into our psyche'; the 'staggering amount of poetic violence from such an exquisite poison pen' would inform Cale's own lyric writing in his solo career.

The rivalry with Dylan and his camp was not only artistic but personal as well, as the to-ing and fro-ing with Nico and Edie Sedgwick had already shown. Dylan associate Bob Neuwirth was linked with Edie at a time when she was spiralling downwards into heroin addiction, and he would later re-emerge in Cale's solo career. On the return of the 'Exploding Plastic Inevitable' from California, the Dylan rivalry also entered the realm of business when the group, expecting to return to their residency at the Dom, found that their lease had been taken over by Dylan's manager Albert Grossman and his employee Charlie Rothchild. The venue had also been renamed the Balloon Farm. Although the Exploding Plastic Inevitable continued to perform until May 1967 and did play at the Balloon Farm, the perfect world that it had briefly inhabited at the Dom no longer existed, and the shows that had been put on there would never be equalled.

Cale went on to use visual elements to interact with his music during his solo career, but when these elements reappeared they would be very different in form and scale. Although he continued to toy with the idea, a return to any real mixed-media performance did not occur until the late 1980s and then it would be a much cooler, more carefully planned exercise.

Adding to the strains in the Velvet Underground, Lou Reed had been arguing with Andy Warhol about money, and the band were beginning to pay the price with the gradual removal of his support. Warhol was already losing interest in the 'Exploding

Plastic Inevitable' and turned down a potentially lucrative offer to take the show to Paris. For him, film was now becoming his most important activity, and he would spend most of the summer working on what would become a landmark production, *Chelsea Girls*.

In June the 'Exploding Plastic Inevitable' played at Poor Richard's in Chicago, without Lou Reed, who was in hospital in New York with hepatitis. The shows were well received. The songs had been reworked to fit Cale's keyboards rather than Reed's guitar, and Cale had worked hard on his vocals. For Cale, finding acceptance in the unaccustomed roles of vocalist and front man was an important development, although it was an experience that he would not capitalize on for several years yet.

At this time he was usually an approachable figure, friendly enough but also intense, with a seriousness that he might suddenly interrupt with a joke. He was generally uninterested in talking about music. He had a sense of honour, not necessarily shared by others at the Factory, and had no problem in standing up for someone who was being badly treated. He was decidedly non-macho, despite the gay culture around him that might have exaggerated his heterosexuality. The scene at the Factory did not phase him at all, but it did not necessarily make it any easier to relate to the women there, who by and large were 'sewn up too tight', as he describes them, although 'some did come running'. Cale was more elegant than Reed and was a more flamboyant if always tasteful dresser; he had a moody attractiveness that rivalled his partner's more up-front appeal. Kenneth Jay Lane, the costume designer, had asked Warhol for help with PR, and in return some of the Factory crowd had been allowed to choose items of his jewellery. As Cale remembers, 'We got to take our pick from his store . . . Edie had a lot . . . I got a snake necklace and a vinyl wristband.' Cale would combine his usual black clothing with an outrageous piece of jewellery, such as the necklace or a rhinestone choker, to striking effect. He had been christened 'Black Jack' by Sterling Morrison and was also known by Warhol as 'Welsh Rarebit'; Lou Reed was 'Lulu'. Cale, too, often came up with ideas that were either vetoed by Reed or incorporated by him into his own songs and, with the band attracting more attention, a certain amount of animosity began to grow up about how it should be divided.

With the Californian débâcle still fresh in their minds and the loss of the Dom adding to their disappointment, the Velvet Underground were frustrated still further in August when release of their recently finished début album was postponed by Verve, the company with which they had finally signed a hard-won record contract. More delays were to come, possibly owing to a desire within Verve to leave the way clear for a strong promotion of another of its new bands, Frank Zappa's Mothers of Invention. For Cale, having already seen many months of work with La Monte Young fail to produce any commercial outlet, this was another in what would prove to be a long line of frustrations with the music industry's inability successfully to convert his art into product.

On 6 August the Velvet Underground recorded 'Noise', a small contribution to the Hiroshima Day edition of 'electric newspaper' the *East Village Other*, putting a subversive musical commentary to some breathless reporting on the marriage of the US president's daughter Lucy Johnson.

During that summer the members of the Velvet Underground regularly attended Max's Kansas City, a club which had opened in late 1965. Andy Warhol had started to hold court in the backroom there, often paying the bill for a night's entertainment with one of his own paintings. Although the working side of his relationship with the band was on the wane, his milieu was one that the band would continue to share for some time.

In September the 'Exploding Plastic Inevitable' rolled into Provincetown, Massachusetts, to play two dates at the Chrysler Art Museum, which was housed in an old church. Although their reception was mixed, the Massachusetts location was a sign of things to come; before long nearby Boston would become a second home for the Velvet Underground. Boston was the base of Steve Sesnick who, with Warhol fading out of the picture, was angling to become the band's new manager. Sesnick would soon start to separate Lou Reed from the rest of the group – and particularly from Cale.

In October the Velvet Underground returned to 'their' venue, the Dom, now the Balloon Farm. Under its new ownership, however, it was an arrangement they could not tolerate for long. Not only was it no longer the perfect place to play, but it became a source of constant resentment against the people who had 'stolen' it from them, for whom they were now working.

In October and November another conflict between Reed and Cale developed when the latter very briefly moved in with Nico at her Upper West Side apartment. Reed and Nico had had a short affair earlier in the year, which had ended acrimoniously. Her presence in the band had always been a bone of contention, but for Cale now to be living with her after she had rejected Reed helped to undermine the relationship between the two men. As it was, the arrangement only lasted a couple of days, Cale describing his stay as 'harrowing'. In a November 'Exploding Plastic Inevitable' performance in Cincinnati the Velvet Underground refused to let Nico sing with them.

Although she returned in April and May, these would be her last appearances with the band. In the meantime she performed downstairs at the Balloon Farm, initially to a backing tape that Reed had recorded for her and then with a series of accompanists including Cale, Sterling Morrison, Tim Hardin and Tim Buckley.

In December reviews started to appear of the first Velvet Underground single, 'All Tomorrow's Parties', but there was little promotion from Verve and no sign of the kind of momentum that could have led to a successful launch for the eventual release of *The Velvet Underground and Nico*.

4
1967–1968

In March 1967, when the Velvet Underground's album finally emerged, any chance of its making an impact was almost immediately scotched. A dispute over the rights to a photograph of Factory member Eric Emerson on the cover resulted in the record's removal from the shops. While Emerson's image was airbrushed out and the sleeve reprinted, a more damaging problem was that, because of the hard-edged lyrical content of some of the songs, no New York radio station would give it airplay. What attention it did get occurred at a time when the record itself was impossible to buy, and when a new version did eventually appear the moment had passed. The album, of which so much had been expected by the band, failed to register.

Cale's contributions to *The Velvet Underground and Nico* are entirely in keeping with Lou Reed's exploration of desperation, the subconscious, subversive drives, decadence and different kinds of love. A one-not, rumbling bass guitar, primitive and elemental, anchors 'Run Run Run', while on 'I'm Waiting for the Man' Cale hammered away at the fifth on his piano 'for as long as I could before changing' and then, hands flattened across its keyboard, smashed out a pounding discord. On 'Venus in Furs' evil yelps highlight the cruelty of the insistent drone of his viola; his playing combines with the ritual smack of the tambourine, the funereal pace of Sterling Morrison's bass and the circling arpeggios of Reed's guitar to produce an atmosphere of unnatural pleasures, of hidden urges rising to the surface. For 'All Tomorrow's Parties' Cale made a 'prepared piano' by putting a chain of paper-clips between the instrument's strings. This conjured up a bell-like tone that brings an atmosphere of both purity and mystery to the song; his repetition of the piano's chord figure creates a hypnotic feel, too. Cale's viola on 'Heroin' maintains a constant drone throughout the song's initial changes of pace before erupting into screeches of feedback and what sounds like the screams of an overdriven jet engine; after the song's apocalyptic climax it shrugs off a last squall of feedback before returning to the drone and a final harmony with Reed's guitar. The closing pair of songs on *The Velvet Underground and Nico* both feature revolutionary interjections from Cale. In between the verses of 'Black Angel's Death Song' he attacks a microphone with venomous, resolutely finite hisses — the sound of a wild animal ready to fight or of water hurled on to red-hot metal. At the end of the first verse of 'European Son' he can be heard running a chair at high speed across the studio floor before sending it crashing into a glass panel. The song itself quickly becomes an anarchic tapestry of noise that is a brief taste of the band's live improvisations of the time, as well as being a foretaste of 'Sister Ray' — and a blueprint for the future of innovatory rock music.

Cale's bass-playing on *The Velvet Underground and Nico* has little in common with accepted practice and can be best heard on 'European Son', where it is everything it should not be: arrhythmic, it proceeds in pulses, runs and loops before launching a punishing assault of hammered notes and distortion and then accelerating to the climax of a trademark 'thunder machine' explosion.

Cale received a few co-writer credits for the album. The whole band was listed as composers of 'European Son', but he and Lou Reed were jointly responsible for 'Black Angel's Death Song' (which had been worked up between the two of them in Ludlow Street from Reed's lyric) and 'Sunday Morning'. Cale was gradually edging himself into song-writing and before long would add to his tally of recorded compositions on Nico's first solo album, *Chelsea Girl*.

This was titled to cash in on the success of Andy Warhol's film *Chelsea Girls*, which by January had been doing such good business that it had moved uptown from the Cinematheque on 41st Street, where it had opened. The song 'Chelsea Girls', which was featured on the album, had been scheduled to appear in the film, but with the Reed/Warhol disagreement this had not happened. The album was recorded in April and May at Mayfair Sound Studios in New York and included the first solo Cale song to see the light of day, 'Winter Song', along with a co-credit with Lou Reed for 'Little Sister' and a share of 'It Was a Pleasure Then' with Reed and Nico. Much of the album was marred by unfortunate arrangements, but 'It Was a Pleasure Then' was, despite the absence of Sterling Morrison and Moe Tucker, more a Velvet Underground song than a Nico one, having been taken from the band's live set. On this piece, one of the best the three ever worked on together, Reed and Cale provide Nico with the accompaniment and collaboration missing from the rest of the album – the kind of setting Cale would give her on her first 'proper' solo album, *The Marble Index*. Nico's voice is used here almost as an instrument, and it blends perfectly with Cale's viola and Reed's guitar, the three creating a space large enough for them to interact perfectly together. Sadly, although another such collaboration would later be considered, it never happened.

'Today, Noise triumphs and reigns supreme over the sensibility of men.'
(Luigi Russolo, The Art of Noise)

In May Cale and Sterling Morrison recorded 'At About This Time Mozart Was Dead and Joseph Conrad Was Sailing the Seven Seas Learning English', later to appear on *Stainless Steel Gamelan*. On this they shared viola and guitar, and Cale manipulated the 'instant pause' control on his Wollensak tape-recorder. Nothing like anything the Velvet Underground ever produced, this is a maniacal mélange of electronic machine and (what sounds like) insect noise. Here are the throbbing of a factory, the droning of a giant bee, percussive batterings like the drumming of the wings of a thousand giant insects, an aeroplane losing power, a helicopter taking off.

By June the Velvet Underground was rapidly returning to its previous integral shape. Nico had departed, the 'Exploding Plastic Inevitable' had run its course, and the cooling of Reed's relationship with Andy Warhol meant that Warhol was officially no longer the band's manager.

Over the summer Lou Reed and Sterling Morrison lived at a communal apartment on West 3rd Street, known as 'Sister Ray House', and Cale occasionally stayed there, too, although sleeping arrangements were pretty relaxed. As its name suggests, it was here that the band concocted the poisonous mixture for what would be their most extreme musical statement, 'Sister Ray'.

In July the Velvet Underground played at a benefit for Merce Cunningham at Philip Johnson's Glass House in Greenwich, Connecticut. This was the last occasion on which Cale recalls seeing John Cage's 'giggling face'. After the gig the band travelled back to New York and made the decision to appoint Steve Sesnick as their new manager.

Sesnick had identified Reed as the prime commercial force behind the band and, once installed, began to pursue a strategy of boosting Reed's self-image and isolating him from the other members. The idea was to increase the band's moneymaking capacity and also to ally himself with Reed, who was the key to that increase. Sesnick would effectively create a new power-base that would bring the band under the control of the two of them. Although the Velvet Underground was now back to its 'original' creative form, its balance was nevertheless changing again. Feeding on the other tensions already apparent, it was a change that would see Cale forced out in not much more than a year.

At the end of January 1952 Dylan and Caitlin Thomas moved into the Chelsea Hotel.

Another of these tensions arose from the results of a second meeting, in May 1967, between Cale and Betsey Johnson. Betsey was living in the Chelsea Hotel, making costumes for the Edie Sedgwick film *Ciao! Manhattan*, and this time the two hit it off together. Cale later moved in with her at the Chelsea, before sharing a loft she rented on La Guardia Place; by August they were engaged. Betsey made a few clothes for the members of the band, and Cale wanted her to make masks for him to wear on stage. This never happened, but it was an idea that would surface again early in his solo performing career. In her closet Betsey still has a fencing outfit that Cale had bought for use as a stage costume.

During the second week in September the Velvet Underground began recording their second album, *White Light/White Heat*, again at Mayfair Sound Studios. It was the height of the 'Summer of Love', and the streets were deserted — everyone had headed off to the West Coast to join in the celebrations. In the studio the atmosphere was rather different. Fuelled by amphetamines and volume levels that they were told were impossible to record, the band created their most uncompromising album. A month or two earlier Cale and Reed had seen Jimi Hendrix play at the Salvation Club in Sheridan Square. Cale recalls walking along 4th Street listening to the BBC World Service on his short-wave radio when he heard 'Hey Joe', 'with all the standing waves sweeping the music and blistering guitar in and out of tuning for the BBC . . . Lou couldn't believe it.' Inside the club Hendrix 'had a heckler in the crowd, whom he shut up by commenting that "Polly Parrot was in the audience tonight"'. Maybe some of Hendrix's musical extremism permeated the sessions, because there was feedback, distortion and leakage everywhere. When the album was finished the band were all agreed that it was a 'technical failure' — but then recording technique never had been their strong point. What was more important was that it was a hugely powerful and groundbreaking piece of work.

Much of *White Light/White Heat* consists of musical improvisation. There are only six songs, compared with the début's eleven and, of these, two last less than a couple of minutes each. The tracks were recorded live in the studio with a minimum of embellishment, and this album says more than their début does about the spontaneous creation of music that was at the core of the band's live performances. This really was their essence and what Cale, in particular, had been aiming at all along. Despite this, there was still plenty of formal experimentation: Cale's suggestion of combining a narrated short story with an instrumental for 'The Gift'; the spoken interjections and sound effects in 'Lady Godiva's Operation'; the sheer length of 'Sister Ray'; not to mention the album's black sleeve with a faint outline of Billy Name's skull-and-crossbones tattoo.

With Nico gone, so, too, were the 'and Nico' songs. This was an uncompromising depiction of the Velvet Underground's worldview and, in 'Sister Ray' in particular, of the various tensions that had been building up within the band. Despite this, the abiding impression is of the sheer pleasure they took in playing together, with everyone contributing ideas and making room for each other (even on 'Sister Ray') to express themselves. Blasting the roof off the studio was a great way to release the pressure inside it.

Cale's influence is evident even more here than on *The Velvet Underground and Nico*, with every song indisputably bearing his mark. Reed's guitar-playing bares his soul as never before, but there is the strong impression that being in the same room with Cale at his most forceful and combative pushed him towards his achievement.

Cale gives the *White Light/White Heat* album much of its distinctive sound, from some demented 'Jerry Lee Lewis' piano poundings to viola sawings, slabs of distorted bass and abrasive organ assaults. On 'The Gift', his bass guitar produces a sound so fat that the listener can almost see the speaker bulging from its cabinet, and the riff is repeated over and over again before its pattern changes to slide back up the guitar's neck, as protagonist Waldo Jeffers's excitement increases. On 'I Heard Her Call My Name', his bass pumps frenetically with the song's momentum but also provides subtle pulses and darts that are sometimes almost subliminal; there is also an amazing and brief lead break from him that, in a high register, whips around at a breathtaking speed quite alien to the rest of the bass part.

The idea of putting something like 'Sister Ray' on a 'rock 'n' roll' album in 1967 was outrageous, and a record company more involved with their band than Verve might well have refused to release it. The band was like a group of soldiers in training for months who are suddenly given the chance to show the world what they are made of. The track is a musical battleground, but the battle is not really one for control between the (male) members of the band; it is more a competition between them to see who can lay waste to the most territory. With Moe Tucker at the back pounding out the rhythm that anchored them, one by one, each of the other band members moves ahead of the rest before one of the others pulls him back and takes his place. The final victory, however, was Cale's, and it was the result of a conscious strategy: 'I kept everything low until a certain point then unleashed the volume I'd been saving,' he says

White Light/White Heat contained Cale's first vocal performances on record. On 'The Gift' this took the form of a narration, telling the story of Waldo Jeffers, which, although generally matter-of-fact, also manages to express a certain amount of both sympathy at Jeffers's state of mind and relish at his violent end. Singing on the gruesome 'Lady Godiva's Operation', Cale manages a misleading tone of innocence. This track was also furnished with some distinctive sound effects: heavy breathing, demented purring, secretive whispering and shuddering sighs.

In the autumn of 1967, although each member of the Velvet Underground was living separately, they were still playing and socializing together regularly. Against this background, Lou Reed wrote Cale a four-line poem,'Forewarned Is Forearmed', threatening to kill him should he ever emotionally desert him. Back in 1965 Cale had written his own poem, 'Curse', to Reed; Angus MacLise had read it and retorted, 'Hey John, far fucking out. This is a love poem!' Reed asked whether it really was a curse and, if it were, would Cale please remove it.

In September Andy Warhol's film **** was finished, and Cale appeared in one of its segments, 'Philadelphia Story', as a Western 'bad guy', a masked outlaw. In stills he can be seen brandishing a rifle, a cannon ball and a pitchfork. In December, while in Spain, he bought a swordstick and his first gun.

In October the Velvet Underground played in what was now becoming their second home, Boston, and would never again play New York with Cale in the band. New York, which had seemingly rejected the band by banning its records from the radio, was now in turn rejected by being banned from seeing it play live.

During December Cale and Reed were interviewed by Tom Wilson to promote the upcoming release of *White Light/White Heat*. Cale, it was revealed, having recently moved into Betsey's loft in La Guardia Place, had begun putting together the beginnings of a studio there. All his instruments had been gathered together: not only the viola, organ and bass but also all the bowed instruments he had been able to find, including Eastern ones such as the sarinda, the serongi and the dilruba. Cale thought that record albums should be released together with colouring books and toys and that music should be created which, by using both ultra-high and ultra-low frequencies, could be made to create weather. Tapes might be compiled that would consistently regulate the heat around the listener.

Cale used the loft in La Guardia Place for plenty of experimental solo recordings, while he continued to listen to the music of La Monte Young and Terry Riley there. 'Sun Blindness Music', from the CD of the same name, was recorded in the loft in late October and is almost a continuation of the 'Sister Ray' that had been recorded a month earlier, with a harsh, overdriven sound, mixtures of different sustains and volume surges. 'After the Locust', which would appear on *Stainless Steel Gamelan*, was taped there, too, and has more echoes of *White Light/White Heat*, featuring remorseless noise from the 'thunder machine' (operated here by Tony Conrad) and the sound of explosions and air-raid sirens — all set to a beat. 'The Second Fortress', from the same period, features electronic drones veering towards the edge of feedback and slight pitch shifts, together with a wider palette of sounds in its middle section. 'Ex Cathedra' and 'Carousel', also of similar vintage and both later to be included on *Dream Interpretation*, see a further shift towards pulses and effects, particularly echo, and some high-register synthesizer-like repetition.

In December Cale and Betsey took their first holiday together, visiting the Virgin Islands and Spain in search of the sun. In Cádiz Cale purchased two Barcelona football shirts and combined them into one piece. This would later appear as a dress on a 'tiny' model in a fashion show for Paraphernalia. They also visited Wales together, where they stayed with his parents over Christmas.

On 30 January 1968 *White Light/White Heat* was released. Like its predecessor it received almost no radio play, owing to its lyrics. Unlike *The Velvet Underground and Nico*, however, there was no longer a Warhol connection to make up for the lack of commercial attention. Production-wise it was seen as pretty much impenetrable and, although the title track was released as a single, it had none of the commercial potential of even the failed singles from the first album and made no headway. The album consequently died a commercial death.

If the recording of *White Light/White Heat* was a victory for Cale over Steve Sesnick, the tide of that particular battle effectively turned after its failure to sell. Sesnick's base in Boston now took over from New York as the band's centre, and Sesnick pushed Lou Reed towards writing more commercial material, telling him that he had what it took to become a successful rock star. While Reed began heading in this new direction, Betsey Johnson was pushing Cale in a divergent one, persuading him that his talents were deserving of more attention than they were getting. She also began designing more clothes for him, with the result that he began to cut a more flamboyant figure on stage, something that increasingly developed into a problem for Reed.

Touring became a way of life now for the Velvet Underground and brought with it the tensions of a life on the road to add to those already present.

On 9 March 1902 Gustav Mahler married Alma Schindler.

In February Cale and Betsey Johnson, engaged since the previous August, announced that they were about to get married. For Reed this seemed a formal declaration that the Velvet Underground was now no longer Cale's number-one priority. Soon after the announcement, however, the wedding was postponed, as Cale was, once again, diagnosed with hepatitis and spent the next four weeks in hospital, but it went ahead in April, and Lou Reed was there in a suit and carrying flowers.

In January, before *White Light/White Heat* was released, Cale had played two nights of Terry Jennings's music at the Steinway Hall in New York with La Monte Young, Terry Riley, Tony Conrad and Jennings himself, organized by Young. On 8 February Cale had recorded what would later be released on the *Dream Interpretation* set as 'A Midnight Rain of Green Wrens at the World's Tallest Building' with himself on viola and Conrad on violin – an eerie piece, mournful and almost melodic, with the two instruments slipping in and out of harmony. Conrad recalls that he and Cale recorded five separate amplified sets in February, with Conrad playing 'limp-string' and Cale on guitar. He was keeping his hand in.

In February the Velvet Underground recorded two new songs, 'Stephanie Says' and 'Temptation Inside Your Heart', both commercially orientated, although the former is in the mould of the 'Nico' songs from the first album. The idea had been to try to record a single, and this was pursued further at the end of May when, surprisingly, they recorded two takes of the decidedly non-commercial 'Hey Mr Rain' back at TTG Studios in Hollywood – the last song Cale would record with them.

By now the Velvet Underground's live shows were often furious affairs, the band's strengthening demons being exorcized temporarily on stage.

In the spring Nico moved in with Fred Hughes, Andy Warhol's business manager, on East 16th Street, just across from the Union Square site of Warhol's new Factory. Here she would lie in the bath with all her clothes on, surrounded by candles, and sing songs from what later that year would become *The Marble Index*. Occasionally, she would also stay with Cale and Betsey – living underneath the sink.

On 3 June Andy Warhol was shot by Valerie Solanas and came close to death, an incident that Cale and Reed wrote about more than twenty years later on *Songs for Drella*. When Warhol recovered and returned to the Factory his way of living and working had changed, and the freedom, experimentation and 'open door' policy of the 'Warhol 1960s' were effectively over. Reed was deeply affected by the shooting but nevertheless allowed the complications of their relationship to prevent him from visiting Warhol in hospital. For him the incident and its aftermath was perhaps a signal that he should bring an end to the first phase of the Velvet Underground's career. Three months later he would push Cale out of the band.

In July the Velvet Underground played at the Hippodrome in San Diego, and the performance featured the first live outing for a song called 'Sweet Rock and Roll', also known as 'Sister Ray Part Two'. Cale's keyboard part carried the song to the extent that it was never played again after he left. The band also featured 'What Goes On', which would later be recorded and performed live without him but which would never capture the intensity of his organ-driven version. Another new song was 'Ocean', which had a strange afterlife when Cale would return 'from the dead' to play on a version recorded in 1970. All of these songs had Cale at their core, but it was a core that would soon be ripped out; musical exploration in the Velvet Underground after his departure would take more and more of a back seat.

He played his last shows with the band at Sesnick's Boston Tea Party on 27 and 28 September 1968. Reed had told Moe Tucker and Sterling Morrison that either Cale went or the band ceased to exist, and they had been effectively forced to go along with him. Backstage photos show both Cale and Reed as sombre figures – one of the most innovative partnerships in rock music had been dissolved.

On 9 March 1918 the Russian Bolshevik Party became the Communist Party.

Part 3
Calembour
(a pun)

On 9 March 1942 the last radio episode of *Superman* was broadcast.

By October 1968 Cale was already working on his first production assignment — and also had a solo recording contract with CBS in the bag. The album he was working on at Elektra Sound Recorders in Los Angeles was Nico's *The Marble Index*. Only a month after his ejection from the Velvet Underground it seemed as though Cale had landed on his feet and had immediately set off at a run. In fact this momentum would soon falter and, used as he was to immersing himself in music throughout his waking hours, the next five years would simply not bring him enough work. Unwilling as yet to make live appearances as a solo artist, his post-Velvet Underground solo career did not really take off in this period, while production work would prove to be only inter-mittent. Before long, restless and bored, Cale was to split up with the successful, per-manently busy and often absent Betsey and, in order to to compensate for the absences in his life, was to renew a relationship with heroin that had lapsed during his marriage. The Velvet Underground had occupied his waking hours for four years, and without the band members he would soon be surrounded by an empty space that was crying out to be filled. At the end of 1968, however, in his and Betsey's large loft he con-tinued to play music and to experiment. He now began to turn himself into a songwriter. This would be necessary if he was to build on his years with the Velvet Underground.

Jac Holzman, head of Elektra Records, had offered Nico the chance to record her new songs for his label, and she had called on Cale to arrange her compositions, origi-nally written for harmonium and voice, and effectively turn their two dimensions into three. Over a mere four days he would do just that, recording her parts first and then returning to the studio alone to push the songs out into the atmosphere.

Cale and Nico were both outcasts from the Velvet Underground, anxious to prove themselves on their own merits, and *The Marble Index* is an album of songs and music from two people with individual visions creating a new world together. It is almost a polar opposite to the work of the Velvet Underground: European not American, ancient not modern, more 'female' than 'male', with no backbeat and no electric guitars. Completely lacking in street realism, it exudes a different kind of displacement from that felt by Lou Reed, one affected by the past and by memory.

Nico had never really been able to express herself in the Velvet Underground and never really seemed to be respected there. Reed had used her more as an instrument than as a performer, but now Cale had allowed her to make a more substantial and highly distinctive artistic statement.

Although *The Marble Index* was recognized in some critical quarters as a groundbreaking work, it was more typically misunderstood and would have to wait until the post-punk area for a full acknowledgement of its worth.

In February of 1969 Cale and Terry Conrad recorded 'Dream Interpretation' – later to appear on the CD of the same name – which featured a low, distorted viola drone that picked up from the point at which the Velvet Underground had left it. Cale and Conrad would also make a temporary return in 1969 to La Monte Young's Theater of Eternal Music for both rehearsals and performances. This time each would sign contracts stating that the music that they would play had been written by Young. Cale also played some Chopin for the soundtrack to Tony and Beverley Conrad's film *Coming Attractions*, which was completed in 1970. Betsey Johnson designed the costumes, and Tally Brown, who had once been approached by Andy Warhol to join the Velvet Underground, acted in it.

Jac Holzman at Elektra was impressed with Cale's work on Nico's album, however, and would soon enable him to add the perfect name to his producer's curriculum vitae, the one that, taken alongside that of Nico, would both have the appropriate cachet and show that he could produce pretty much anything: the Stooges. In June Cale produced *The Stooges* – at the Hit Factory in New York – in half the time it had taken to record *The Marble Index*: two days. Nico would sit next to Cale as he worked in the studio. He wore a black cape with a large collar, and Nico knitted.

Cale's production of the Stooges concentrated on clarity and straightforwardness, the production of a man intent on pursuing this line of work professionally, as a serious source of income. It was an intent that would bear fruit but not for some time. Meanwhile he had a couple of underground 'names' under his producer's belt.

There was also some session work in 1969 to bring in a little money: acoustic guitar on one track of Earth Opera's *Great American Eagle Tragedy* and viola on the début album from a short-lived folk-rock band, Chelsea.

At the end of the year Cale had five poems published in *Aspen* magazine: 'The Fish', 'Boys', 'Stolen', 'Lightening' and 'Sebastian'. Rooted in Europe rather than in the USA, where he had now been living for six years, these pieces are sombre and quietly menacing, and depict landscapes and people merging with people, people whose lives are ruled by tyranny, war and compromise. History lies behind these poems and a sense of its tragedy spreading through the past into the future. The characters in the poems are psychologically complex, their motivations often mysterious and at odds with those around them. Mental battles are fought as well as military ones. Children are knowing victims who plan revolts against their parents, progress is made only through contemptuous perseverance and thoughts of escape, which permeate the poems, seem to be almost drowning in a thick syrup of corruption, treachery and inertia. There is plenty of Cale's life to be read into these texts, although not in explicit terms: the childhood frustration weighed down by opium, the flight from

Wales into the further snare of heroin use, the feeling of betrayal after being forced out of the Velvet Underground, a kind of bewildered paralysis about the future. There is a hint of Dylan Thomas's presence in the bleak landscapes and the mining of the dark night of the soul: it is his imagery, rather than the use of Dadaist and Surrealist juxtapositions, that lies behind the style of Cale's writing at this point.

In the 1860s Privates John Cale and John McClure were both members of the 3rd Kentucky Cavalry Regiment: Cale in Company D; McClure in Company M.

In 1970 John McClure was director of the CBS Masterworks programme, but the job was starting to frustrate him. Having worked with figures such as Igor Stravinsky and Leonard Bernstein, he now found himself handling already familiar pieces of music for a second and sometimes a third time. Clive Davis from CBS gave him the chance to extend the remit of Masterworks to include minimalism, jazz and rock, and he was only too willing to take it. McClure was an admirer of John Cage and also knew visual artists such as Robert Rauschenberg. McClure worked with Cage for a while and, among other projects, tried to reproduce the famous 'Cage versus Duchamp' chess match for recorded release, but the results were unsuccessful. The Rauschenberg and Warhol circles mingled together to a certain extent and, with Cage also as a connection, McClure and Cale had soon came to know one another. Previously McClure had enjoyed seeing the Velvet Underground play and had tried to sign them to Masterworks but had been rebuffed by the label. When Cale was ousted from the Velvet Underground McClure almost immediately offered him a two-album record deal, which Cale was happy to accept. McClure had been responsible for releasing the first big-label record for minimalist composer Steve Reich as well as Terry Riley's début and wanted to give Cale a similar opportunity. For MacClure, these signings were, he says, 'a way of formalizing an interest in that whole genre of music and just hoping that something would strike, some spark would happen'. For Cale here was a chance to develop his solo career in two directions at once – there could be an instrumental album that commercialized the work he had done with La Monte Young and an album of songs that would launch him as a singer and songwriter.

McClure suggested that Cale join forces with Terry Riley, whose revolutionary *In C* album CBS had already released. Cale and Riley had worked together in La Monte Young's Theater of Eternal Music, and the pair had also collaborated together outside this group, sometimes with Angus MacLise. Cale wanted MacLise – and Sterling Morrison, with whom he was still hanging around – to play on what was to become *Church of Anthrax*, but, as it turned out, neither was in town when the sessions were recorded, and the plans came to nothing.

It was decided that for *Church of Anthrax* to be able to cross over to any real extent into the rock 'n' roll market there would have to be a definable rock beat behind it, and so drummers Bobby Colomby from Blood Sweat and Tears and Bobby Gregg, who had played with the Hawks, were brought in. For Cale, the album would be an opportunity to bring together the work of the Velvet Underground and that of the Theater of Eternal Music.

Another quick-fire production, *Church of Anthrax* was recorded over three days at CBS Studio, a converted church on East 30th Street. The album was completely improvised, apart from one Cale song, 'The Soul of Patrick Lee', and co-produced by Cale, who took care of most of the mixing and editing while MacClure concentrated on the logistics.

Church of Anthrax features sustained tones, La Monte Young-like saxophone, insistent, often pounding beats and hypnotic keyboard sequences. The long tracks allow enough time to develop improvisations, and, in a melting pot of sounds, there is plenty of overdubbing.

Cale worked on the album's post-production after Riley had left, and Riley was unhappy with the result. The sleeve is dominated by Cale, with his short prose piece 'Caricature' and lyrics to 'The Soul of Patrick Lee' on the back. The front cover featured three separate images of Cale to a single, repeated and colourized image of Riley (à la Warhol) in a picture frame.

'The Soul of Patrick Lee' shares a similar English folk-song feel with the early versions of 'Venus in Furs' and also a similar guitar line. Lyrically it draws upon the Welsh landscape and the past and deals with death and tragedy.

Cale's prose pieces, such as 'Caricature' here and 'Beirut', which would appear in *Creem* magazine in 1973, are Surrealist in nature. They have incisive titles that collide with the texts, strident and contradictory images, disjointed sentences and unconscious narratives. Their meanings are derived from the juxtapositions and sounds of words and phrases, and their intention is to shock, disrupt and destroy. In an interview for *Sounds*, on 4 September 1971, he would say that his short stories 'end up as maps and charts' and that the songs he writes run into the stories.

After finishing *Church of Anthrax*, which was not released until February 1971, Cale began rehearsing with Garland Jeffreys's band Grinderswitch, working with them on the songs that would appear on the *Vintage Violence* album which, despite being recorded after *Church of Anthrax*, would actually be released first.

Vintage Violence is full of short songs, 'about things I'd thought about that morning', he says in the *Sounds* interview, with instrumental development kept to a minimum. Musically reminiscent of Van Morrison and the Band, the lyrics are mainly in the mould of Cale's prose pieces of the time, some British in tone, some American. Room is made, nevertheless, for a song about lost love in 'Amsterdam', the wistfulness of 'Big

White Cloud' and even, in the catchy 'Cleo', a potential hit single. Cale's vocals are sometimes hesitant and coated with reverb, but the material was undoubtedly strong, particularly considering the fact that Cale was known, where he was known at all, as an instrumentalist, arranger and producer rather than as a writer. Promoted well, it could have been a success, but CBS did not seem to understand the album's strengths. It was almost as if no one had actually listened to the record and had considered only instead the title which, like many of Cale's song and story titles, was not meant to be a literal description of its content. CBS allowed the album to go out with a ghoulish cover, and their press advertisements for it featured the phrase 'It's been a long time bleeding'. Andy Warhol had come up with a cover for the album, but it had been rejected. It had featured Cale with long hair; by the time the album was ready his hair was short and the image out of date.

Cale's intentions for the album, too, seem to have been contradictory. He had written it as an exercise in song-writing and had limited his experimentation to a proportion of the lyrics. Having succeeded in producing a commercial record, he had gone a long way towards dooming it by its title and cover – and by being unwilling to tour in support of it. Still not confident enough in his abilities as a solo performer, it would be another four years before he began his first tour.

At the end of July Cale was in London, finishing off work on Nico's *Desertshore* album, which he had begun a couple of months earlier at Vanguard studios in New York. The recording was completed at Sound Techniques, a studio just off the King's Road in Chelsea run by John Wood, with whom Cale would work extensively.

Joe Boyd, who was running his own Witchseason production and management company, featuring artists such as Nick Drake and Fairport Convention, had heard that Elektra, disappointed with the sales of *The Marble Index*, were dropping Nico and had decided to offer to make her next record. He managed to convince Warner Brothers to sign her and got in touch with Cale, purely on the basis of his work on *The Marble Index*, and told him that he would only go ahead with the project if Cale agreed to produce it. Once again Cale was happy to do so.

Living opposite Sound Techniques on Old Church Street at the time was Kate Heliczer, Piero's wife, and she was friendly with Marianne Faithfull, whose own house was near by. Faithfull used to bring her mother around on visits, and sometimes these resulted in drunken brawls. Kate Heliczer lent Cale an eight-millimetre camera, with which he made a short film, *Police Car*. 'I was interested in getting dim pictures with the flashing lights from a street repair trench near the Chelsea Bridge. The film was left with someone in Fluxus who then included it in a box of Flux-stuff which I totally forgot about until I got a call from someone saying my "movie"'was mentioned in the *New York Times* review of the box.'

Joe Boyd was working extensively with John Wood and introduced Cale to him.

Wood specialized in folk music, but Cale and Boyd fed him a diet of rock 'n' roll, and he soon began to develop a taste for it, too. Wood went on to work on *Academy in Peril*, under the alias 'Jean Bois', and all Cale's albums for the Island label.

Boyd remembers Cale and Nico maintaining a distant but respectful relationship during the recording of *Desertshore*. Cale would roll his eyes at some of Nico's suggestions, which he sometimes vetoed. After he had returned to New York Nico made a few changes to what had been done and Cale was not pleased. *Desertshore*, like *The Marble Index* before it, was an artistic success that met with a mixed reaction critically and a blank one commercially, but it was unequivocally another positive indication of Cale's arranging and production talents.

While in London Cale and Boyd got to know each other well and became friends. Cale expressed interest in the other artists Boyd was working with, and the latter played him some tracks that had been recorded for Nick Drake's *Bryter Layter* album. Cale demanded Drake's address and went over to see him that same afternoon. The next morning, as Boyd remembers, 'Cale called up and ordered a celeste and a Hammond to be delivered to the studio I had booked and came in dragging a bemused Nick behind him. The result was "Fly" and "Northern Sky".'

Boyd also played Cale some of the solo album by the Incredible String Band's Mike Heron, *Smiling Men With Bad Reputations*, and Cale went on to play all the instruments bar one on its 'Feast of Stephen' and to appear on three other tracks.

The performance of Antonin Artaud's play *Les Cenci*, on 6 May 1935, was the first occasion on which stereophonic sound was used in the theatre.

Back in New York, over the summer, the tensions between Cale and Betsey Johnson had increased, and they now separated, with Cale moving to a new apartment on 28th Street between Madison and Lexington Avenues. He was now working on a job that John McClure had 'improvised' for him, mixing existing CBS back catalogue material for quadraphonic sound. Quadraphony proved to be an idea whose time had yet to come; none of the systems used was able to come up with the goods in terms of a finished product mastered on to disc, the one developed by CBS being 'invented' in the back of a taxi after hearing the demonstration of a rival system. Cale's work provided a steady income, but there was no real creative input for him to make, and he felt himself on a treadmill. Partly to cope with the boredom of his new employment, he began using heroin again – and found the work becoming increasingly necessary to fund his habit.

Cale spent Christmas 1970 at his parents' house in Wales and travelled up to London afterwards to work on Mike Heron's album – and also to play his first gig as a solo artist.

On 17 January he performed on the same bill as Nico and Pink Floyd at the Roundhouse in Chalk Farm. Cale, dressed casually in turtleneck jumper and shirt, played viola and piano for Nico and was then joined by Mike Heron for a selection of songs from *Vintage Violence*. A low-key one-off, the performance was nevertheless proof to Cale that he could perform his own material live. While in London he revealed that he now had his own production company, Hit and Run Productions, to which Nico was signed. He expressed a desire to back her with the English Chamber Orchestra.

By now Cale's New York lifestyle, with Betsey gone, had become claustrophobic and deadening, and he jumped at an offer from Joe Boyd to work with him on film music at Warner Brothers Records headquarters in Los Angeles. Cale had also been offered a job as an executive producer in New York by CBS, but he now turned it down. The thought of escaping from everything that was dragging him down to work on a project with real artistic possibilities, far away in the regenerative sunshine of the West Coast, was too good an opportunity to waste.

Early in 1971 Cale forsook New York and heroin for Los Angeles — and cocaine. As soon as he walked into the Warner Brothers offices there, the smell of pharmaceuticals was in the air and it was to prove an irresistible lure.

Cale was originally supposed to be concentrating on film music, but before long the focus of his work shifted exclusively to rock 'n' roll. Joe Boyd had felt that he would be perfect for soundtrack work, a judgement that would be borne out in later years, but the directors brought together with Cale did not know what to make of him. He 'auditioned' for the soundtrack to *The Omega Man*, improvising an accompaniment to a five-minute scene, but director Boris Sagal was not sympathetic to his approach, and Cale was not taken on.

He had moved into his own apartment on arriving in Los Angeles and then into a house in the Hollywood Hills. Before long, however, he was sharing Joe Boyd's house on Woodrow Wilson Drive. Boyd was living there with his girlfriend Linda Peters, who later married Richard Thompson. On one occasion Cale, Boyd and Linda Peters went to Santa Monica Civic Auditorium to see the Bee Gees play with a full orchestra, an experience that all three enjoyed immensely. Cale's work was not onerous, his environment pleasant, and he had just bought himself a Shelby 350 GT Mustang, having recently learned to drive. Life seemed pretty good. Set against the benefits of his new lifestyle, however, were a number of drawbacks: a rapidly forming cocaine habit, a feeling that he did not really fit into this new environment and the nagging suspicion that he was not achieving enough in his own right as an artist. Soon to be added to his list of problems would be the arrival in his life of (Miss) Cindy, an ex-member of Frank Zappa's groupie band the GTOs, whom he would marry.

During an interview for *Rolling Stone* in February 1969 Cindy had said: 'I'm the chronic liar of the group . . . I can't remember anything . . . I don't know how old I am, I'm from everywhere.' The article described her as 'gentle and sad'. Cale was attracted by Cindy's combination of beauty and volatility, but his efforts to bring stability to her personality through marriage were to prove tragically ineffectual.

Since leaving the Velvet Underground Cale had wanted to write a symphony and, following the commercial failure of *Vintage Violence* and *Church of Anthrax*, the time seemed right time to do it. In early 1972, after another Christmas in Wales, he was temporarily back in England, recording at the Manor in Oxfordshire.

Academy in Peril took three weeks to write, record and mix and, despite Cale's intentions of writing a symphony, featured only three orchestral pieces. These had originally been intended to form the basis of the symphony, but what Cale saw as the lack of development between them meant that the idea was shelved. That and the fact that on arrival at the studio he had begun with a piece of shuffling rock 'n' roll, 'King Harry', and enjoyed the experience so much that he wanted to do more. With two weeks to wait until the orchestra was booked in at London's Church of St Giles's Cripplegate, he used the time not only to work up his three orchestral pieces but effectively to distract himself with a mixture of other material, particularly when friends Ron Wood, then of the Faces, and 'Legs' Larry Smith from the Bonzo Dog Band turned up to help out on a track each. 'Legs' Larry was himself recording in Oxford at the time, and the two worked on several other pieces, none of which were regarded as successful enough to be used. When the time arrived for Cale to begin work with the Royal Philharmonic at Cripplegate, he already had his three 'movements' scored and had also recorded a piano piece, 'John Milton'. Cale had to listen to this piece on headphones as he conducted the orchestra accompanying it. He had been inspired to write 'John Milton' after watching a BBC *Omnibus* documentary. It was only when the session had begun, however, that he found out that Milton was in fact buried at Cripplegate. Cale knew a few members of the orchestra already – including Berian Evans – as they had previously been in the National Youth Orchestra of Wales with him, and they told him to watch out for the principal violist, who was liable to exploit any signs of weakness in the rookie conductor and who would attempt to dominate the session. When Cale found out that this was Frederic Riddle, a hero of his, he introduced himself. From this point on, Riddle helped to run the session for him. Cale noted that the mentality of the orchestral players was the opposite to that of rock musicians and that they enjoyed having discipline imposed on them. The principal cellist, he discovered, was in fact a moonlighting mathematician.

The end result is perhaps Cale's most wide-ranging album. His orchestral pieces and piano work are slow, even mournful, reflecting his stated disenchantment with the frenetic life and music of New York. Of the rock 'n' roll material, 'Days of Steam' is an out-and-out, feel-good instrumental, but the other pieces rebel against their upbeat tempi: 'The Philosopher' (originally entitled 'Woodwork') with its wind effects and footsteps, 'King Harry' with its sinister whispered vocal and 'Legs Larry at Television Centre' with its surreal juxtaposition of a camp 'monologue' from 'television producer' Smith and a mournful viola duet.

The Academy in Peril is the sound of a man not yet able to express his unique vision satisfactorily — but that would soon come. In the meantime Warners seemed happy enough with something that was never going to make them much money but which would receive a certain amount of appreciative attention in influential quarters.

On 29 January an unlikely reunion took place at the Bataclan club in Paris between Cale, Lou Reed and Nico. With Cale and Nico both well into their solo careers, although not selling large quantities of their albums, and Reed just starting his own, it made sense for the three to join together again and grab some exposure. Since Cale's departure from the Velvet Underground, Reed had gone out of his way to praise his former band-mate's talents, and the two had undergone a certain rapprochement; this kind of encounter was certainly no threat to anyone. There had been talk of Cale producing Reed's *Lou Reed* album, and the actual production by Richard Robinson would end up sounding very similar to that on Cale's *Vintage Violence*. The trio played a mixture of solo material and Velvet Underground songs to an ecstatic French audience that had never been able to see the original band. Originally, it had been intended that there be a British follow-up gig, but this never materialized. The next year both Cale and Reed would turn to Europe for new albums,— Cale to *Paris, 1919*, and Reed to *Berlin* — and their careers would continue to track each other's closely over the years.

Cale's production work continued throughout 1972, exclusively for Warner Brothers artists now that he was under contract to them, and this resulted in albums by Jennifer Warnes and Jonathan Richman's Modern Lovers, for whom he also provided some pounding Velvet Underground-style vintage piano on 'Pablo Picasso'.

When Cale had begun work for Warner Brothers as a producer he had still been under contract to CBS, and a potential single, 'Dixieland and Dixie', was recorded in Los Angeles for possible release by CBS. The track was produced by Ted Templeman, who brought along young guitarist named Lowell George to play on it. Cale was so impressed with him that he asked George and his band Little Feat to play on what was to become *Paris, 1919*.

In the spring of 1972 Procol Harum had released their orchestra-backed *Live at Edmonton* album. Cale heard it, was impressed with its sound and got in touch with Chris Thomas, its producer, to ask him, too, to work on *Paris, 1919*.

In the winter of that year sessions at Sunwest studios in Los Angeles began. By this time Cale had, in what would be an almost unique situation in his career, already written all the songs that would appear on the album, and it proved to be one of his most professional, with the accomplished band picking up the material almost immediately and playing it with the minimum of rehearsal. Chris Thomas used to work late into the night refining what had been recorded. The result was the first complete statement of Cale's solo career, a stronger, more unified piece of work than *Vintage Violence* but one that built on that album's accomplishments to establish a solid base for him as a songwriter. The basics had now well and truly been understood and implemented, and from this period on Cale's experimentation in the field of rock 'n' roll would have a firm foundation. This was comparable to the grounding that his classical education had given to his work with the Theater of Eternal Music and the basis that it had given in turn to what he had gone on to achieve with the Velvet Underground. A not inconsiderable factor in these successive foundations was the provision of an accepted practice that could then be subverted.

Cale, Thomas and the band used to go into the studio at midday every day and work until six in the evening, the short working day a testament to the ease with which the musicians learned and interpreted the songs. On one occasion Chris Thomas happened to walk past the music stand of Wilton Felder from the Crusaders, who was bass guitarist on the session. The band had been played the song they were working on only once by Cale; Felder had immediately memorized both the song and the part he would play for it and was using the 'spare' time to read the Bible.

Despite the fact that Cale had first been attracted to the idea of using Thomas as producer after hearing the combination of strings and rock band on *Live at Edmonton* – and that he had recently finished *Academy in Peril* with its extensive use of the Royal Philharmonic – Cale did not initially intend to use an orchestra on *Paris, 1919*. Once Thomas had overcome his initial reluctance, however, and it had been decided to use strings after all, he revealed himself as a skilful orchestrator. This time around, the emphasis was different. On *Academy in Peril* there had been pressure to come up with a symphony; here the orchestra had not been even considered at the beginning of the project, and was to provide a backing to the songs rather than complete, stand-alone instrumental pieces. On *Academy in Peril* time had been tight, resulting in both the scaling-down of the orchestral suite and what Cale felt was a failure to achieve a high enough quality in the resultant material produced. For *Paris, 1919* the string parts were to be added to what had already been recorded rather than being cut down from an envisaged whole, and there was to be plenty of time to accommodate them.

In 1919 Paris was the setting for the Versailles Peace Conference, which had attempted to impose a lasting settlement on war-ravaged Europe. One of the tracks on *Church of Anthrax* had been called 'The Hall of Mirrors in the Palace of Versailles', a reference to the venue for the signing of the treaty which finally laid out the terms which were to imposed by the victors on Germany. *Paris, 1919* deals with an uncertain world through the filter of Dada and Surrealism, the revolutionary artistic movements which had grown out of a hatred for the old order that had spawned the Great War. The city of the album's title was the adopted home of these two forces that were to exert such an enormous influence on twentieth-century art — and on Cale himself. The Paris of 1919 therefore was effectively the birth of Cale's approach to art, and now became the starting point of his solo career proper. From the heart of a blasted continent and a ruptured civilization emerged shell-shocked displacements of time and place, anger and sorrow and a universal concern with war and its effects on the lives and minds of men.

The Great War was not the only conflict to inform *Paris, 1919*; Vietnam is a shadowy presence, too, one that would continue to be a part of Cale's song-writing. On 27 January 1973 by which time *Paris 1919* had been finished, the Paris Accords finalized the Vietnam ceasefire. The month of the album's release was the month in which the last US troops returned home.

Part of the sense of dislocation to be found on *Paris, 1919* comes from its largely European settings and references coupled with their expression via a quintessentially American group of musicians. After eighteen months of living in Los Angeles, Cale was still no closer to fitting in. He had the *Guardian Weekly* sent over from Britain, and the novels he was reading were by writers such as Graham Greene and Eric Ambler. There are also references on the album to Dylan Thomas and James Joyce.

Towards the end of the *Paris, 1919* sessions, with much of the work done and the results pleasing, Cale began to indulge himself a little more. On one occasion, coming out of the Japanese restaurant underneath the Château Marmont where Chris Thomas was staying, he and Thomas waited for their dinner guests to emerge. Thomas sat on the bonnet of Cale's Shelby Mustang, and Cale began driving him slowly round the car park. Before Thomas knew what was happening they were out on Sunset Boulevard and Cale was accelerating fast, with his producer grimly holding on to the bonnet vents. After a mile Cale turned the car round and drove him back again. Thomas was convinced he was going to die. By the next day he had pulled himself together enough to make a furious phone call to Cale, shouting at him: 'Do you realize you could have killed me?' 'Do *you* realize I could have lost my licence?' Cale replied.

On another occasion Cale drove Thomas to Santa Monica in roughly eight minutes, a journey that Thomas remembers as 'seriously terrifying' and 'probably impossible — even if you go by spaceship'. Despite this, Cale was unsatisfied with the Mustang and wanted something faster. Still new to driving, another worrying habit of his was to keep the car in second gear most of the time.

"DENSE JAIL HAVOC"

One night, with the recording very nearly complete, Thomas brought two bottles of champagne into the studio, with the idea of sharing them with Cale at the end of the session. Growing bored, Cale drank them both himself and started to attack Thomas underneath the table, biting his legs. Cale then announced his intention of going out for a six-pack and disappeared. The next time Thomas heard from him was when Cale phoned from the local jail three hours later, having been stopped for drink-driving. Cale had accelerated hard away from a Stop sign on a wet road and attracted the attention of a member of the California Highway Patrol. He asked Thomas to get him a bail bondsman, but the ex-Velvet Underground road manager, Phil Schier, who was engineering the session, shouted out 'Leave him there!' By coincidence, Little Feat were recording their own material in the studio next door, and Thomas went over to try to organize a whip-round for the $100 Cale needed to get out of jail. He told the band members what had happened, to which they responded by telling him where to go. Cale eventually rounded up the money from another source and at around three the next morning turned up at the château with the six-pack under his arm, having driven all the way back.

Lowell George and Cale, each very much his own man, had clashed in the studio, and George stopped working on the album halfway through. At one point Cale passed Thomas a note referring to George as a prima donna. Cale's lack of self-confidence was still apparent, however, and this expressed itself in continuing worries about his vocal prowess. Thomas, however, was laid back about what he saw as a minor problem and managed, in the event, to elicit a stronger performance from Cale than the one he had given on *Vintage Violence*. On the track 'Antarctica Starts Here' Cale had to whisper his guide vocal track to the band, who were playing very quietly in a small room, in order to make sure that his voice did not bleed on to the other tracks. Thomas listened to the whispering, thought it would be perfect for the finished album, and they decided to leave it in place. Thomas also whistled the 'bird song' in the middle of the title track, an idea that he had taken from the Beach Boys.

For Thomas, used to loading tracks with different instruments and sounds, *Paris, 1919* was a fairly straightforward project. With the images in the songs providing enough colour on their own, the rest of the work was to add a shade here and there to balance them, almost as if he was 'painting by numbers'.

Paris, 1919 had an appreciative response from the critics. Cale had made his first really positive statement as a solo artist. In press interviews to publicize the new album, he talked of working on the scores for two films, although *Caged Heat*, for Roger Corman's studio, would be the only one to reach fruition. Directed by Jonathan Demme, whom Cale had met while working at Warner Brothers, Cale improvised its music, accompanied by harmonica player Peter Ivers and guitarist Shuggie Otis. They played while watching a print of the film, recording the whole soundtrack 'live'.

Demme would prove to be a useful contact, and Cale later wrote the soundtrack for his television film *Who Am I This Time?* and contributed to that of his feature film *Something Wild.*

In the interviews Cale mentioned discussions he and Lou Reed had recently had to reform the Velvet Underground. In September Reed's *Berlin* album was released. On the track 'Men of Good Fortune' the narrator would profess not to care about money or its absence. On 'Half Past France', from *Paris, 1919,* Cale had already written:

> Back in Berlin they're all well fed
> I don't care
> People always bore me anyway.

When Cale married Cindy, a few months after meeting her, he was making a doomed attempt to give some stability to an irredeemably imbalanced personality, and the effort would draw deeply upon his own reserves of strength. For the marriage ceremony he had originally expressed a desire to be dressed in tennis gear, the sport having become a regular recreation of his, while he recited the vows in imitation of a polar bear and Cindy pretended to be a dog.

After the wedding Cale and Cindy moved into their own house in the San Fernando Valley. On one occasion Cindy went out shopping and Chris Thomas was left at home with Cale. The phone rang and Cale asked Thomas to get it. Hearing what he thought was a familiar female voice on the other end, Thomas was surprised to be asked to pick the caller up from the airport and replied that he thought she had only gone shopping. Once the phone call had become bogged down in non-sequiturs, Thomas handed the receiver to Cale, saying that he could not figure out what Cindy was going on about. Cale took over the call and discovered that it was actually Nico on the phone — and Thomas realized where Cindy had got her unusual speaking voice.

On 5 November Miss Christine, also formerly of the GTOs, was found dead of a drugs overdose at a house that the Modern Lovers were renting and Cindy, heart-broken, fell to pieces. For Cale this would be the beginning of a long period where life was largely ruled by her psychiatric problems.

After finishing *Paris, 1919* Cale was sounded out by Bryan Ferry as producer for the second Roxy Music album. Ferry asked him which studio in London he would use, and Cale replied that he would choose AIR studios, where he had mixed *Academy in Peril.* AIR was already Chris Thomas's studio of choice, and in the end the production job was given to him rather than Cale, beginning a professional rivalry between the two men that would continue to run parallel to their long-term friendship and working relationship.

Cale began rehearsing musicians to promote *Paris, 1919* but thought better of the idea as time went by, believing that he had acted too late and that a series of proper live shows would have to wait a while longer. Interviews at the time reveal him still lacking the confidence necessary for a tour; in another year he would be sufficiently self-assured to head out on to the road for the first time.

6
1973—1974

By early autumn 1973 Cale's contract was up with Warner Brothers. Back in London, Richard Williams had recently begun working in the A & R Department of Island Records. In his office he had a framed print of a shot from the Bataclan gig, which had been given to him by photographer Mick Rock. Williams had been one of the few early admirers of the Velvet Underground in England; back in 1967 he had led his regular column in a Nottingham weekly paper with a review of *The Velvet Underground and Nico*. In 1971 Williams had interviewed Cale while he was producing *Desertshore* in London, and the two had got on well. Williams received a call in the autumn of 1973 from New York journalist Lisa Robinson, a friend of his, who told him that Cale was no longer under contract and that this would be the perfect time to try to sign him. Williams took her advice but, before taking the idea any further, asked Phil Manzanera from Roxy Music, who were signed to Island at the time, whether he would be interested in working with Cale. He was as excited as Williams at the prospect, and Williams then went to see his MD at Island with a proposal that emphasized Cale's recent artistic and critical success with *Paris, 1919* and also the Roxy Music connection. Williams and Cale exchanged several phone calls, during which the possibility arose of Nico signing to Island as well. Williams flew over to Los Angeles to meet Cale, whom picked him up in the infamous Mustang at the Continental Hyatt House, and the two went off for a drink. Cale talked about tennis, and Williams met Cindy, who he remembers as beautiful but 'clearly with an unusual temperament'. A deal was soon done, with Cale given a three-album contract. There would be a budget of £30,000 for each album and anything left over afterwards would be Cale's to keep. He would also be on a 10 per cent royalty on records sold. Williams had no knowledge of what kind of album Cale would come up with, apart from knowing that it would be a collection of songs rather than instrumental work, but he was more than happy to allow him free rein to produce whatever he wanted. Cale, for his part, wanted to make an album that would capitalize on the success of *Paris, 1919* while not being 'another Procol Harum album'.

This would be another chance to escape an environment within which it had been impossible to avoid the regular use of drugs. He had never really been suited to Los Angeles, and the offer by a young adventurous record label to sign him and return him to London, where he could make another clean start, was just what he needed. He had been given another opportunity, too, to become a solo recording artist in his own right — he was no longer a record company employee. With the new opportunity, however, would also come a new challenge — he knew that this was going to have to be the start of his career as a solo performer.

By April 1974 Cale was living in Britannia Road, Fulham, south-west London, in a well-furnished, comfortable and elegantly decked-out house rented for him by Island. While staying here he began writing what would become *Fear*, on which he would work again with his favoured engineer, John Wood, at Sound Techniques in Old Church Street.

In 1915, Antonin Artaud signed his poem 'En Songe' with the pseudonym 'Eno'.

Phil Manzanera had already met Cale briefly in Los Angeles, as Roxy Music shared his US record label Reprise — and was also acquainted with him through Chris Thomas. Manzanera was enlisted as Cale's executive producer for *Fear* (Cale would produce it himself) and set about finding the right musicians to play on the album within the budget that he had been set. He brought along the rhythm section from Kevin Ayers's band, the Whole World, and before long would also recruit Eno, who had recently left Roxy Music, to recruit his assistance. Other guest appearances were by Eno associate Judy Nylon, Richard Thompson (a friend and work colleague of John Wood's), Brian Turrington and Michael Des Maris from Eno's band the Winkies and slide-guitar player Bryn Haworth.

The musicians began rehearsing at a small demo studio on the King's Road before moving round the corner to Sound Techniques. By the time everyone gathered here Cale had written most of the material for the album, with the exception of some of the lyrics, and played them to the band on the piano. Manzanera settled down to finding a musical context for them, and this evolved over the course of the sessions with little predetermined sense of what it would be. Manzanera often found himself working alone in the studio; one of the reasons for Cale's absences was that his relationship with Cindy was proving more and more tortuous as her behaviour deteriorated, and he was trying to escape from it by seeing another woman. Cindy would phone the studio and be told that Cale had just 'popped out' for something. There was plenty of alcohol around, too. For Cale each day was an unapologetic mixture of real life and music.

Manzanera felt the need of assistance in the studio and now enlisted Eno, who, at a low ebb following his departure from Roxy Music, was happy to lend a hand. Unsure about how to begin carving out a career for himself, he was on the look-out for new, interesting projects; collaborating with Cale, the man behind the sound of the Velvet Underground, was an exciting opportunity. In the studio Manzanera and Eno would work together whether Cale was there or not. Even if he was there, Cale was often preoccupied and might sometimes only be glimpsed, horizontal, at the back of the control room. They would add overdubs, sound effects and treatments, but their contributions were not major factors in the songs themselves — those had very much been established by Cale at the writing stage. Manzanera began the sessions in awe of Cale's talents, an awe which grew to envelop also what Manzanera calls Cale's 'wonderfully erratic' but unpretentious behaviour. He also noted Cale's huge appetite for pouring out ideas and for sharp, humorous and well-informed conversation, often on current affairs and politics — he was much more likely to be reading the *Wall Street Journal* than *Rolling Stone*.

Cale was happy to share work on the album's production, open to Manzanera's and Eno's suggestions and not remotely precious about his own role. Musically he had the confidence to accept suggestions but also to overrule them where he thought necessary. Phoning up Eno at five o'clock in the morning to discuss a new production idea that had just occurred to him was also part of the process, and similar demands would be made on other collaborators in years to come.

The production on *Fear* gives it a distinctiveness that Cale has said he had wanted for *Paris, 1919* but never achieved. The sound is uncluttered, sharp and punchy with just the right amount of unusual effects and textures to give it an edge. On each of these songs something unique is happening. On 'Fear Is a Man's Best Friend' Manzanera's guitar plays behind the beat, and Cale's bass is treated at the end to turn it into a lead instrument; Eno's synthesizer makes an odd entrance late on in 'Ship of Fools' and way back in the mix to greet the arrival of Dracula; Cale pronounces 'Orgy' with a hard 'g' and hisses on the opening line of 'Momamma Scuba'; his viola adds a dizzying and deadly attack to 'Barracuda'.

Fear followed *Paris, 1919* in its assured song-writing, its use of Surrealist techniques and its sense of a fractured whole. The romanticism evident on *Paris, 1919* is taken to further lengths on the impossibly pure 'Emily' and ends in tragedy on 'Buffalo Ballet'; sex is tied in with death on 'Barracuda' and 'Momamma Scuba' and with repression and inadequacy on 'The Man Who Couldn't Afford to Orgy'; 'Fear Is a Man's Best Friend' is a depiction of paranoia that is both frightened and frightening. On *Fear* there is a more pronounced mixture of beauty and violence ('Gun' forming the antithesis of 'Emily'), and the two are also intertwined in a way that would now become symptomatic of Cale's writing.

On 'Gun', Phil Manzanera and Eno used a technique that they had already employed with Roxy Music and on experiments at Eno's flat over recent months, which was the 'two-man' guitar solo — although this was the only time they were to use it on someone else's album. It involved Eno 'doctoring' the sound from Manzanera's amplifier through his VCS3 synthesizer and effects such as a Revox echo unit.

'The Man Who Couldn't Afford to Orgy' featured some sultry spoken interjections from Judy Nylon. Painting the walls at Eno's house one day, she had answered the phone to find herself speaking to Cale and, during the conversation, had agreed to come up with some suitable lines to accompany the song.

The album's greatest achievement is perhaps 'Ship of Fools', a song that had actually been written much earlier. Here, the universality of the original concept is used as a lattice to frame a journey between America and Wales, across time zones and through a web of human inadequacies, failures and inanities.

During one of the *Fear* sessions Eno's house keys disappeared. When recording finished for the night, at three in the morning, they were nowhere to be found. Suspicion immediately fell on one of the Island press officers, who seemed to have it in for Eno at the time. Tony Secunda — ex-manager of the Move, the Moody Blues and T. Rex, who became friendly with Cale and would soon become his manager — was in the studio at the time and rounded up a posse consisting of Cale, Manzanera and Eno, which proceeded to drive to the press officer's flat. Secunda smashed down his door, marched into his bedroom, grabbed him by the scruff of the neck and shortly afterwards returned downstairs with the keys. While the others chalked the incident down to 'rock 'n' roll', Eno was very upset by it and had to be pacified over breakfast later that morning by Chris Blackwell, head of Island Records.

Tony Secunda had a reputation as a successful music business hustler and seemed to know his way around the industry. Cale looked to him to take care of the kind of business things that he himself either could not or did not want to do. Secunda took control of the logistics of Cale's life and 'paid' him, but in the event his mark on Cale's career was not a strong one. His wildness, together with Cale's own — a double dose of excess — did not leave room in the relationship for enough stability to make it effective.

Richard Williams remembers everything being right about *Fear*: the songs, the production, the Roxy Music connection, even the cover, which was, literally, in your face, an extreme close-up of Cale in black and white that was striking and unnerving but which at the same time drew the listener in. The first song that Richard Williams was played from the *Fear* sessions was 'Buffalo Ballet', and he knew straight away that the album would be fine. The Island management were pleased with it, too. Despite thinking it unlikely to sell in large numbers, they believed that it might produce a hit single in 'Buffalo Ballet' or 'The Man Who Couldn't Afford to Orgy', which might, in turn, boost album sales. The latter track was actually released as a single in the UK, but without any success, even though it got a few radio plays. DJ copies were pressed, but the Island Marketing Department believed, probably rightly, that the BBC would not play any record with the word 'orgy' in the title. As a result the radio station copies were all labelled 'The Man Who Couldn't Afford to . . .' so that any disc jockey playing it would not have to say the offending word. The single and its B-side, the non-album cut 'Sylvia Said', were both, unlike the album, given the production credit 'John Cale with Eno and Phil Manzanera'. When it was released in September *Fear* received a positive reception from the critics, and Cale was immediately in the position of selling between twenty thousand and thirty thousand records. This was a total he had never achieved before but one that was par for the course for Island, who looked to shift that many for all their artists.

The album was entitled *Fear* for good reason: Cale's day-to-day life revolved around its presence and his attempts to banish it. His inability to eradicate drug-taking was now exacerbated by an increasing reliance on alcohol. Cindy was careering around and away from him, and he had the added pressures of knowing that he would soon have to make his first full-scale live performances as a solo artist.

Kevin Ayers had been due to perform at the Rainbow Theatre in London's Finsbury Park on 1 June 1974, and it had been decided to turn the gig into an event. Richard Williams took Ayers, Cale and Eno to lunch at a restaurant in Kensington, and they discussed turning it into something like the 1972 Bataclan reunion of Cale, Lou Reed and Nico. Everyone was keen on the idea, and it soon developed into an album project as well with the revolutionary idea of recording the gig and, with it fresh in public memory, almost immediately reproducing it on to vinyl and getting it into the shops. There would also be two provincial dates a month after the Rainbow gig, one in Birmingham and one in Manchester. Cale decided not to take part in a scheduled free show in London's Hyde Park after Eno was taken ill and unable to perform.

Nico had also agreed to be involved in the project. She, Cale and Eno each performed a small selection of their own songs in the first half of the Rainbow concert, with Ayers, whose gig it was, playing his material in the second half. Each of the main participants would also perform with each other. Mike Oldfield and Robert Wyatt, who were old friends of Ayers's, formed part of the back-up band. Outside in the Island mobile recording studio Richard Williams and John Wood sat watching a video feed and recording the music. They were to mix the sound the next day, ensuring that all the artists were kept out of the studio, and send it off for pressing immediately: a process that would prevent the performers raising objections as to how the album would sound.

For Cale this was the first time he had taken to the stage with a full band as a solo performer, and it was therefore a highly significant occasion. The pressure on him to become a performer rather than just a recording artist had been building ever since the making of *Vintage Violence*, and with this concert the psychological ground was taken, paving the way for his first solo tour the following year.

Cale, with his back to the audience most of the time, as in his Velvet Underground days, performed 'Gun', 'Buffalo Ballet' and a revolutionary reworking of 'Heartbreak Hotel' that has stayed in his live set pretty much ever since and is preserved on the album *June 1, 1974*. 'Heartbreak Hotel' was the first in what would become a series of cover versions. These are devastating reinterpretations of the original recordings, breaking down and then remaking them, laying bare their previously hidden souls in the process. 'Heartbreak Hotel' was certainly starting at the top; the original arrangement is completely dispensed with (not something that had happened very much to Elvis Presley's songs) and the full extent of the despair at its heart tapped from its underground well. Cale's vocal performance is restrained here, compared with some that the song would receive from him over the years, but he gets into his stride about two-thirds of the way through. Some of the emotion released on this occasion may have been due to the fact that Cindy had gone off with Kevin Ayers the night before. This was an episode that Cale would later refer to in the song 'Guts', with Ayers the 'bugger in the short sleeves' who 'fucked my wife'.

Judy Nylon had tried to persuade Cale that the two of them should perform 'The Man Who Couldn't Afford to Orgy' together on stage at the Rainbow, but he had refused. She had envisaged something 'after Jane Birkin and before Donna Summer', she recalls, but live collaboration between the two would have to wait. Nylon had seen Cale perform in the 'Exploding Plastic Inevitable' at the Boston Tea Party and had also seen him around in New York in the mid- to late 1960s, while she had been pursuing her interest in performance art. At the time of *Fear* she was in an art-performance group called Moodier, whose shows were seen by future Sex Pistols manager Malcolm McLaren and his partner Vivienne Westwood, among others. Nylon and Cale shared a background in both art and music that was rare in the pop world at the time. Cale, who had proved himself in the Velvet Underground, and with Nico subsequently, to be much more open than many of his contemporaries to artistic collaborations with women, offered her a rare chance to work, and to be respected, in the medium of rock music, and the two would work together again before long.

As well as contributing to *Fear*, Nylon also hung around with Cale occasionally at this time at his Britannia Road house. To her he was 'charismatic with no feminine aspects to his face . . . one of very few guys around that could be honestly called "handsome"'. He was 'smart and impatient', but underneath his apparently unconcerned recklessness she saw 'an art monk outsider with more energy than outlets'.

A studio version of 'Heartbreak Hotel' was recorded after the Rainbow gig, at Basing Street in London's Notting Hill, with the idea that it might become a single. Cale and Secunda brought it in to Richard Williams once it was finished, but the idea was shelved, the version eventually appearing on Cale's next studio album, *Slow Dazzle*.

The week after the Rainbow gig rumours began to circulate in the music press of a 'new Velvet Underground' being lined up to tour in the autumn – with Nico returning and Eno 'replacing' Lou Reed. Nico's manager, Jo Lustig, was said to be in the USA negotiating with Sterling Morrison and Maureen Tucker, but nothing came of the story.

After completing *Fear* Cale began work on another Nico album, *The End*. Cale had managed to get Nico the record contract with Warner Brothers that had resulted in *Desertshore* and had performed the same feat again by getting her on to Island.

Richard Williams had been almost as excited about getting hold of Nico as he was when he signed Cale and also had the benefit of knowing Jo Lustig, an ex-Broadway publicist of the 1950s and now heavily involved in the British folk-rock scene (managing Richard Thompson among others). Lustig had first met Nico at a party back in 1965 when she had made her first single 'I'm Not Saying'. Nico had been on the look-out for a good manager, and Lustig had fitted the bill. The fact that he already knew Richard Williams made it that much easier for Island to sign her.

The End was recorded, like *Fear*, at Sound Techniques with John Wood engineering, and the now familiar pattern of Nico recording first with her harmonium and Cale coming in afterwards to arrange her songs was employed again. This time Phil Manzanera and Eno were on hand to help out. Manzanera remembers Nico advising him: 'Don't do anything he says. Ignore everything. Play whatever you like.' Cale and Nico seemed to spend most of their time together fighting, but the result was another artistic high, even if it was once again critically misunderstood. Nico also sold her twenty to thirty thousand copies.

'The spectacle we are watching must be unique, it must give the impression that it is as unprecedented, as incapable of repeating itself as any action in life, any event brought on by circumstances.'
(Antonin Artaud)

In August advertisements appeared in the music press for 'The Music of John Cale', a show at London's Victoria Palace Theatre that was to be his first full-scale live performance as a solo artist. He had spent a lot of time discussing the format of the show with Tony Secunda and others and wanted it to fit into a new kind of pattern. Instead of touring conventionally he wanted to perform a couple of shows a year that would be real 'events', containing enough surprises to consistently transcend the boundaries of a normal rock 'n' roll show. The show at the Victoria Palace was scheduled to take place on 22 September and feature the St Paul's Cathedral Boys' Choir (with whom he had already worked on the Jennifer Warnes album) on a version of the Beach Boys' 'Surf's Up'. There would also be a performance of the yet-to-be-released *Guts* that would feature half a side of beef held by two assistants in lab coats. Cale was to illustrate the song by pointing to various parts of the cow, and the song would end with him throwing the contents of a bucket of entrails at the audience. The show was postponed and never rearranged.

Around this time the Austrian artist Hermann Nitsch was doing something similar in theatrical spaces, by playing loud music and bringing a slaughtered animal on to a stage, disembowelling it and pouring the intestines over a nude woman or man. For Nitsch the intention was to reintroduce primitive rituals into society, to try to bring back into modern life the catharsis that these would have brought to early human social groups. Part of Cale's motivation, as a now adept and successful songwriter and rock musician with a musical form buttoned down, was to subvert that form, as he had with classical music. His own background in Dadaism and performance art from the Goldsmiths' days was still deep within him — as was the experience of having been shown a local slaughterhouse in Wales as a child. The killing of animals was something accepted by but hidden from most people in the modern, 'civilized' world, something that he felt needed to become a recognized part of life once more. There were other reasons, too, for this intended assault: the impending break-up of his marriage, his drug and alcohol use, a continuing paranoia and lack of self-confidence, despite his achievements, and a massive head of steam built up after the years working in record company offices and dingy quadraphonic mixing-rooms.

In August Richard Williams had been trying to set up a Berlin concert for Nico, backed by Cale and Eno, and an appearance at the Meta Music Festival there was duly arranged. They were to play, the night after Terry Riley, in the Neue Nationalgalerie, a beautiful glass construction built in the 1960s by Ludwig Mies van der Rohe, set on a concrete terrace underneath an overhanging roof. While in Berlin for the concert Williams, Cale and Eno went through Checkpoint Charlie into the East. Nico, as a holder of a West German passport, was unable to go. Cale looked fairly unconventional to the East German border guards, but Eno's green hair really threw them. The three headed off for a wander along the Unter den Linden.

During the concert itself Cale played 'I'm Waiting for the Man' and 'Fear Is a Man's Best Friend'. He and Eno accompanied Nico — Cale on grand piano and Eno on his VCS3 synthesizer. Eno had prepared a table with a line of water-filled glasses which were miked up and during Cale's performance he proceeded to smash them, sending glass and water across the stage and a wave of explosive sound into the auditorium. Nico insisted on playing the whole of 'Deutschland Über Alles', including the imperialistic words that had been banned since the end of the Second World War; Cale played piano over the top and Eno created the noise of a thousand-bomber air raid. The spotlights suddenly looked like searchlights, and the audience revolted *en masse*, throwing their white plastic cushions towards the stage in a blizzard of giant snowflakes.

Afterwards the musicians retired to the festival producer's house and listened to tapes of Terry Riley and the Tibetan monks who had performed at the festival the previous evening.

Eric's

9 MATHEW
LIVERPOOL
051-

on Thurs 21st April

JOHN
CALE

THE COUNT BISHOPS
THE BOYS

bers £1 40p Guests £1 80

Part 4
Calescence
(increasing warmth)

On 9 March 1942 the German 'Tank Destruction' badge, the 'special badge for the destruction of tanks by a single man' was founded.

"CAJOLE SHAVEN ID"

During December 1974 Cale's next album for Island, *Slow Dazzle*, was recorded at Sound Techniques. A few months earlier he had listed some of the songs slated to appear on it: 'Heat the Heat', 'Guts' (originally to have been called 'Bugger'), 'The Queen of Tarts Laughs Last', 'It's the Man That Smells the Burning Calls the Law', 'There's a Honey of a Moon Out Tonight,' 'Television, Television, TV' and 'The Jeweller'. By the time it came to recording, however, almost all of these were replaced by material written in the studio, with the addition of the already recorded 'Heartbreak Hotel'. By now, too, another project had already slipped over the horizon. A proposed album of cover versions with the St Paul's Cathedral Choir that had yielded an unfinished reggae version of the Beach Boys' 'God Only Knows' and was due also to include interpretations of 'Jerusalem', the Byrds' 'Eight Miles High' and the Who's 'I Can See for Miles' would never be completed.

Phil Manzanera's only appearance on *Slow Dazzle* was on 'Heartbreak Hotel', and Eno appeared only on this and 'The Jeweller'; by this time both were busy on other projects. Cale assembled a new cast of musicians for the album, the core of which would become the basis of the touring band that would go out on the road later in the year to promote it.

Chris Spedding was a highly successful session guitarist who had also played with the Island band the Sharks. Richard Williams knew him through the Sharks connection and brought him into contact with Cale. Spedding was initially booked to record only one session with Cale. At the beginning this was just another job for him, one session among many. Spedding might record with Petula Clark in the morning and Cale in the afternoon, and if he had come up with a riff he particularly liked he might use it with both artists, even if they were musically dissimilar. Spedding was joined by Pat Donaldson on bass and Timmy Donald on drums, both of whom had played with Sandy Dennis and Richard Thompson. There was no such thing as a 'John Cale Band' at this time, however, just what would become a series of self-contained projects, both live and studio, in between which the musicians were free agents and worked with other artists. Cale liked what he heard on the initial recordings, particularly Spedding's mixture of professionalism and spontaneity, and rebooked them. The relationship would continue on the same *ad hoc* basis over two tours and another album, *Helen of Troy*. Cale's partnership with Spedding would then be renewed in the 1980s, when they would temporarily become brothers-in-law, a formalization of what had already become a close relationship.

Chris Thomas was still hanging around with Cale at this time. Cale would often pick Thomas up from AIR studios, where he worked, or meet at his house for dinner, although this would sometimes involve Cale watching Thomas dine while scouring the kitchen for something to eat for himself. The evening, more often than not, would end at the Marquee club. Sometimes during the day the two would meet at Cale's new basement flat in Sinclair Road in Shepherd's Bush, where they might listen to Beach Boys records and talk about Brian Wilson. They would also listen to Queen's 'Now I'm Here' time after time in admiration of its Beach Boys-like harmonies. Cale sometimes admitted to being 'homesick' for Los Angeles, where he still had a house, and looked forward to possible American tour dates that would allow him to holiday in California. Thomas also contributed to *Slow Dazzle*, playing electric violin, and would later gladly accept Cale's offer of a place in his touring band. Thomas had agreed to produce another album for Cale after *Paris, 1919*, but schedule clashes and miscommunication (problems that were to recur in their relationship) meant that nothing came of the proposal. Another misunderstanding had occurred when Thomas had turned up at the Rainbow Theatre on the night of 1 June the previous year and had been rebuffed by a highly distracted Cale. What seemed like a personal slight in fact had more to do with the pressures of Cale's first solo gig with a band, in front of a sold-out audience, and the disappearance of his wife with Kevin Ayers the night before.

Although Cale was writing much of *Slow Dazzle* in the studio, by the time the musicians came into the equation he knew pretty much what he wanted and would direct them through the songs. Spedding would have been happy to improvise extensively with the material, but Cale was keen to keep control over what he had written, allowing musical ideas to come through from the others but only within the framework he had already set.

Slow Dazzle was an attempt to make a commercial album with several tracks that could be released as singles. Another aspect of this new approach was the creation of a Cale 'image', with his impending entry into the world of performing. Both the album sleeve for *Slow Dazzle* and his turn-out on stage would feature a distillation of Lou Reed's Velvet Underground and *Transformer/Rock 'n' Roll Animal* personae. If Reed could attract attention by drawing on the mystique of the Velvet Underground — and capitalize on it by commercializing it — then so could Cale.

Cale's private life continued to be often chaotic, with an increasing reliance on alcohol and cocaine and a decreasing ability to restrain Cindy's wildness. On *Slow Dazzle* he took on what was happening to him, turning it into one of his most personal albums. Two of the songs in particular, 'Dirty Ass Rock 'n' Roll' and 'Darling I Need You', which follow each other, start out from the same premise – waking up in the morning to an awareness of a collapsing life. Despite this, it is in its own way as surreal as *Fear*. Love, sex, faithlessness, betrayal, degradation, despair and a touch of ecstasy are all mixed together, heightened and skewed by a subtle use of oblique angles. These place Brian Wilson and Harold Wilson in the same song and throw up images of Texan faith healers, an 'undercover Sigmund Freud', 'garbage on garbage, right up to the sky', a 'twelve-bore in the corner . . . quite operatic in its self-disgust' and – the culmination of the album – the transformation of an eye into a vagina. The jaunty and easy-paced rhythms of many of the songs conceal lyrics of heartbreak, violence and desperate sex. The epic strings, ethereal backing vocals and soaring lead guitar that all signify 'love song' are used for its antithesis: 'I'm Not the Loving Kind'. Songs in major keys hide minor-key middle-eights and codas; improvised and only semi-intelligible lyrics are whispered in 'Mr Wilson' and roared in 'Rollaroll'. The hissing Cale of 'Black Angel's Death Song' returns as soon as he opens his mouth on 'Heartbreak Hotel'. Here, too, a 'heavy metal' guitar sound combines with Eno's *Psycho*-like synthesizer strings, with lyrical excisions and a Lugosi-like vocal performance, to bring out the real desperation, the terrible closeness to death of the song.

'No one knows how to scream any more in Europe . . .'
(Antonin Artaud)

Slow Dazzle is the album on which Cale starts screaming. He screams against deceit and betrayal on 'Rollaroll', in despair on 'Heartbreak Hotel', in an exorcism of violence and revenge on 'Guts'. 'Guts' is in B flat, which is the approximate key of the 'sixty-cycle hum', the frequency on which American (but not European) electricity supplies operate. It is the ideal environment, therefore, for this tale of a domestic hell created in London after forsaking Los Angeles.

The album ends bravely with 'The Jeweller', another Cale short story, but, in its depiction of unconscious desires, Surrealist rather than Dadaist as 'Caricature' and 'Beirut' had been. Narrated in the same matter-of-fact tone as he had employed on 'The Gift', the bizarre is once again given a setting of normality. Sexuality and the rationality of observation grow together and apart, fighting with each other for control of mind and body against a background of cool electronic tones.

Several songs were recorded at the *Slow Dazzle* sessions that did not make it on to the final album; 'All I Want Is You' and 'Bamboo Floor' would see the light of day on *The Island Years* two-CD set in 1996, and 'Willow Weep for Me' (a version of Ann Ronell's song of how 'love has sinned') which would be recorded several times but never released. (Some of these versions were recorded in unused studio time at the end of production sessions for other artists). 'Bamboo Floor' includes the third reference on the *Slow Dazzle* songs to looking in mirrors: this one is 'dull', another 'broken', the third has 'rusty veins', and all are testimony to Cale's inability to see clearly into himself.

In March Lou Reed was in London to play at the Hammersmith Odeon, and he met up with Nico, who was hoping at the time that he would write an album of songs for her, at Blake's Hotel. Photographer Mick Rock was there, too, and Reed made a phone call to Cale suggesting that he, Nico and Rock come round to Cale's flat in Holland Park, west London. Nico never made it, but Reed did, and Rock was on hand to document the meeting with his camera: two figures in close proximity moving in different planes. Cale's new flat was over the road from Keith Moon's local pub, the Dog and Duck, and Rock remembers seeing 'a flash of him in a giant white Borsalino with a camel-hair coat thrown over his shoulders in the back room'.

Cale's new band prepared for his first tour as a solo artist with two days' rehearsal at Island's studios in Chiswick, west London. Chris Spedding turned up expecting to be taught all the earlier Cale songs that he would be expected to play and found out that he was expected to have 'done his homework' first. He proceeded to 'fake it like crazy', a procedure that he would have to repeat many times during his work with Cale. On stage Cale would often launch into the introduction to a song from *Paris, 1919*, the audience would cheer in recognition and the band, with the exception of Chris Thomas, would stare blankly at each other. Picking up the key, they would begin to play and hope for the best.

When Chris Thomas was asked by Cale to join his new touring band he happily said yes, keen to grasp what, as a studio-bound producer, would probably be his only chance of rock 'n' roll fame. He had assumed that he would be playing the only instrument on which he was proficient, bass guitar. About three weeks before the tour was due to start Thomas learned that Cale did not want him to play bass at all; he wanted him to play keyboards — and Thomas had never played these. He had to sit down for four hours a day and learn scales and arpeggios in every key. It had to be every key, because he knew that Cale would be liable to just shout out a key live on stage and expect him to be able to play in it — which, sure enough, he did.

On 9 March 1697 Tsar Peter the Great began his tour of Western Europe.

Cale's first solo tour began with warm-up dates in Europe in April, including visits to Marseilles and Paris, while the tour proper, ten British dates, began in Colchester on 3 May. In Marseilles the band put on a surprisingly professional performance, despite their lack of preparation and Cale having unnerving problems getting his guitar in tune. There was some dispute about what key 'I'm Waiting for the Man' was to be in, and the song's meandering conclusion was cut abruptly short by a crashing, discordant piano chord from Cale. On 'Antarctica Starts Here', in particular, everyone apart from Cale sounded pretty hesitant, but the show as a whole was a success. Two days before Colchester Cale and band had been at the BBC in London, recording three songs, 'Taking It All Away' and 'Darling I Need You' from *Slow Dazzle* and *Fear*'s 'You Know More Than I Know', for *The John Peel Show* on Radio One.

In mainland Europe Cale had felt less open to scrutiny than he knew he would be in Britain; to a certain extent he could hide behind the language barrier — away, too, from the attention of the British music press. Colchester was not exactly a media hang-out, however, and he felt free, therefore, to experiment a little. Essex University had provided a grand piano for the occasion, and Cale pounded it with his fists during 'Fear Is a Man's Best Friend' and crawled underneath it to sing 'Guts', which goes:

> The bugger in the short sleeves fucked my wife
> Did it quick and split
> Back home fresh as a daisy to Maisy — oh Maisy —
> The twelve-bore that stood in the corner
> Quite operatic in its self-disgust
> Blew him all over the living-room floor
> Like parrot shit, parrot spit, parrot shit was shot
>
> Now maybe it was someone familiar
> Someone that we all would know
> An embarrassing dénouement, n'est ce pas
> Or familiar hyperbole
> And there would go the secret plot
> The piss that missed the hole and the pot
> Like some ancient teenage dream
> From soul to poisoned soul to poisoned soul
>
> Guts, guts — got no guts
> And stitches don't help at all
> Guts, guts — got no guts

Holes in the body, holes in the head
Holes in the forehead, holes in the legs
There should never be holes at all

So kill all you want or more – make sure – do it right
Dead is dead and doornails forget
Then you'll notice how the waster and the wasted
Get to look like one another in the end . . .

During 'Gun' Cale crawled across the floor on his stomach, screaming and hitting his head against the floorboards. For the first English date of his first solo tour he had invited his parents along and got them seats near the on-stage monitors. Chris Spedding had never really caught the exact opening line of 'Guts' before, as Cale had usually garbled it up to this point, but this time he caught every word loud and clear; he remembers thinking at the time that this must have been for the benefit of Cale's parents.

Cale had agonized long and hard about what form his first proper stage shows were going to take. Gone now were the projected theatrical extremes of the can- celled Victoria Palace show; in their place were the shades and the leathers and, at the Theatre Royal in London's Drury Lane on 11 May, a dummy dressed in a nurse's uniform. Inside the dummy's knickers was a capsule filled with fake blood. The idea was for Cale to attack the dummy at the end of the gig, but that all changed when during the course of the performance he broke a string on his guitar. The roadie whose duty it was to fix the string was unprepared, so Cale had to take some decisive action if the momentum of the set was not to be lost. He grabbed the dummy and bit at its crotch, but the hidden capsule refused to burst, and he had to resort to a frenzied attack on the lifeless figure. During this assault, in the course of which Cale hit the floor, the capsule did eventually burst, and he continued the gig with 'blood' over half of his face, with some people in the audience convinced that he had broken his nose. As a result of this performance Cale and the other members of the band are banned for life from the Theatre Royal.

The Drury Lane gig also marked the only appearance so far of what would briefly become a Cale trademark: a white plastic ice hockey mask which, with two eye-sockets and a grid of holes over the lower face, gave the wearer a distinctly horrifying aspect. Cale had been interested in wearing masks on stage ever since his Velvet Underground days. Adding a layer of mystery, they were also, like dark glasses, a way of hiding from the audience. Sometimes Cale would add more layers, with more masks and shades worn over a stocking mask. Cale would admit to hiding behind the band on the early dates of his first solo tour, and he certainly still had a lack of confidence about performing live. This would dissipate slowly over the next few months as he gathered more shows under his belt, heard and saw the appreciation of audiences and garnered good press reviews.

Cale had been worried about how to communicate with his audiences and had even considered talking to them about matters that interested and concerned him. Rejecting this as impractical, he decided instead to use the theatrical devices of props and disguises, together with musical improvisation, that would feed off his inter-action with them. The props and disguises would continue to be used into the early 1980s.

The Drury Lane gig was the high point of press interest for the tour, and Cale's performance certainly attracted plenty of attention. The presence of Eno on stage for a guest appearance on 'The Jeweller' helped, too. As a result of this attention, how-ever, Cale felt under the most pressure in the UK at this time and considered that his performance suffered as a result. Still very much feeling his way as a solo live per-former, he was happier perfecting his performances away from the glare of the media and of London audiences. There was one more of these to face over the course of the summer, but, at the bottom of a shared bill, the pressure would not be so great.

On 7 June Cale and band performed a short set at the Crystal Palace Garden Party. Cale, in white shirt and dark glasses, made a good visual foil for Chris Spedding in his black leather jacket, and the band were impressive. Their version of 'Fear Is a Man's Best Friend', which was now becoming a centrepiece of their show, ended with a repeated shriek of 'Say fear!' Cale gave Spedding a false lead on the piano, but Spedding, completely unfazed, continued as if nothing could be more normal. In fact it was pretty normal, as Cale would often do things like this to the band, as well as starting one song and almost immediately playing something else, changing keys, playing songs that had been written a few minutes earlier at the sound-check, even walking off the stage, leaving the band not knowing when or if he was going to return. Cale's exits from the stage were sometimes a result of improvisations that were not working out — in which case he might just leave the band to get on with it.

Antonin Artaud performed at the Roman amphitheatre in Orange in the summer of 1922.

Over the summer Cale had hoped to be touring major US cities such as New York, Boston and Los Angeles, but this mini-tour did not materialize. Instead, he and his band ended up playing at the Roman Amphitheatre at Orange in France in mid-August. By this time Cale and Chris Thomas had undergone another of their periodic misunderstandings, and Thomas was out of the band. On the first European dates earlier in the tour Nico had supported Cale, and she and Chris Thomas had 'hooked up together'. Thomas had stayed with Nico in Paris afterwards, and Cale had phoned him there in order to summon him back to England for rehearsals. When he did return, it turned out that there was no rehearsal — Cale had a proprietorial attitude to Nico that did not sit well with her having relationships with members of his bands. Thomas remembers meeting up with Lou Reed around that time and thinking that he sounded just like Cale and Nico and that they must have taught each other to 'play this particular game'. He told Reed that he spoke just like his fellow ex-members of the Velvet Underground, and Reed replied: 'Yes, but there's one difference. I've got talent.'

During the gig at Orange Cale, although putting on a performance that Richard Williams remembers as 'very, very exciting', seemed on the verge of losing control. At one point he swung a microphone stand at the photographers' pit, narrowly missing the head of an employee of Island's press office. The performance ended when Cale did one of his running-off-stage tricks; this time, however, he kept running and did not stop until he reached the car park. When he did try to return to the stage, he came up against an armed security guard who could not believe that the strange-looking apparition in front of him was one of the performers and refused to let him back in. Meanwhile the band continued to play, looking around in vain for any sign of Cale. Not only were they in the middle of a song, they also had a sizeable portion of the set still to play. Spedding eventually brought what he remembers as a 'long, embarrassing guitar solo' to an end, and the song fizzled out. The band made a sheepish exit from the stage and went to rescue their leader from the irate guard.

Later that month Cale and band were back in the studio, recording what would be his last Island album, *Helen of Troy*. The band's live performances had reached a peak by now, and Spedding assumed that Chris Thomas would produce the album and translate the power of their live shows on to vinyl. Thomas had assumed no such thing, however, and was not surprised when he was not even asked to play on it.

By this time Cale's relationship with Island had started to deteriorate. When they had signed him, they had wanted him to concentrate on his own work, without the distractions of producing other artists, and he had been happy to agree to this initially. Another part of the Island deal was that he would receive £30,000 per album and that anything left over after each was made was his to keep. As a result, it was tempting to keep costs down in order to maximize this sum; by the time of *Helen of Troy* he was spending less than was necessary on recording. *Fear* had featured, in all, fourteen musicians; *Slow Dazzle* nine; *Helen of Troy* used seven. Not only would hiring Chris Thomas as producer have taken some of Cale's control of the project away, it would also have added another large fee to the wages bill. By this time he was spending more money on cocaine than ever before. When he received a call while working on *Helen of Troy* from Jane Friedman, Patti Smith's manager, to ask whether he would produce Smith's début album, money was certainly part of his reason for saying yes. *Horses*, Patti Smith's album, was due to be recorded in New York during August and September, with sessions and mixing for Cale's own album having to fit around it. *Helen of Troy* would therefore suffer both from lack of time and lack of money.

Many of the songs on *Helen of Troy* were written in the studio and have short lyrics with little development. The exceptions are 'Sudden Death', 'Cable Hogue' and two songs that the band had already featured in live sets: the title track and 'Leaving It Up to You'. Of these the last three, tellingly, would be the ones that Cale would return to regularly in later years. 'Sudden Death' was more a studio-based track, difficult to reproduce on stage; it would effectively be replaced later on by some of the material on the *Honi Soit* album, to which it bears strong similarities. The other song on the album that would feature regularly in Cale's live shows in later years is 'I Keep a Close Watch'. This was the song about which Cale expressed a hope, half seriously, that one day it would be covered by Frank Sinatra. It is a gorgeous ballad, beautiful and melancholic, but very short — only two verses. The final minute and a quarter of its three minutes and twenty-seven seconds is purely instrumental.

There is a strong atmosphere of claustrophobia on *Helen of Troy*, an awareness of being trapped, as if the world in which Cale was living was closing in on him. There is also a deep sense of the magnetic power of sexual attraction and its ability to corrupt and the pull of degradation. Alongside these is a suggestion of the lack of true friendship and of the distance that must be travelled to find love.

The lack of development in many of these songs gives the album an edgy feel but also a sense of mystery. Songs such as 'My Maria', 'Engine' and 'Save Us' hint at hidden depths, inaccessible to the listener.

The title track was one of the songs that Cale and his band had worked up on tour, and the arrangement that they had come up with featured a Chris Spedding guitar line that sounded like a trumpet part, as if it might have come from the film *Spartacus*. In the event this was not used for the recording, and a real trumpet was introduced instead. Added to the version they had been playing live were three spoken verses, voicing Helen as a very camp homosexual; another surreal touch was added by Eno's synthesizer. This track has one of several interesting arrangements on *Helen of Troy*. The songs that suffer most from a lack of musical development are 'Engine' and the slide-guitar-driven cover versions, 'Pablo Picasso' and 'Baby, What You Want Me to Do'. 'Pablo Picasso' was a Jonathan Richman song from the original Modern Lovers days, recorded in 1972 and produced by Cale but shelved and yet to be released by the time *Helen of Troy* came out. The result of this delay was that it became known first in Cale's reinvented form as a howl of outrage at the artist's success with girls and only later in the way Richman intended it, as a plea for integrity and artistry to be valued higher by the opposite sex than selfish, 'macho' behaviour.

Helen of Troy also shows the first real signs of Cale's interest in world politics, war and intrigue. 'My Maria' and 'Sudden Death', in particular, deal with these subjects, ones to which he would increasingly return.

Before *Helen of Troy* was completed Cale flew to New York to produce Patti Smith. As Spedding remembers it, one day he was simply not there.

Horses would not only be another important entry in Cale's producer's CV, in the same column as the Nico projects and the Stooges and Modern Lovers albums, but would also mark a new development for him. Here Cale got Patti Smith to reinvent her poetry as a new form of rock 'n' roll, and the result was one of the landmark albums of the 1970s. On at least one occasion during the sessions the verbal battles between Cale and Smith over the form of the album turned physical, with Smith hitting Cale. He was also seen crawling along the floor and head-butting a wall. Once *Horses* was completed, however, what was revealed on the master tapes was nothing less than a new landscape.

Island Records were not happy with Cale's disappearing to New York and the problems they felt it was causing with *Helen of Troy*. On his return to London he had to burn the midnight oil to get a finished version of his album ready in three days before he began a European tour in October. There were arguments with Island about its content; the label tried to release a version that did not include the title track and substituted an outtake, 'Coral Moon', for 'Leaving It Up to You', which had a reference to the murder of Sharon Tate. These arguments would ultimately result in Cale leaving Island, although that would not happen for several months yet.

"HAVOC JEAN SLIDE"

On tour in Europe Chris Thomas was back in tow, and the band were playing better than ever; the members all believed that they were on the verge of a big breakthrough. After a Dutch gig they found themselves in a bar in Leuven, and Cale got into an argument that turned into a fight, during which a broken bottle was produced. Cale fell on to the floor and landed on the bottle, the glass puncturing not just his skin but, more important to him, the brand new pair of leather trousers he was wearing. Thomas escorted him to hospital, where, as a doctor stitched him up, Cale 'howled' but meanwhile noticed something on the shelf the other side of the room. When the doctor left, Cale said to Thomas: 'See that shelf up there? Get some of those bottles.' Thomas weighed up the probability of getting caught, having his passport confiscated and ending up in jail, called on his Dutch courage and grabbed the bottles.

The next day the band were back in the van, driving to Brussels for a television performance in the afternoon and rubbing the stolen Xylocaine into their gums, hoping that it would enhance their journey. As they piled out of the van in Brussels the television director came over and attempted to engage them in conversation, but all he could get out of them were paralysed mumbles. Mouths frozen solid, none of them could get out a single intelligible word.

Soon after returning from Europe in November, and only days away from the start of the British leg of his tour, Cale found that Cindy had been detained by the police on suspicion of shoplifting. This was to prove the final straw for him. After he managed to get her out of the police station where she was being held, she left for Los Angeles where Cale still had his house, and that was the end of their marriage.

8
1975–1979

For Cale a chance to escape another period in his life that had brought him a good deal of misery and pain now beckoned. The success that his band was enjoying was not enough to hold him in London, and he decided to head back to New York. Here he would move in with Jane Friedman, Patti Smith's manager, who would now look after his career as well. If Cale had hung on for a few more months – and hung on, too, to the band, whose time together was starting to show such strong indications of paying off – he would have caught the momentum of the emerging British punk movement and been in a good position to capitalize on it. Six months later Chris Spedding was having his clothes made by Malcolm McLaren and producing the first demos for McLaren's band, the Sex Pistols – all of which would have added another huge dimension to his already considerable capacities in Cale's band. In 1977 Chris Thomas would produce the Sex Pistols' *Never Mind the Bollocks . . .* It must have been extremely galling for a cutting-edge producer such as Cale to miss out on the biggest band of the punk movement and see them picked up by both his guitarist and key-board player. Cale, with his work in the Velvet Underground, his iconoclasm, his eagerness to take risks and his solo albums for Island – not to mention his produc-tion work for the Stooges and the Modern Lovers – was ideally placed to be a major player in the London of 1976 and 1977. As it was, while punk took off in Britain Cale was back in New York, the place from which he had fled five years earlier. It was to be another three and a half years before he released a new album, by which time punk in England was over, and Cale, one of its 'godfathers', had barely contributed to it. The years from 1976 to 1979 were, effectively, lost years.

At the end of December 1975 Cale played a couple of songs with the Patti Smith Group at New York's Bottom Line, where he met up again with Lou Reed, who had been in the audience, and went on to tour with her band in the summer of 1976. For these shows Cale was the opening act and would improvise with Smith before her band came on, returning to stage at the end of her set for its regular encore of 'My Generation'. On 1 January Cale played 'I Keep a Close Watch' at a St Mark's Church Poetry Project Benefit in New York and was then joined by Reed on 'I'm Waiting for the Man'. The two would continue to keep in contact, with Reed joining Cale on-stage again in July at New York's Ocean Club. Other special guests on that occasion were Patti Smith, Alan Lanier of Blue Öyster Cult, David Byrne of Talking Heads and Mick Ronson. The material was basically the set that Cale had toured with the previous year, but the guest musicians certainly attracted plenty more attention for him, and he played to an all-star audience of music-business cognoscenti.

Jane Friedman's company, Wartoke, rented space to two of the Copeland brothers,

Miles and Ian, and this would prove to be a profitable connection for Cale. Miles ran the record label, IRS, which brought him a fair amount of production work, while Ian's booking agency, FBI, would get him gigs on the concert circuit. Miles's and Ian's father, Miles Sr, had worked for the CIA in a variety of capacities and intrigued Cale enormously – for him the world of espionage and security services was a fascinating one. On the road the previous year he had expressed the conviction that he was being watched and followed, and he would continue to believe that he was being spied on for several years. The paranoia-inducing effect of cocaine was at least partly responsible for these feelings, and it was a common observation among those who knew him that Cale took the drug out of a compulsion to create a way of life that had drama and that was appropriate for the kind of artist he was.

Cale was kicking his heels through most of 1976 while trying to escape from the remains of the Island contract, unable to record. The summer gigs with Patti Smith and the appearances at the Ocean Club helped restore his profile a little in the USA and kept his hand in on the performing front, but with no record label there was little opportunity to capitalize on the activity and advance his career. Jane Friedman had certainly brought him some public attention, but what he needed more than this was regular live work and a functioning record contract. By the end of the year he would at least have the former.

"I SHAVE COLD JANE"

In the autumn of 1976 Cale finally put together a new band for a month-long tour of continental Europe. On guitar was Bob Kulick, who had recently played on Lou Reed's *Coney Island Baby* album, and alongside him were bass player Mike Visceglia, drummer Joe Stefko and David Labolt on keyboards. Chris Thomas would join them occasionally as a second keyboard player and also hung out with the band. The tour, playing mainly theatres, was a big success with audiences and went off relatively smoothly – despite the band having been warned beforehand that Cale had an almost schizophrenic 'split personality'. The 'other' Cale, they were told, would be released by drugs and alcohol. In Brussels, early on in the tour, the after-show conversation, which had been on the subject of the night's gig, changed as if at the flick of a switch. Cale's facial expression darkened, and his voice dropped low as he asked: 'Do you know what a rocket is? Do you know what a *rocket* is? It's what is *left behind* . . .' Later that night, on the stairs of the band's hotel, Cale made a noisy appearance, naked, with a frightened-looking Jane Friedman. The band pulled her into a bedroom and locked Cale out, but he opened a window in the hall, hauled himself through and climbed from balcony to balcony until he was outside the room. It had been raining; Cale stood with one bare foot in a pool of water and the other planted right next to the transformer for the neon lights of the hotel. Jane was ushered out of the room and Cale dragged in – literally inches from death. From this point on, he became known on the tour as 'the Fiddler on the Roof'.

Before another gig Joe Stefko turned up early to find Cale on his own on stage at the piano. Solitary and unwatched, he had been playing a classical piece and seemingly pouring his soul into it. Once he realized that he had an audience he immediately stood up and walked away.

At the end of the tour in October the band was in the French capital for a final high-profile gig at the Pavilion de Paris with the Patti Smith Group, who were also winding up their tour. Both bands, with their crews, got together to celebrate the final show at a restaurant where they had booked a private room, but Cale decided to leave early. Outside he hid in a doorway, convinced that a parked car contained members of the CIA who had been following him. While in Paris Cale and his band also played at a private club which had scaffolding on the stage. During the show Cale scaled the scaffolding and hung from it. The set itself consisted solely of one long improvised song, with Cale shouting out chord changes as it went along.

Back in New York Bob Kulick and Dave Labolt decided enough was enough and left the band. They were replaced by Ritchie Fliegler and, from the Patti Smith Group, Bruce Brody. This new formation played more gigs with Patti Smith, including one at the Palladium that also featured Television, who were being managed by Jane Friedman at the time. They also played many shows in their own right, including several at CBGB, where guests such as Lou Reed, Ray Manzarek from the Doors and Television's Tom Verlaine would join them on-stage.

The new band soon left New York for a West Coast tour. Cale started to introduce a little new material at this point, including 'Hedda Gabler', which would shortly be recorded. At one show, in Palo Alto, he grabbed the microphones from the other members of the band and crawled underneath the piano with them. He wrapped the cords around his neck and lay there, growling into the mikes and refusing to come out. A roadie who reached towards him to try to help was bitten.

The band played a week-long stint at CBGB in December, returning there again in March of 1977. Each time there were queues of people around the block. CBGB would become a regular venue for Cale and an important hang-out for checking out the burgeoning American punk scene. In February, he and his new band were supported by the up-and-coming Blondie for four sets over two nights at My Father's Place on Long Island. Here they played a version of Chuck Berry's 'Memphis' – which Cale would soon record, too – in another of his radical reinterpretations he would reveal its protagonist as a desperate paedophile. At CBGB in March, Lou Reed and Alan Lanier joined Cale on-stage. After the gig was over the three returned to jam together until five or six in the morning, watched by a 'crowd' of around a dozen.

Cale had already made other use of CBGB — he had been exercising regularly in its gym, and this had helped him to qualify at the end of the previous year for *New York Rocker*'s 'Most Put Into It' performance award of 1976.

Interviewed in spring in *New York Rocker* Cale talked of having written new material and looking forward to recording it when a new record contract could be sorted out. He also had hopes for live shows that were more theatrical or were 'special events' and talked of putting together a project that would involve the proper integration of a rock band and orchestra, maybe including a choir and a cathedral organ. In the meantime a return to Britain was looming, as part of a new European tour.

While Cale had been away in the USA everything had changed in Britain. It was almost as if, as soon as the arch-revolutionary's back was turned, the revolution had begun. Suddenly there was music with real edge again — and anything regarded as lacking it was completely disowned by the insurgents. Cale, ironically, was about to be caught on the back foot by this. His reaction in America to the conservative musical climate that he had left behind in England had been to take the sound of the Spedding band to new extremes — to go heavier . . . and hairier. Punk's natural affinity with Cale would not be consolidated, therefore, when he arrived back in Britain with his new band. Audiences and the new critics who had recently taken over the most influential parts of the UK press were about to be presented with what looked and sometimes even sounded like the kind of American heavy rock band that the new culture most despised.

Cale and his band arrived in Britain in April to a pretty sharp culture shock, playing their first gig the day after they arrived, having had no time even to attempt to assimilate what was going on. Chris Spedding could not believe what Cale's musicians looked like when he first saw them, with their long hair, headbands, tie-dyed T-shirts and flared jeans. They could not have contrasted more sharply with the spiky-haired punks in chains, leather jackets and drainpipe trousers. These British dates were to have featured front-line English punks the Clash, but they pulled out, saying that the Cale-led tour, which also featured the pop-inclined Boys, was 'not radical enough'.

Cale's response to the image problem, which he made after the early provincial English gigs, was to ask his band to get their hair cut. Ritchie Fliegler agreed, but Joe Stefko, who had the longest hair of them all, refused. Cale would not take no for an answer, however, and made a series of attempts to change his mind — including summoning Stefko to his room, where he was waiting with a pair of scissors. The two had been 'road buddies' up to now, but with this stand-off the relationship began to cool — and Cale started actively looking for ways to upset him.

After the provincial dates the band played two shows at London's Roundhouse, supported by Generation X as well as the Boys. With a punky Chris Spedding joining the encore of 'Baby, What You Want Me to Do' on the first night, the gigs were received reasonably well, despite their tendency towards hard rock. Most of the problems were seen as being ones of presentation.

Cale's attempts to upset his drummer reached a peak as the band made its way back through the English countryside back towards London at the end of the tour. Whenever they passed a farm Cale would call a halt and the road manager would climb out of the van and disappear into the farmhouse. Stefko, a strict vegetarian, was seated in the back of the van and kept asking what was going on. Cale would turn round and say: 'You shut up.' At the third or fourth farm Cale himself got out and returned with a live chicken, which he put in a box in the van. Stefko asked what he intended doing with the chicken and was told once more to keep quiet. When they finally reached the Portobello Hotel, where they were staying, he rang Cale's room and said that if Cale was going to do anything untoward to the chicken he wanted nothing to do with it. Cale responded: 'Trust me. I'm just going to have some fun.'

The next gig on the tour was at the Greyhound in Croydon, south of London, and Stefko asked one of the road crew, a friend of his, to check all the band's gear while he was setting up the stage beforehand. If he found the chicken he was to release it. The crew member searched thoroughly and reported back that everything was fine. There was no chicken to be found anywhere.

At the Greyhound the band went through almost the whole show without incident, and by the time they began the closing song, 'Heartbreak Hotel', Stefko started to think that everything was going to be all right. As the guitar solo began, however, Cale left the stage, returning in a butcher's uniform, holding the chicken by its feet, with his right hand behind his back. As he passed the drum kit Stefko saw that the concealed hand held a meat cleaver. Moving up to the microphone Cale sang: 'I could be so lonely — you could be so lonely, you could die', put the chicken on the floor and decapitated it. Throwing its head out into the audience, he started swinging the bird by its feet. Blood spurted out of its neck, and its body hit Stefko's drums. He stopped playing, threw down his sticks and walked off the stage. Cale followed him. In the wings, while chaos raged behind him in the theatre, he accused Stefko of desertion. The drummer responded that he had made no secret of what he would do if something like this happened. Meanwhile, the sound man, another friend of Stefko's, had pushed all the faders up to ten, drowning the hall in feedback and adding to the atmosphere of anarchy. Cale told Stefko that the chicken was already dead by the time he had brought it on stage, that it had been killed beforehand, but the drummer refused to come back on-stage. As the gig ended in mayhem the band returned to the Portobello.

In the restaurant downstairs at the hotel Stefko met up with Miles Copeland, who was promoting the tour, and Jane Friedman. Stefko told them that he was leaving the band and asked for his ticket home. Copeland refused to hand it over unless he finished the tour. Stefko then headed for his room, together with bassist Mike

Visceglia, the sound man and the crew member who had searched the equipment at the Greyhound. Here they locked themselves in and barricaded the door, uncertain of what was going to happen next. After a while it became clear that in fact nothing was going to happen. Stefko decided to lay low until early the next morning.

At the crack of dawn, while Cale, Fliegler and Brody, who were travelling on to the next gig in Swansea, were still asleep, he left the hotel.

Later that day, while the other members of the rebel group phoned the USA and arranged with their parents for pre-paid tickets to enable them to get home, Stefko resolved to stay behind in London and devise a strategy for rescuing his drums, which had been packed up with the rest of the band's equipment. Cherry Vanilla, who had a recording contract with RCA and an association with Miles Copeland's band the Police and who was also a friend of Stefko's, heard of his plight and offered to put him up in her London flat.

Where things had been going pretty much to plan for Cale in the USA Britain was already proving a different story — he had never been called 'not radical enough' before. When he beheaded the dead chicken on-stage and threw the head into the audience, it was an act of frustration more than anything else. Urged on by his management and old friends in the music business to live up to his image as the 'godfather of punk', while finding himself in the bizarre situation of being behind rather than ahead of the times, he found himself taking desperate action.

After the Croydon gig, Chris Spedding received a phone call in the middle of the night from what he describes as a 'very down-in-the-mouth' Cale.

'Chris, do you know any good drummers?'

'John, what have you done?'

'Well, I kind of chopped a chicken's head off on-stage and my drummer is kind of a vegetarian . . .'

In fact, Cale needed a new bass player as well, as both had quit. He somehow managed to find new musicians in time for the final dates of the tour, which culminated in a performance at London's Marquee club on 2 May, at the end of which the band managed a fearsome, magnificent noise on 'Gun' and 'Pablo Picasso'. After the encores Cale ripped open pillows and showered feathers on the audience.

Joe Stefko's story was eventually to have a happy ending. He, along with Cherry Vanilla's roadies (who were also the Police's), took a van up to the Marquee after the show in order to try to 'steal back' his drums. However, it turned out that Cale had just had all his equipment confiscated, having not paid the rental company from whom he was hiring it. Although Stefko's drum kit was taken by them as well, he later managed to reclaim it and take it back to the USA. The incident led to him coming to the attention of Meatloaf, just in time to become a part of the hugely successful 'Bat Out of Hell' band.

While in London Cale took time out to record an EP in Chalk Farm, *Animal Justice*, which included a new song, 'Chicken Shit', that featured the voices of Jane Friedman and Ritchie Fliegler. This dealt with both the Croydon incident and its aftermath and reproduced some of the telephone conversation that Cale and Stefko had had at the Portobello Hotel.

'Hedda Gabler' was recorded here, too, and Chris Spedding made another guest appearance on the third song, Cale's reworking of 'Memphis'. On the cover Cale was a condemned man, blindfolded and ready for execution by firing squad. Also recorded at Chalk Farm was another projected and later rejected single, 'Jack the Ripper', which would finally emerge years later on the *Seducing Down the Door* boxed set, and 'Ton Ton Macoute', which has failed to surface.

Miles Copeland was by now working hard in the punk scene in London and had started the Step Forward label, which released *Animal Justice* on its Illegal imprint. Although still based in New York, Cale began working alongside him temporarily as house producer at London's Pathway Studios, where he produced singles for Sham 69, Squeeze and Menace, among others. Although still without a record contract that would enable him to get an album of his own out, *Animal Justice* and production work in 1977 would bring him at least some of the punk kudos that he had missed out on in the previous months. The year before had not just been a lean one in terms of recording projects, there had been not a single piece of production work either; 1977 would make up in part for that and also bring in some much needed cash.

Through the Miles Copeland connection Cale began work on what would turn out to be an abortive session with the Police before embarking on a more successful project with Squeeze. He produced their début album, with John Wood as co-engineer, and although his radical ideas for it, which included calling it *Gay Guys* and having it half full of instrumentals, were rejected, he succeeded in forcing the band to jettison many of the songs they wanted to record and to write new material instead. The album was a success, spawning a Top 20 hit in 1978 with 'Take Me I'm Yours'. At the end of 1977, Julie Covington's 'Only Women Bleed', which Cale had arranged, reached number twelve in the charts. In the middle of all this production work, when asked who he would really like to produce, Cale replied that it was Captain Beefheart, rock 'n' roll's arch-surrealist.

In 1930 André Breton and Paul Eluard began to study at first hand images drawn by the 'insane'.

Cale managed a short European tour in June and returned there again from New York at the end of the year. *Animal Justice* was released in August, by which time he was on the point of following the example of Miles Copeland and other punk entrepreneurs by setting up his own record label. This would be called Spy, and he announced that he was looking for new talent in 'borstals and asylums'. Spy's first release was an EP by Harry Toledo, five thousand copies of which were released in the UK. By September Cale was working on a possible album of short stories.

Cale's transatlantic travels continued again in November when he played two gigs in Paris, moving on to Germany and then Holland in December. By now Judy Nylon had joined his band. While Cale was in London she had picked up books for him at the International Institute for Strategic Studies in Covent Garden and at the Institute for the Study of Conflict in Soho's Golden Square, which he remembers as being 'manned by old biddies with colonial or Sandhurst backgrounds/accents'. Nylon had also enjoyed discussions with him on their shared interests, such as mercenaries, spy toys and military and political strategy. Cale had given her a copy of *The Last Adventurer* by military leader and mercenary Rolf Steiner. At a meeting in the restaurant of the Portobello Hotel, exhausted after a year of flu and about to undergo an operation to remove her tonsils, Nylon nevertheless jumped at the chance to work on stage with someone she regarded, she says, as 'an intuitive Celtic poet', whose work was 'like a telepathic electric bolt that rarely misses its mark'. Nylon had known many of the major players in the English punk scene, with which she had been closely involved. With that scene now decaying, however, she felt that it was time to move on; after the operation she 'slugged back liquid aspirin for two weeks' and joined the tour. While in Germany she taped pre-recorded telephone messages used to solicit information on possible members of the Baader-Meinhof terrorist group. These she would later use for her band Snatch's 'R.A.F', a song that would appear on the flip-side of Eno's 'King's Lead Hat' single.

By now Ritchie Fliegler had left Cale's band (although he was later to return), and it now consisted of guitarist Davey O'List — who had been a member of the Nice and had also played with Roxy Music — Jimmy Bain on bass, Peter Oxendale on keyboards and Pete Nicholls on drums. O'List would in due course be replaced by Ollie Halsall, who would go on to work with Cale more extensively in later years. The intention was to have the band play the same material for several nights in a row, get it tight and record it for a live album. This would eventually happen but not for another eighteen months and with another band. Under-rehearsed at the start of the tour, they nevertheless managed to make some memorable performances, not least of a new song, 'Even Cowgirls Get the Blues', for which Nylon had written a 'scat sequence' that she sang through a Roland Space Echo effect box. As well as singing Nylon played bass on 'Pablo Picasso'. She and Cale would improvise different lyrics every night to Dutronc's 'Et Moi et Moi et Moi'. A female counterpoint to Cale, Nylon brought a parallel spontaneity to the shows, sometimes provoking him into life by taking centre stage away from him. Tattooed and strikingly made-up, each night she would cut up a different Snatch T-shirt (from a box she took on tour with her) and wear it with with black leather trousers and sneakers. She maintained, she says, 'a posture of warrior strength at all times on stage'. In Hamburg, without warning, Cale produced a gun and shot at her, and she fell to the floor. Realizing that the gun was in fact a starting pistol and had only burned the back of her T-shirt, she threw a punch at him from the ground, still managing to land it in the middle of his chest — in time to the music.

Less than a week after the final gig in Holland Cale was back in London again and being interviewed at the Portobello Hotel, accompanied once more by Tony Secunda. Back in 1974 Cale had prowled the corridors on all fours here, biting Cindy, who had rushed screaming to the front desk begging for a separate room. This time, he prowled again — naked. On an attempted return visit to the hotel three or four years later he would be refused entry. During the interview he announced an intention to give his imagination free rein in his forthcoming production work — success in this would see him eclipse the achievements of Phil Spector.

One final transatlantic crossing took him back to New York for Christmas.

The following year, 1978, would be another without a record contract and one also of little live activity. The new live band featuring Judy Nylon was put on hold, and the new material (including 'Evidence', 'Baby You Know' and 'Don't Know Why She Came') would be left to gather dust. Cale would make guest appearances on stage with Chris Spedding, Jonathan Paley, Harry Toledo and Nico and in the studio with Ian Hunter and Mick Ronson, but in terms of his own music the year he could have been capitalizing on the impact of punk was a dead year. Instead he worked on Spy and on immersing himself in a certain kind of New York life.

Spy was housed in Cale's 250 West 57th Street office with, for a while, a sister company called Cheap and Nasty Productions, which distributed some of Illegal's records in the USA. Spy was formed in partnership with Jane Friedman and also with Michael Zilkha, who would go on to found the Ze record label, for which Cale would both record and produce in the early 1980s. One of Cale's first projects for Spy was to take over the mixing and release of rock critic Lester Bangs's début single 'Let It Blurt'. Cale had got to know Bangs through living near him and took over the project when Terry Ork's Ork Records ran out of money before completing it. Spy also put out an EP by the Model Citizens and a single by the Necessaries (featuring Ernie Brooks, late of the Modern Lovers). Bob Neuwirth, who Cale had known since Velvet Underground days, was also lined up to record for the label, although nothing came of the plan. A similar fate befell projected releases by ex-Labelle star Nona Hendryx and actress and cabaret star Geraldine Fitzgerald, who was meant to put out a version of Cale's 'Antarctica Starts Here' produced by himself. There were also proposals, later shelved, to release Spy's singles in limited, numbered editions on coloured vinyl and to back them up with limited tours for the label's artists, extending from Toronto across to and down the East Coast. Spy would turn out to be most useful, however, as the vehicle for the release of Cale's 'Mercenaries (Ready for War)' single and *Sabotage/Live* album.

"CIA DELVE AS JOHN . . ."

The New York that Cale immersed himself in was one steeped in politics and political intrigue, guns and missiles, mercenaries, terrorism, espionage and the on-going Cold War. He subscribed to a variety of publications unavailable on news-stands, including mercenary magazines — the kind of thing that would arrive through the post in photocopied form. mailing lists for these magazines attracted the atten-tion of the CIA, and Cale appeared on their files as a result. This fact bore out his claims to have been followed by them — being paranoid did not mean that they were not out to get him. Cale had been fascinated by the CIA's involvement with LSD pro-duction and experimentation in the 1960s. Its ongoing, wider activities — particularly in destabilizing foreign countries — would continue to absorb much of his thinking. He was also developing a network of personal and correspondent contacts who were informed about the subjects in which he was interested and through whom he would collect and trade current information from all parts of the world. Cale's concerns ranged far and wide — wherever the cutting edge of world affairs could be found. In later years he would know about AIDS from New York mortuary personnel while it was still being diagnosed as 'Green Monkey Disease' and would predict both the eruption of the Iran–Contra affair and the start of the Gulf War months before they happened. Many people would go on to regret their tendency to doubt his information and to put his theories down to paranoia.

In the summer of 1978 Cale entered Big Apple Studios, where Spy's material was recorded, with Mick Ronson, Ian Hunter and ex-Mountain drummer Corky Laing. A late-night session of alcohol, cocaine and mayhem ensued, led by Cale, from which the participants somehow stumbled with a tape of four completed tracks of raw rock 'n' roll. A take of 'Shakin' All Over' was intended to appear on the B-side of 'Mercenaries' but would, in the event, mutate into the four-track recording, 'Rosegarden Funeral of Sores'. Cale was also to play on a track from Ian Hunter's 1979 album *You're Never Alone With a Schizophrenic*.

On 2 September Cale, accompanied by Chris Spedding, joined Harry Toledo on stage for a version of 'Pablo Picasso'. Cale played guitar with his microphone stand and took part in a 'guitar duel' with Spedding, which ended with him wrestling Spedding to the floor. The latter had recently arrived in New York, which he had decided to make his new base, and the Welshman was one of the first people he had called once he arrived. Cale was surprised to hear that he was there, telling him what Spedding had told Cale more than two years earlier — that he should have stayed in

England. Cale welcomed his old sparring partner to New York, however, introducing him to all the club doormen so that he could get in free. Cale seemed exactly the same to Spedding as he had been back in England — just as crazy. A common topic of conversation would be Miles Copeland Sr, and years later it would be Cale who told his former guitarist that there was now a Spedding in MI6, refusing to believe that he was no relation.

In October Cale joined Spedding, who was playing his first American solo gig, at Max's Kansas City, on versions of 'Pablo Picasso', 'Baby What You Want Me to Do' and 'Mary Lou' — all songs from the *Helen of Troy* sessions. Later on in the month the pair played live for a second time — a 'manic' Cale and 'delinquent' Spedding, as they were described in *New York Rocker*, with Jonathan Paley, again at Max's Kansas City.

By the end of the year Cale had a new band ready, one that would soon be able to stand comparison with his 1975 band and allow him to break new ground. This one was young, hungry and smart and would have the capability, finally, to capitalize on the punk scene — the one now gaining ground in the USA — and also on what was by now post-punk in Britain. After more than three years of relative inactivity Cale was finally about to start mattering again.

Over four nights of the 1978/79 New Year weekend a John Cale scratch band, consisting of Ritchie Fliegler on guitar and Bruce Brody on keyboards (both from the 1977 band), together with Judy Nylon on vocals and the Patti Smith Group's bassist Ivan Kral and drummer Jay Dee Daugherty, played at CBGB. Cale was dressed in a white shirt, a loose black tie and black leather trousers — a return to a much sharper image suggested to him by Jane Friedman — after the rugby shirt and jeans he had worn in 1977. With the inclusion once again of Nylon and the addition of the two members of the Patti Smith Group, the 'punk' quotient was adequately high. The set was a mixture of material from the Island years, together with unrecorded but no longer new songs such as 'Don't Know Why She Came' and 'Baby You Know', plus more recent songs, 'Casey at the Bat', 'Salome' and 'Even Cowgirls Get the Blues'. 'Salome' is one of many Cale songs of this era showing sex leading to corruption and violence, but here the setting is a very specific one, a mini-opera telling the story of Salome's Dance of the Seven Veils, which leads to the decapitation of John the Baptist. Judy Nylon had come up with what she describes as an 'obsessive rant' for the song, 'following four recurrent lines to reel it back in' when she was 'at the very edge' of her ability to ad-lib. Musically it builds slowly to a frenzied climax with Salome 'dancing to the beat of the rhythm of death'. The version played at CBGB led directly into its companion piece of historical sex, corruption and violence, 'Helen of Troy'. 'Even Cowgirls Get the Blues' follows a pattern of songs with borrowed titles that usually have little or nothing in common with their sources, this one taken from the book by Tom Robbins. As is the case with his Dadaist prose pieces, titles can be very

much part of a song for Cale, creating contradictions and, through them, new meanings. Nylon's unearthly coos and howls, together with a clunking, shuffling rhythm
that eventually builds to a series of heavy, descending chords in a minor key, tell as
much of the story of dislocation and despair as Cale's slow, melodic vocal line. 'Casey
at the Bat' takes the famous nineteenth-century story of a baseball hero's failure at
the plate and shifts its timescale so that the action takes place after the end of the
baseball game, with Casey pursued by a murderous mob. They howl for revenge at a
show of cowardice, a failure of nerve that, for them, is the failure of mythical
America, for which the price is death.

On 28 January Lou Reed was interviewed on the radio by WPIX FM. Cale joined
him on air to hear Reed call 'Hedda Gabler' a 'beautiful record' and tell his audience
that a good way for an artist to defy a record company was to bring Cale in as a producer. Cale talked a little about Spy, which was finally about to get off the ground,
and about the tour he was due to begin on 23 February and for which he was audi-
tioning two bass players.

On 17 February Cale was backstage with Nico to see the Clash at the Palladium
Theater; also present were Andy Warhol and Blondie's Debbie Harry. Two days later,
after a couple of rehearsals at the Chelsea Hotel where she was staying, Nico played
at CBGB, a gig arranged by Jane Friedman, and Cale accompanied her on viola. Half
the bands in New York seemed to be represented in the audience, and Cale's star was
rising again. Also in the audience was David Bowie, and he and Cale were to
collaborated briefly on stage and in the studio in October.

Cale's new tour took place over the course of nearly three months and forsook
the familiarity of the Big Apple for a massive haul across huge swathes of the USA and
Canada, peaking in June, back at home in New York, in the recording of his first
album in three and a half years — Sabotage/Live.

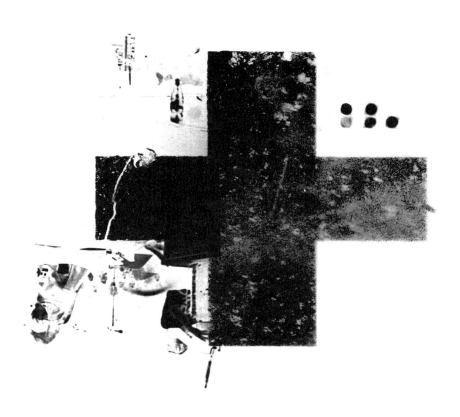

Whisky a Go Go
8901 SUNSET BOULEVARD • LOS ANGELES, CALIF.

JOHN CALE

Sat., March 29, 1980

9:00 P.M.

$6.50

WHISKY A GO GO
8901 Sunset Blvd. — Los Angeles, Calif.
Phone 652-4202

ADVANCE SALE
GENERAL ADMISSION
NO REFUND — NO EXCHANGE

ADMIT

DATE

SOURCE

Part 5
Calenture
(a delirium which convinces the afflicted that the sea is made up of green fields)

**On 9 March 1942 the San Bernardino Chemical Warfare
Service Plant produced its first incendiary bombs.**

**On 9 March 1942 Vannevar Bush wrote to President Roosevelt
advocating the building of an isotope separation plant that
could produce enough U235 to make one atomic bomb a month.**

Cale and the 'Sabotage' band (the personnel would undergo several changes on the
road) travelled thousands of miles across America in a nine-passenger station-wagon
in the early half of 1979 and set out again on a Midwest tour in July. In December
they started a third tour that would last for three months. There would be other gigs
between tours, too, the best of which often took place back in New York in front of
home crowds — playing these was like performing in front of an audience of friends.
This schedule was by far the most exacting of Cale's performing life and represented
a determined effort to establish himself as a performer in the USA. The tours were
booked by John Huie of FBI, and many of the venues Cale played were small bars and
clubs in out-of-the-way places, often to people who had never heard of him. In these
situations Cale and band were effectively a guerrilla outfit carrying on a war against
the parts of America that punk had yet to touch. War, terrorism and subversion were
a large part of Cale's subject matter now. This was both a conscious departure and a
reflection of the campaign ahead, and his songs would be informed by some of the
people, including Vietnam veterans, that he encountered on his way around the USA.

For his early stage shows Cale wore the white shirt and black leather trousers that
Jane Friedman had suggested for him, but before long he rejected these in favour of
continuing a habit begun in the Island days of wearing flying suits (he would pick
these up from army surplus shops on his way around America) and dark glasses. He
would also for a while adopt a yellow hard hat — turning him into a construction
worker concerned more with destruction, or a futuristic miner, a displaced version
of his father. There would be more dummies, as well, subjected to various kinds of
violent treatment, including decapitation.

Cale had a wealth of new material, and more songs were written on the road and
between tours, before near-identical sets were recorded over several nights at CBGB
in June of 1979 and edited to become the *Sabotage/Live* album.

The band that Cale had put together by the end of February consisted of Marc
Aaron on guitar, Joe Bidewell on keyboards, Tony Shanahan on bass, Doug Bowne on
drums and backing vocalists Cindy Black and Deerfrance.

Joe Bidewell's father had been an FBI agent, which fascinated Cale, but Bidewell had also known Jane Friedman since 1975, had backed Nico for a while and had auditioned for the Patti Smith Group when keyboard player Richard Sohl left. Tony Shanahan would later join the Patti Smith Group and Cindy Black was the girlfriend of Smith's drummer, Jay Dee Daugherty, who had recently played with Cale. Deerfrance had been a fixture on the New York punk scene for some time, having been the girlfriend of Television's Fred Smith and having also worked on the door at CBGB. All this meant that there was a strong sense of 'family' about the new band, which would survive the various personnel changes that it would nevertheless undergo.

Deerfrance had a striking presence on stage even before she sang – tall, beautiful and wild-looking in a punkish way. When she sang, she had an ethereal, little-girl voice that was at the same time both perfectly unaffected and otherworldly. Street-smart and feminine, she was the ideal female presence in Cale's band of intelligent young punks; self-confident and easy-going enough to be 'one of the boys', she was able at the same time to retain her identity as a woman. She was also the kind of woman who did not put off the women in the audience. As Joe Bidewell describes her, she had the 'radiance of a Lower East Side charm and grace', and for many of the female members of the audience she was a role model. She would soon establish herself in the band and was given her own spot in the show, where she sang songs such as 'Only Time Will Tell', 'Sunday Morning' and 'Rape'. She was also a constant reminder that songs such as 'Mercenaries' were far from being testosterone-filled macho posturing. Set to music by Cale, with lyrics by Deerfrance, the lyrics to 'Rape' were a real-life account by Deerfrance of an incident that had happened to her. The idea behind the song was to dramatize the ordeal it described, get it out in the open and by 'replaying' it provide a cathartic release for her. Cale would watch her supportively while she sang and, for the band, neither the song nor its performance were things they had to think twice about.

Rehearsals began at Cale's 30th Street rehearsal studio in preparation for the band's first tour and, with the members new both to each other and to the material, were initially long and intensive. Cale had wanted to capitalize on the punk scene that was now starting to grow in the USA and which had opened up the music business, making it easier for spontaneity and inspiration to flourish. He wanted to mould a band with some degree of permanency to it, which would be able to use that cohesion to move outwards into areas of improvisation and experimentation. Some of the songs he wrote now – 'Mercenaries (Ready for War)', 'Evidence' and 'Dr Mudd' – were rawer than ever, propelled by primitive chord sequences. There was no protective skin here, just bare, open flesh from which blood would flow in the solos. On all of these songs Cale played rhythm guitar in a very basic punk style. He would sometimes bring little more than the germ of an idea for a song to these rehearsals, maybe just one line with a melody, and allow the band to contribute their own musical ideas. These would be edited by him as the sessions went along, and he would add to and refine the lyrics until the song was complete enough to be used in live performances. Here it would often go on to gain further new life. Cale would improvise lyrics on stage in a 'stream-of-consciousness'. He and the band would try out musical ideas, too; these would be assessed later when tapes of the live shows were played back and either rejected or worked into the song. Cale was as keen as ever to pull ideas out of the air and find forms for them in his songs. He would seize upon certain 'mistakes' in the band's playing, not to admonish the player responsible but in order for them to be repeated. Such mistakes could be used as a departure point for a journey into the unknown and would sometimes lead to a breakthrough of the sub-conscious into the conscious world. It was a journey that might lead to the magical and the beautiful.

Rehearsals usually began at Cale's loft (which also became his home) around four in the afternoon, by which time he would have been at the piano for a while, working on his own. Acoustics in this space were poor, but the band's morale was high, and there was genuine excitement about the material on which they were working.

'When the conversation turned to politics and war, without warning he suddenly went into a raving fantasy . . . His talk . . . became disconnected, violent, maudlin and obscene.'
(From Dylan Thomas in America by John Malcolm Brinnin)

One of Cale's new songs that the band was playing at the start of the tour was 'Mercenaries (Ready for War)', the most obvious indication yet of his interest in politics and the make-up of war, and it would usually begin the band's live shows. With a martial bass line, heavy two-chord riff and menacing delivery, it would draw an audience immediately into a world ruled by war — a world that Cale saw all around him. In January 1979 the Chinese leader Deng Xiaoping had visited the USA and had talked of the two countries uniting against the USSR. Soviet-allied Vietnam had recently invaded Cambodia, and Deng now threatened to take direct, unilateral action in response. Two weeks after his visit he did just that, launching an invasion of Vietnam. The Shah of Iran also abdicated that same month, leading to the take-over of the country by the Ayatollah Khomeini. Khomeini supported the Mujahedin of Afghanistan, who were fighting the Soviet-backed government there. The Mujahedin were also being clandestinely supported by the CIA via Pakistan's dictator Zia ul-Haq. The Cold War seemed to be spreading, with the USSR being marginalized in the

The School Play, *Strife*, Amman Valley Grammar School, 1958
(Cale fourth from left)

Playing at the School Dance, Amman Valley Grammar School, 1959
(Cale at piano)

In New York, mid-1960s

In the band's station-wagon,
spring 1979

Shortly after leaving the
Velvet Underground in 1968

At CBGB, New York,
Christmas 1976

Ready for war, in the dressing-room, Holland, 1976

In the van, somewhere in Europe, 1976

With Joe Stefko on stage in Holland, 1976

In Paris, at the end of the tour, with Jane Friedman and guitarist Bob Kulick, 1976

Nico visits the Paris dressing-room, 1976

A poster for a gig at Eric's, Liverpool, 1976

Bum notes: playing piano for the Patti Smith Group, Paris, 1976

Erics

9 MATHEW ST
LIVERPOOL 2
051-227 5645

on Thurs 21st April

JOHN CALE

with THE COUNT BISHOPS
& THE BOYS

Members £1.40p Guests £1.80

Wearing Joe Stefko's glasses
in the dressing-room,
Paris, 1976

The doctor will
see you now . . .
Denmark, 1976

Belgian–French border,
paperwork incorrect . . .
1976

In the dressing-room with his parents, Will and Margaret, Paris, 1976

In the garden of the Portobello Hotel, London, 1977

With the 'Sabotage' band, San Francisco, May 1979 (Left to right: George Scott, Cale, Mark Aaron, Doug Bowne, Deerfrance, Joe Bidewell)

At the Whisky a Go Go,
Los Angeles, 30 April 1979

On stage in New York,
1987

Life Underwater, 1989

Wonderland USA, 1993

Behind the scenes,
UK tour, 1999

Rehearsing with the Velvet Underground before the first gig of the reunion tour, Edinburgh, 1993

With Sterling and Martha Morrison's daughter, Mary Anne, at rehearsals for the Velvet Underground reunion tour, Big Mike Productions, New York, 1993

In New York, 2001

With Sterling Morrison and Moe Tucker of the Velvet Underground at the Beverly Wilshire Hotel, Los Angeles, 1967

Middle East and at loggerheads, by proxy, with the USA in Africa, where the mercenaries backed by each of the two superpowers fought against one another. In January Britain and Germany had now accepted the installation of American missiles on their soil. Cale was instructing his audiences to be ready for war for good reason.

'Mercenaries (Ready for War)' incorporates words from Machiavelli for its introduction and a quote from 'The Last Post' as a musical motif; in an atmosphere of mounting hysteria the world is seen to be in the hands of 'soldiers of fortune'. In a performance in Pittsburgh in March the mercenaries were described as 'tired of listening to the Colonel in the back of the bus': heading for the airport, they say that they 'love the Kremlin . . . love Vietnam'. During the travels of the 'Sabotage' band across the American Midwest in the next few months Vietnam vets would sometimes turn up to the band's gigs, feeling a connection to what was being presented on stage. On one occasion, in a manifestation of the kind of world he was talking about, one of these men came up to Cale after a show, inviting him back to his house where he had a present he wanted to give him: a Luger. Cale declined the offer.

Tony Shanahan left the band in April, and George Scott, who had been playing with James Chance's 'No Wave' band the Contortions, was flown in to take his place. The evening Scott arrived Cale gave him live tapes of the songs he was expected to play the next night at the Opry in Houston. He had no problems learning them in time and became a seamless fit in the band, both on stage and off, where he was a riot. Cindy Black soon left the band, too, leaving Deerfrance as the only female vocalist.

"JANE. CHAOS. DEVIL . . ."

Through the months of March, April and May the band journeyed across the USA, playing big cities and small towns, ballrooms and bars. Despite living, working and travelling together, usually within the closest of confines, they managed to enjoy each other's company. Cale could be authoritative when necessary, and the other members respected his right to be so. He could also be morose and withdrawn but, to balance that, hilarious and silly and charming, too. Interviewed in Austin in April, he said that he had done little sightseeing on the tour but was enjoying the opportunities it afforded to lie in the sun doing nothing. Despite admitting to suffering from the long hours cooped up in the station-wagon, he seemed to be enjoying life on the road as much as the younger members of his band. He would take two bags on tour with him, one containing clothes, the other a backpack full of books — many of the long hours travelling were spent reading voraciously.

While in Austin Cale met up with Sterling Morrison, who was working there as a tugboat captain, and Morrison came on-stage at the Armadillo World Headquarters that night to join the band for a version of 'Mercenaries (Ready for War)'. After the show both were interviewed on local radio station KWT. The gig had been a huge success, with people hanging from the rafters, and four weeks later the band returned to play a hastily organized repeat performance, with equal success. On this occasion Cale and Morrison repaired to Cale's hotel and spent three hours in conversation, mainly on politics and academic subjects. These were highly enjoyable meetings for both men, who had barely seen each other since 1970. Morrison wore a T-shirt bearing the slogan 'I Kill Moonies', which Cale insisted that he give him.

There were other people who joined the band on stage from time to time. Judy Nylon occasionally turned up and sang a song in her own guest spot, and Chris Spedding also played if he was in town. Nico, too, performed at the odd show. One night Timothy Leary appeared backstage; another night Betsy Johnson was there, giving some wholehearted support; and ex-members of Andy Warhol's Factory — such as Paul Morrissey, Joe Dallesandro and Viva — sometimes attended. Cale and his band were well received everywhere they went, even in less obvious places where the audience might not even have heard of him. People might turn up out of curiosity about 'New York punk' or simply because there was nothing else going on, but they would usually leave satisfied. The band would always put on a real rock 'n' roll show, one that was entertaining and energetic, even crowd-pleasing — but with another layer, for those who wanted it, of subtler, more subversive pleasures. Cale, although always himself on stage, with no hint of pretence, was nevertheless refining the way in which he tried to communicate his ideas, and the approach worked. After one particularly success-ful gig he asked the audience: 'Where have you been?'

Interviewed in mid-April, Cale lamented the fact that the band had only had the chance to rehearse enough songs for one set and said that he had plenty more new material to be worked up when they got the chance. By the end of April they had begun playing 'Chorale' and also 'Sabotage', the title track of the live album to be recorded at CBGB in June. A prime example of the way Cale's songs would change through live performance, the lyrics were originally quite different from those on the version that would appear on *Sabotage/Live* . Here a lost file, an intelligence failure, leads to a 'broken-hearted man' burning down villages 'to find his way around' — an act of sabotage indicative of worse to come. The audience was urged to arm itself against impending disaster . . .

After more gigs throughout May, during which the band worked on more new songs, Cale was interviewed on 3 June and announced his intention to put together a live album from tapes of his upcoming four-night stint at CBGB. He cited the fact that his band was much better in live situations than in the studio as a reason for not recording his new material in the conventional way.

The four nights at CBGB, 13–16 June, were the culmination of three months of touring and, although Cale would later comment that the band's playing suffered as a result of knowing that the pressure was on to get a live album out the shows, there were some fiery performances. Each set concentrated largely on the same songs, with the intention of getting versions of them all good enough to put on the album. Although performed, 'Rape' did not make it on to *Sabotage/Live*. At the mixing stage Cale had consecutive performances of each of the same songs lined up on tape and listened song by song to each take before selecting the best for release.

Sabotage/Live was Cale's first and only album on Spy, although he would talk about reviving the label in later years. Various record companies had approached him in the 'wilderness years' between 1975 and 1979, and in 1980 Jane Friedman arranged a deal with A&M, after which Spy was put on hold. The projects that Cale had wanted to pursue with other artists on his own label went by the board, too, and this included a 'non-commercial' disco record, 'Equus'. Here the conventional disco vocals had been replaced with various pianos, a remixed version had been spliced on to the end and the noises of thunder, rain and whinnying horses overdubbed: a narration had then been placed over the whole.

'To let culture mature, one should close the schools, burn the museums, destroy the books, smash the printing presses.'
(Antonin Artaud)

Sabotage/Live depicts a world on the edge of war, but it is a world that needs a war, a world that needs to be destroyed and built anew. At the end of the Great War the Dadaists wanted to destroy all art because it had contained the elements that had combined to create that war. Now, on the brink of the Third World War, Cale was warning of three stark choices: either go with the war that seems inevitable and prepare to live with it and work out how you are going to deal with it; hand the world over to the mercenaries; or do the only thing that will prevent the war — destroy the culture that has made it inevitable.

In between the warnings and instructions of 'Mercenaries (Ready for War)', 'Dr Mudd' and 'Sabotage', 'Baby You Know' describes dishonesty and deceit in personal relationships (in live shows it would sometimes go straight into 'Guts', with its famous opening line), while 'Walking the Dog' relates a doomed attempt to escape the world by taking heroin. Cale had noted that the influence of heroin on blues could be detected by looking at the heaviness of the bass line — and this song would always feature two bass guitars. In 'Evidence' there *is* no evidence, no reason behind anything, no accountability: just gaps in the middle of real life that no one can fill. Some of these gaps occur in personal lives that lack meaning and humanity, others are created by people destroying the evidence or by those who can see it but ignore it.

On 9 March 1500 Pedro Cabral left for India with a fleet of thirteen ships.

'Captain Hook' deals with the legacy of imperialism, and the way it could break those acting for it as well as its victims. 'Only Time Will Tell' looks to a time when, as the Dadaists hoped, with war over and a new world order, art would be free from the corruption of the old world and free to create anew. 'Chorale' finds a similarly faint hope in fragments of love surviving in a broken world.

The title track, 'Sabotage', practises what it preaches and creates some of the most extreme music that Cale had come up with since leaving the Velvet Underground. Here the band, with Cale leading from the front on fretless bass, launch a guerrilla assault on music itself, with melody and conventional rhythm kept to a minimum and distortion, discord and noise joining the percussion of gunfire and explosions in a maelstrom of revolutionary activity.

Although *Sabotage/Live* was fairly straightforward to put together, it was not to be released until December. Meanwhile in July the band set off on another tour, this time concentrating on the Midwest and including dates in Minneapolis, Milwaukee, Detroit and Chicago. By 4 August they were back in New York again, playing at Irving Plaza.

With the autumn came time for recuperation after their travels, but on 22 and 23 September Cale, without the band, played at McCabe's Guitar Shop in Santa Monica. On 5 October he was back in New York at Ciarbis Studios, where he and David Bowie recorded a couple of demos, 'Velvet Couch' and 'Piano-La', neither of which have been released. Both feature Bowie singing, accompanied by Cale on piano. The first sounds almost as though it could be a ballad from Bowie's 'Ziggy Stardust' era, while the second, musically as pleasant, has Bowie improvising vocally without words. Cale and Bowie were also to appear together at a benefit concert at New York's Carnegie Hall. The two chatted beforehand backstage. Bowie had a violin with him, so Cale invited him to appear on stage with him, which he did, on a version of 'Sabotage'.

Cale played at the Squat Theater on 20 October and then, at the end of December, what was now a different version of the 'Sabotage' band played another four nights at CBGB, publicizing the release of *Sabotage/Live*. Dougie Bowne, following a misunderstanding with Cale, had been replaced by Robert Medici, and in place of George Scott, who was suffering from drug problems, was Peter Muny. Medici was a well-liked and respected, very professional percussionist, with a large drum kit that was heavy on the cymbals. At the sound-check for a gig at the Mudd Club Cale made the roadies remove all of his cymbals, the sound of which was, he said, obscuring the clarity of his vocals. Medici objected, but Cale refused to budge, and the drummer played the gig without them.

M.

Thanx for
Everything

Best Wishes

J.C.

The CBGB gigs were the prelude to what would be another heavy touring schedule, promoting the newly released live album, that would last through most of the first half of 1980.

Sabotage/Live was given further impetus early in 1980 with the release of a specially recorded single version of 'Mercenaries (Ready for War)'. By now the band had a new guitarist, too, Sturgis Nikides, who had played in Joe Bidewell's band and had also, with Bidewell, backed Nico for a while. Marc Aaron had left in the wake of George Scott's departure, so Cale was looking for a new guitarist, and Bidewell introduced Nikides to Cale in the dressing-room at Max's Kansas City. Cale was impressed with Nikides's appearance (saying that he 'looked like Sid Vicious') and offered him an audition, which he passed. The original intention was for him to rehearse with the band with a view to being ready for the start of the next tour in March, but Cale wanted to record the single version of 'Mercenaries (Ready for War)' and asked him if he felt he was up to it. If not, he would ask Chris Spedding, who continued to jam with Cale's band throughout the 'Sabotage' era. Nikides was not about to turn down the opportunity and joined the band for the recording session at Radio City Music Hall's Plaza Sound. 'Rosegarden Funeral of Sores', which was the single's flipside, was recorded on a home studio in Arizona, with Cale on bass, piano and vocals, accompanied only by producer Michael Mason's drum machine.

After playing at the Cellar Door in Washington in February the band were back at the Armadillo in Austin, Texas, on 9 March. Once again Sterling Morrison came on stage for 'Pablo Picasso', borrowing one of Nikides's guitars as he no longer had his own – his fingers, unused to playing, bled on to its body. By now sets could last up to two hours and were full of guitar work-outs; 'Pablo Picasso' alone could last more than half an hour. At the end of March, the band was back in New York for two nights at the Bottom Line before travelling to Los Angeles for three nights at the Whisky a Go Go. While in Los Angeles (gigs for which Jane Friedman and the rest of the New York office flew out) the band stayed at the infamous rock 'n' roll haunt the Tropicana Motel on Santa Monica Boulevard. Here, for once, they enjoyed the excesses of a traditional rock 'n' roll lifestyle. Normally the members of the band were fairly quiet off-stage, not the kind to attract groupies – more likely, in fact, to settle back with a good book. On one occasion, in Cleveland, the band found themselves on the same floor of the Holiday Inn as Mötorhead. At the Mötorhead end windows were being broken, doors kicked in, and drunken, drugged-up girls were sleeping in the hall. At the Cale end everything was deadly quiet, with the boys in their rooms either taking a nap or reading.

In Los Angeles representatives from A&M records had seen the band play, having been brought along by Jane Friedman, and this contact was shortly to lead to Cale signing a record deal with the company. From Los Angeles the show moved off to San

Diego, Costa Mesa, San Francisco, Berkeley and on to the Midwest again, dates in Seattle and Vancouver having been cancelled. At the Cuckoo's Nest in Costa Mesa someone in the audience threw an object at Cale. Louis Tropia, who was both road manager and a long-time friend of Cale's, the two having roomed together on tour, reached down and grabbed the assailant by the throat, dragging him the length of the stage and out of the door. During the band's sojourn in the Midwest, US embassy staff in Tehran, capital of Iran, were taken hostage and in the atmosphere of renewed international tension *Sabotage/Live* began to seem even more significant. Back at Irving Plaza at the end of April Cale and his group performed over two nights, billed as 'Sabotage Surprise'.

'Rest in peace, Louis. You were my friend.'
(Sturgis Nikides)

On 24 and 25 May Cale played two shows entitled 'The Nine Lives of Gordon Liddy' − a reference to the charmed existence of the ex-Watergate burglar − at New York's Squat Theater. Nico was living there at the time, having moved down the street from the Chelsea Hotel, and, like the Mudd Club and CBGB, it was a regular venue for Cale's New York gigs. A melancholy song cycle, 'Nine Lives' gathered material old and new into a suite characterized by melancholy and despair. This was a look at personal relationships that echoed the pessimism of *Sabotage/Live*'s world view − music for an old society − and also prefigured the substance and tone of the *Music for a New Society* album that would appear in 1982. 'The Nine Lives of Gordon Liddy' linked the two projects by including 'Only Time Will Tell' from *Sabotage/Live*, which might be said to be the cycle's starting point, and a new song, 'Thoughtless Kind', which would appear on the later album. Other new songs included the bleak 'Cold Country Comfort', which opened the set, and 'Coming Around Again', but there was also a reworking of the old cowboy lament 'Streets of Laredo' − twinned with Cale's own 'Cable Hogue' − which would soon be hauled into the present and electrified.

By now the new line-up of the 'Sabotage' band was well into its stride and producing performances every bit as good as those with Scott, Aaron and Bowne. At the Emerald City Club in New Jersey they played 'Let All Mortal Flesh Keep Silence', the liturgy of St James set to a traditional French melody and given a heavy rock backing. The hymn describes the return of Christ to earth, an apocalyptic scenario in keeping with the concerns of *Sabotage/Live*, and the music has a grandeur, beauty and power to match. The hymn is not so much reinterpreted, in the way that Cale had earlier dealt with 'Heartbreak Hotel', but brought back from the past, its original fire burning again nearly two thousand years after the crucifixion. At the Squat Theater 'Let All Mortal Flesh Keep Silence' had been played in an instrumental arrangement for piano that had segued into 'Fear Is a Man's Best Friend', whose opening line 'Standing, waiting for a man to show', had been given new meaning.

The Emerald City Club gig also featured a strong, upbeat updating of 'Sunday Morning'. Transformed into 1980s punk/electro-pop, it was sung by Deerfrance, tall and blonde but a world away from Nico. Two new songs were also figuring in the set, 'Dead or Alive' and 'Magic and Lies', and both would appear on the A&M album, for which recording sessions began at the end of the year. 'Dead or Alive' was written about a disturbed woman who had tried to attach herself to Cale — an experience that would be repeated during this period when another woman turned up to one of his gigs with two dozen roses asking, 'Where's my husband?', genuinely convinced that she and Cale had been married. While in New York Cale was living with Jane Friedman, but it was a relationship that was put under strain once he was away on tour. She would worry about what he was up to and he, in turn, would begin to feel resentful that she was not being supportive enough of his career.

In July the band made a brief trip to Europe. By this time both Joe Bidewell and Deerfrance had left the ranks. Deerfrance, who had gone to live in France, was not replaced; Bidewell would be, but not just yet. The band returned to the USA for what would be a relatively quiet summer. Here Cale slotted back into his New York milieu, renewed his acquaintance with various contacts in the worlds of government, the security services and Vietnam veterans and continued to feed his mind on its regular diet of politics, intrigue and technology.

In October Andy Warhol offered to design the cover for Cale's new album, which was to be called *Honi Soit*. Cale accepted the offer but consequently had, reluctantly, to reject a series of photographs that Mick Rock had taken and which Cale had liked. Rock had shot him, dressed predominantly in white, in martial arts poses. A few weeks after this photo session Rock photographed Lou Reed, and one of the shots was used for his album *Growing Up in Public*. In February 1980 Reed had married his second wife, Sylvia Morales, with whom Cale had earlier had a one-night stand. In October 1981 Cale would also marry for the second time. Musically disengaged they may have been, but their lives continued to intertwine in other ways. Visiting Reed and Morales at their rural retreat in New Jersey, Cale found the two absorbed in video games, oblivious to the presence of their guest.

Towards the end of 1980 Cale and his band began working on *Honi Soit* at CBS Studios on East 30th Street, where *Church of Anthrax* had also been recorded. By now Cale was not only still living part of the time at his crash-pad loft in the same street (which was a complete shambles) but also sharing a penthouse apartment on Barrow Street with Risé Irushalmi, whom he had first met coming out of CBGB in the small hours of New Year's Day. Cale had fallen in love with Risé and saw in her the chance of redemption, the chance to escape a lifestyle that was now beginning to draw on his strength and sanity. This was a time during which, as Sturgis Nikides remembers, Cale would attract stalkers and 'the occasional psycho [would] hit on him'; he was also living with the knowledge that he had 'trodden on a few people's toes'. His was a lifestyle that was deeply embedded inside him, however, and one that he was unable to detach from his inspiration. Working with Jane Friedman now became even more stressful for both of them. For the moment Cale would carry on a schizophrenic existence that seesawed between the future and the past.

On 9 March 1942 *Newsweek*'s cover story was 'MacArthur of Bataan: War's No. 1 Hero'.

Cale had decided to get an outside producer in for the album. This had to be some-one who could be relied upon to be a calm centre at the storm of a Cale recording session and come out the other side with a commercial-sounding record that never-theless would also properly reflect the artistic efforts that had gone into its creation. Although *Sabotage/Live* had been well received critically, it had not sold in large numbers, and Cale was looking for ways of making his songs more widely acceptable in a way that would not compromise their inspiration and intent. He decided that he wanted to work with Mike Thorne, who had recently produced Wire and Soft Cell, so Jane Friedman phoned Thorne in London to gauge his interest. Thorne was positive about the project and spoke to Cale himself before finally meeting up with him at the Molly Gee bar in New York. Here the specifics of work were temporarily ignored in favour of a discussion of mutually admired bands and common friends in the music business. Cale had already established Thorne's ability to do the job, and now it was just a question of whether the two would be able to establish a relationship that would stay the course. Cale already had several songs written for the album, and these were well-constructed and commercially appealing pieces, although lyrically dark; the ones that would make it on to vinyl were 'Dead or Alive', 'Riverbank' and

'Magic and Lies'. He understood himself well enough, however, to know that once he was in the studio it was possible that everything pre-prepared would be thrown out of the window in favour of expressing the creative currents running through his head at the time. What he needed was someone to hang on to some, at least, of what had already been written and to make sense of whatever else was to come.

With the recent arrival of Jim Goodwin on keyboards, Cale's group had now meta-morphosed into the 'Honi Soit' band, and they put in a little rehearsal for the record-ing of the album before the sessions proper began up the road at CBS Studios. These sessions lasted for two weeks and were followed by four weeks of overdubbing, edit-ing and mixing at Media Sound on 57th Street. This was the home studio of recording and mixing engineer Harvey Goldberg, who was Thorne's right-hand man for the project. Much of the hardware at CBS Studios, which had been built and used exten-sively for orchestral work, was old and two-track, and more modern 48-track equip-ment had to be brought in. However, there were also two concert grand pianos which had been played by Glenn Gould, and these were shown due respect (even by Cale). The building housing the studio had originally been a church and had a seventy-foot-high 'cathedral' ceiling and a nave, providing some wonderful, natural reverb. Mike Thorne hung microphones twenty feet above the drums and grand pianos in order to capture this resonance. As the studio had been constructed for classical use it was not capable of handling a full drum kit, with the result that when Robert Medici hit the drums the whole room would shake. It was to Harvey Goldberg's credit that he managed to overcome the acoustic problems and come up with a full, undistorted sound for the percussion.

Miles Davis had been talking about using CBS Studios for recording at this time, which would have curtailed the *Honi Soit* sessions, but, as Thorne recalls, 'Fortunately, he didn't wake up in time.' As it happened, *Honi Soit* would be one of the last albums recorded at these studios, the building being knocked down soon afterwards to make way for a car park.

Instrumental backing tracks were laid down at CBS for songs that had already been written, but Cale also brought poems and lyrical ideas to the sessions, and these were used as the basis of improvisations. Starting from notes, he would free-associate in a stream of consciousness; when he was in his stride, it was almost as if he was aquaplaning. These improvisations might sometimes even be used with dif-ferent music later on; songs such as 'Strange Times in Casablanca', 'Honi Soit (La Première Leçon de Française)' and 'Wilson Joliet' came about in this way. Some of Cale's lyrics would come to him as he sat at the piano with a copy of the *Guardian* newspaper open in front of him. He would also, with a 'mind's ear', be able to call up musical possibilities that might have occurred to him while sitting in a pub before the sessions, and these would be translated immediately into notes on the piano. In this way ideas had the chance to take flight along unusual paths, rather than following the line of least resistance that was otherwise sometimes too easy to follow.

Thorne had been to see Cale play a solo show at CBGB not long before recording began, and Cale encouraged him now to get closer to the songs by joining in with the band and playing some synclavier and piano. This brought him directly into the music and made him a part of it — another element in the very important process of establishing trust between the two of them. The roles of each in terms of production were solid and well defined, however, and Cale never tried to invade what had been designated as Thorne's territory. Recording sessions would last, typically, from two in the afternoon until ten at night — at which point Cale and Thorne would usually agree that the law of diminishing returns was taking effect — and the band might go out for drinks and supper together. Sometimes Thorne and Cale would disappear to talk about the sessions in a general way, often to 1 University Place, which was run by Mickey Ruskin, who had previously owned Max's Kansas City, the Velvet Underground's hang-out.

For Thorne these were very intense sessions, at which he had to hold the centre while Cale thrashed around in every direction. At night Thorne would have to leave the telephone on as Cale would call him one night in two at either three or four o'clock with ideas he wanted to try out on him; this was just part of the job as far as Thorne was concerned. On one day in particular Thorne remembers pursuing Cale around the studio with a quarter-inch jack as he, in a hyperactive fit, tried keyboard after keyboard to get the sound he wanted. Thorne was trying to keep up with Cale while keeping hold, too, of the overall picture of what they were trying to create, and he succeeded — on this particular day they managed to record five separate backing tracks in one nine-hour stint. Thorne recalls being giddy afterwards and unable to walk straight as he headed home on foot — he was so full of the day's achievements that he had to 'walk them off' rather than take a cab as usual and have them still pounding in his head when he got there. This was the day from which two of the album's strongest pieces came: 'Streets of Laredo' and 'Wilson Joliet'.

One particular point of contact that Cale and Thorne had was in the field of nuclear physics — more specifically, for Cale, the way to construct a nuclear bomb. A game of 'raising the stakes' developed. Cale had bought a nuclear textbook, and he showed it to Thorne, asking to be brought up to speed on creating a small device. Thorne paused and said thoughtfully: 'Well, we're going to need a few things.' He explained that the main ingredients were a few pounds of plutonium and a critical mass and that the idea was for the two to come together suddenly — but not while the bomber was within a hundred miles. The engineering involved was very clever, but it would certainly be possible for a renegade state, with a lot of hard work and dedication, to make a powerful 'dirty bomb' and bring it into New York in something no larger than a suitcase. Cale decided that the project would be too time-consuming to be a practical consideration but that a successful end result might be a piece of performance art that could be jettisoned once it had been made.

The final version of 'Strange Times in Casablanca' was the result of several intense raps that Cale poured forth, having propped himself up against a microphone. After each burst of words he would pause to gather breath, before resuming the position and taking off again. Thorne put together a composite of takes over the course of the best part of an afternoon, with Cale's blessing, in an attempt to get an objective view of the song. The one he eventually chose turned out to be one that Cale and Jane Friedman had already earmarked. For the album's title track, 'Honi Soit (La Première Leçon de Française)', which had started as another rap, over an improvisation snippets of tapes of Sturgis Nikides's guitar riffs and other musical sections were pasted together after the fact to create a full musical backing. Cale delivered the song like a lecture, banging on the music stand to attract the attention of his 'students' — its subtitle being 'The First French Lesson'. 'Wilson Joliet', born as an improvisation, became a song only at the overdubbing stage; Nikides initially had to ask Robert Medici's help in assessing when to make his chord changes within the piece's difficult eleven-eight time. The unusual percussion effects heard on the track were made by Cale wandering around with a hammer. 'Russian Roulette', originally to have been the album's title track, is remembered by Mike Thorne as 'one of the craziest moments of the session . . . coming straight at you'. The song was blasted out live in the studio with a vocal that was at first thought unusable owing to the incendiary music around it — until Harvey Goldberg pulled it out of the fire.

One song recorded at the sessions, 'Need Your Loving', had been tagged as a possible single. A big production number with a curious rhythm based on a snare delay on the backbeat, Cale was keen to include the song (in preference to 'Riverbank') right up until the point where the album had been mixed and was ready to be pressed. At this point he made one of his middle-of-the-night phone calls to Thorne and changed his mind. For him the decision rested on the balance of the album; it needed to be commercial, but the inclusion of 'Need Your Loving' would have been a step too far in that direction, tilting the balance away from the main concerns of Honi Soit: war, global politics and their effects on people.

The opening and closing tracks on the album — 'Dead or Alive' and 'Magic and Lies') — are concerned with the cruelty of life on a personal level, the damage done to individual human beings. In between there is a terrible catalogue of the misery wrought by states, political systems and cultures within which war is embedded.

After the deceptively upbeat 'Dead or Alive', with its piccolo trumpet fanfares, 'Strange Times in Casablanca' creates a thick, stifling canopy of sound. Dense with flypast fighter engines, rain, explosions, echoing corridors and a pounding heat, this is the sound of decay and depravity, set to a remorseless beat. Cale comments on the proceedings from the White House, first of all with a devilish leer and a voluptuous snarl but finally with the level, straight-talking amorality of someone who has just washed his hands of what he sees. 'Strange Times in Casablanca' spews forth images from the unconscious and lets them form their own patterns, bypassing conscious agency — automatic writing and remote viewing.

The Second World War 'Fighter Pilot' of the next track is a symbol of war's embodiment in the life of his country. A hero but also a 'terrible man', he has a wife and children and an aircraft that is a killing machine. War is institutionalized in him, and he has to uphold its stature in his country's way of life. He is a symbol and must win the propaganda war as well as the military one. In this he has failed . . . He has been setting a 'bad example' back home, the price for which is death — a penalty to be exacted by both 'angels' and 'bandits'.

In 'Strange Times in Casablanca', part of the White House spokesman's ease with the events on which he is commenting comes from the fact that 'We've turned our back on it once before'. That was in Vietnam. In 'Wilson Joliet', a slow march, two veterans of that campaign, survivors of the 'Death March' of Bataan, are now outcast in the country for which they risked their lives — outcast and in jail, having found another world that was 'without rhyme', just like the one they have fled. They have relived the horror of that war and can find no peace, being forced instead to re-create what they lived through. Having escaped once from the terror of that existence, they now have to escape again — not just from their immediate surroundings but also from the memories that will not go away, memories of mothers who have lost their children, of an existence without meaning. 'Wilson Joliet' is thick with claustrophobia and the sense of people dragging themselves desperately through life. At the end it spirals upwards towards the sky, against an anguished countdown, towards release.

'Streets of Laredo', set to a funereal march, laments the death of a fighting man — a man who has killed but a man for all that. Drastically reduced from the original version's eight verses and pared to the bone as a result, it also has its tune rewritten to avoid the jauntiness that had originally hidden some of its bleakness. This version has nothing but gambling, sex, killing and then death; it ends with ribbons of melancholy viola, a tolling bell and Cale banging on a radiator with his hammer. In the film *Bang the Drum Slowly* this song was used to illustrate the death of a baseball player; here it is wrapped around the death of a Vietnam veteran.

Honi Soit's title refers to 'Honi Soit Qui Mal y Pense', the motto of the Royal Order of the Garter, the highest order of British Knighthood, which is also inscribed on the Royal Coat of Arms. This insignia is found on British government documents, passports and military uniforms — it is, in effect, the British army's licence to kill and a literal embodiment of warfare in Britain's constitution. It is also the message that Britons carry to foreign countries and therefore not only a constant statement of hostility but also a permanent reminder of Britain's colonial past. 'Honi Soit Qui Mal y Pense' is the 'first French lesson', but for some it might be the only one, the only French they need to know. A similarly critical view of French history might reveal that the only thing worth knowing in this context is that France was the first Western invader of Vietnam, before withdrawing and leaving it to its fate. 'Honi Soit (La Première Leçon de Française)' rattles along at a jolly pace, the 'lecturer' happily defining a *coup d'état* as '*la valoir*', glory, and repeating its uncomplicated message before announcing '*C'est fini*', it is finished. The logical extension of 'Honi Soit Qui Mal y Pense' is Armageddon, and when Cale performed the song live over the next few months he would sometimes finish it with an extra section that conjures up the Four Horsemen of the Apocalypse.

'Riverbank' is the most straightforward song on the album in terms of musical arrangement and the most direct lyrically, as well as being one of the most beautiful Cale has written. Partly inspired by the story of Ophelia's suicide by drowning in *Hamlet*, it also refers to the war widows of Vietnam and the mothers of children killed there.

From the innocent victims of war to the big stage: 'Russian Roulette' takes on not just the Russians but also the French, Americans, Germans and Japanese in an apocalyptic ranting rap that hurls blame in all the right places and draws parallels on a variety of levels between all the players on the world stage. Part of the idea for the song had come from a report of a group of left-wing black doctors who had tried to stop a meeting of the Ku Klux Klan, an attempt that ended in shots being fired. This is thrown into the pot along with images of Ronald Reagan, who would take office as US president in January, as John Wayne riding to the brink of apocalypse, a missile circuit as 'the moist vagina of the war', Miles Copeland Sr as 'Miles Underground' and various pieces of word play: 'disgust'/'distrust', 'defecting'/'defective', 'in the rain'/'infiltrated'. Cale seethes through these twisted, entwined analyses and accusations, spitting out his words and raging with the powerlessness of a single human being in the face of battling superpowers. The music rages around him, too, a furious, guitar-led onslaught, howling outrage at the objects of his disgust.

Mirroring its starting point, *Honi Soit* ends with 'Magic and Lies', a song about those worn down by the remorselessness of lives lived under the heel of fate. In 'Dead or Alive' the central figure is an actress in pornographic films; here she is a prostitute. Both have suffered abuse at the hands of unseen men. The men who actually appear in 'Magic and Lies', however, are victims, too. At the beginning of this final song, an old man appears. He is a loser, someone who has failed to live successfully in the world; at the song's end, another man appears, young but already tired, already on the way to living the same kind of life as the old man has led, one that believes in magic and lies.

Honi Soit was released in March 1981, and Cale played some solo gigs to promote it. There was also a band appearance in New York, recorded for a radio broadcast, which featured an appearance by John Gatchell, who had played piccolo trumpet on the album, and Jim Goodwin on saxophone, an instrument that he would continue to play extensively on an upcoming European tour. There were new songs here, as well, including 'How Could You Call Yourself a Lover?' and 'Not With Your Neighbour's Wife', neither of which would make it on to vinyl.

One of Cale's solo gigs in March was at the Edge in Toronto, and the show held the nucleus of what would become his staple solo set in years to come. There were selections that would not stay the course, however: a couple of mainly improvised piano pieces, straight versions of 'Streets of Laredo' and 'Let All Mortal Flesh Keep Silence'. 'Thoughtless Kind' made another appearance, as did another new song that would later appear on *Music for a New Society*, 'Chinese Envoy', here with some quite different lyrics. On occasions throughout the show Cale experimented with a reverb effect on his piano, and he grabbed an electric guitar for a long, heavily distorted version of 'Pablo Picasso'.

The band travelled to Europe in April. On the way to a gig in Paris in the small hours of the morning, the road nearly deserted, Cale had been convinced that the car behind contained CIA agents who were following him. At the next toll stop he jumped out of the station-wagon and remonstrated with the occupants, battering their vehicle. At a restaurant stop everyone got out to eat; Cale disappeared and was eventually found hiding under a bus, refusing to come out.

At London's Lyceum in mid-April Cale wore a black stocking mask and played guitar most of the time, while the band were at their blistering peak: tight, sharp and intense. 'Wilson Joliet', which had undergone so much preparation in the studio, was brought back to life perfectly, shining with a deep, underground light, and, apart for a brief reduction in tempo for 'Riverbank', the energy never let up for a moment – as soon as one song finished the band piled into the next. On 'Fighter Pilot' they were joined by the Mo-dettes on backing vocals. The all-girl band, disguised as the 'Bomberettes', had also backed the song on *Honi Soit*. 'Russian Roulette' reached the same level of inspired mania as the recorded version and was channelled immediately into an apocalyptic 'Honi Soit (La Première Leçon de Française)', telling the story of the man who bought his four sons a horse each on their birthdays, writing the one word 'Ride' on their cards. When they grow up the four horsemen do just that.

'I do not think that I would wish to go through the Middle West, excepting Chicago, again . . .'
(Dylan Thomas)

By the end of the month the band were back in the USA and playing at the Ritz

Club in New York. Andy Warhol attended the gig, having his photograph taken with them in the dressing-room, and Chris Spedding came on-stage for an encore of 'Leaving It Up to You'. In May the group embarked on what would turn out to be another long cross-country trip — the last tour with a band that Cale would make until the spring of 1983.

The itinerary this time took in some smaller venues in even more out-of-the-way places than the ones played by the 'Sabotage' band. The tour was booked once again by FBI's John Huie, and the road manager was Lenny Fico, who had worked for Stiff Records the year before and knew some of the venues that would be visited. FBI's biggest act was the Police, featuring the third Copeland brother, Stewart. Promoters who wanted to book the Police would do deals that also involved them taking on FBI's other acts. In Cale's case this meant that his band was given a variety of often obscure venues to pioneer, to go along with the bigger city venues he needed to play. As a result, the band would play places that had never put on a live band before — tiny clubs and bars in remote locations.

On tour the band was once again cooped up in an unsuitable vehicle for long periods — this time an eighteen-seater airport van — as A&M refused to pay for a proper tour bus. Most of the stage equipment was held together by gaffer-tape — including Cale's Fender Rhodes electric piano. Far away from New York Cale had plenty of time to wonder why the 'office' back home had sent him out into the wilds to slog across country, sometimes through two or three states in a single day, for hours on end, only to end up playing to an audience of ten in the middle of nowhere.

The airport van had bench seats at the back. Cale got to ride shotgun at the front, and Lennie Fico drove. The band members at the back of the van probably had a better deal than Cale, as they were able to stretch out on the wide seats and get some sleep. The van broke down on several occasions, and the band would be stranded on highways all over the country. A typical breakfast for Cale on the tour would be a six-pack of beer, a quart of chocolate milk and strawberries. For lunch he would drink quarts of pea soup. The results were predictable . . . At one gig keyboard player Jim Goodwin fell off stage and hurt his back. Unable to sit, or even to lie down on the van's bench-seats, he was on the verge of having to leave the tour until the band stole a room door from a motel and laid it down in the back of the van for him. More time was spent in this van than in motel rooms. By the time they got to a motel after a gig it was usually around two in the morning, and by eight it was time to get back in the van and travel to the next one. Money was tight, too; whenever they made any at the larger venues, it disappeared almost immediately on paying the motel and food bills at the tiny bars where door receipts would not cover them. The combination of the travelling, lack of money and often tiny audiences, together with the high cocaine intake that was still a large part of his life, meant that at times Cale, now approaching forty, sometimes seemed on the edge of a nervous breakdown. Sitting on the bus, he would bite his fingernails — so much so that they disappeared.

Tour itinerary 14 May — 10 June 1981 [notes by Lennie Fico]

14 May. The Patio, Indianopolis, Indiana.
  Parking facilities: In the street
16 May. Point East, Lynwood, Illinois.
  Load-in area: In parking lot — right side of dumpster
17 May. The Palm, Milwaukee, WI
  Sound: Currently hiring a new system, more information by show time
22 and 23 May. New York Times, Omaha, Nebraska.
  Special notes: Stage manager and promoter have never seen the club . . . club owner says he has a nice club
  Load -in area: Through the front door — Club is upstairs, take the elevator up
  Special notes: Expect anything — act accordingly
24 May. Duffy's Minneapolis, MN.
  Drum riser: No — low ceiling
  Lights: Lights — what lights?
26 May. Destination, Oklahoma City, Oklahoma.
  Special notes: John Cale will be the first national act to play this club. The club is currently under renovation — club and stage may be larger by the time we arrive
27 May. Rocks, Lubbock, Texas.
  Special notes: Where's Waylon Jennings?
29 and 30 May. Club Foot, Austin, Texas.
31 May. Hot Club, Dallas, Texas.
  Capacity: 350
1 June. Agora, Houston, Texas.
3 June. Old Man River, New Orleans, Louisiana.
5 June. Casa Loma Ballroom, St Louis, MO.
10 June. Club Europa, Tucson, Arizona.

At the Patio in Indianapolis, in a performance broadcast on radio and on a stage that was right next to the bar, the band played a new song, 'Wake Up the Boys', about the sailors who died in the Atlantic in the Second World War. At the Channel in Boston earlier in the month they had played another, 'Candy Store'.

At the New York Times in Omaha, Nebraska, Cale attacked Peter Muny on stage during the first song of the set. They rolled off the stage and ended up outside the club. Cale never returned and, although the band tried to carry on playing, the audience started throwing things at them and they had to beat a retreat.

From Omaha to Minneapolis, Minnesota, where the next day's gig was to take place, was probably a ten-hour drive. There were similar journeys from Minneapolis to Oklahoma City and from there to Lubbock, Texas.

'He just could not face the idea of another day's travel that would not be in the direction of New York.'
(From Dylan Thomas in America by John Malcolm Brinnin)

Back in New York in July Cale was suddenly without a manager — or a record contract. Jane Friedman had hoped that they would marry, but when he made it clear on his return from the tour that this was not going to happen — he was by now deeply involved with Risé — the relationship, which had been under heavy strain, came to an end. For Jane Friedman this was not just the termination of their personal association, their working relationship was finished, too. The A&M contract had been overseen by her, and when she parted with Cale any chance of renewing it for another album went with her.

Without anyone to pay for it, Cale was effectively without a band as well. Sturgis Nikides and Robert Medici would in fact play a few more gigs with Cale over the next few months, with a new bass player, Gordon Wands, a friend of Nikides, temporarily replacing Peter Muni, but Jim Goodwin soon left, and the band was now no longer functioning as a full-time unit. With the departure of Jane Friedman Cale had to administer business arrangements himself, and the chaotic results, particularly over money, brought Wands, an accomplished drinker with a short temper, close to hitting him.

On 9 March 1796 Napoleon Bonaparte married Josephine de Beauharnais.

On 14 October Cale married Risé, whose younger sister, Jody, was Chris Spedding's girlfriend and would later become his wife. For Cale marriage to Risé would consolidate a relationship that he needed in order for his life to progress — the chaos had to have some sort of order stamped on it. Cale now knew, too, that he wanted to become a father and would need to provide the stability of a formalized relationship for his child.

By the end of October he was playing live again, at New York's Peppermint Club. The evening had been billed as a combination of two sets, one acoustic and one electric, but in the event it was one long show of band music, finally expiring around three o'clock the next morning. In a mixture of new material and old improvisation tugged at the structures of every song, tearing their surfaces and allowing their subconscious undercurrents free rein. The opening piece dealt with the death squads of the El Salvadorean government and the misery of its people. Using a copy of the right-wing pamphlet *West Watch* (slogan: 'Keep track of the revolution lobby') as an object for his hatred and contempt, Cale ended the song by burning it.

Another new song dealt with the gunrunning political fomentation of 'Uncle Sam in Samoa', and the next went further into improvisation, finding Cale 'losing my words of wisdom' and pleading 'You need friends'. 'Streets of Laredo' squeezed a few more drops of desperation from a now near-skeletal form, and 'All on Board' was the story of a 'broken woman' in a 'burning town'.

Cale sounded here as though his strength was finally ebbing, as though his own surface was cracking and his subconscious emerging into a desiccating light. As he was becoming more aware of his own painful emotional condition, however, he was also being led towards an empathy with the victims of physical and psychological violence. These were not only the war-wronged of 'Strange Times in Casablanca' and 'Riverbank' but also those brutalized in other ways by the world in which they live. This was the state of mind and these were the concerns that would lead to the creation of his *Music for a New Society*.

Part 6
Calean
(an oriental pipe for smoking drugs)

On 9 March 1942 tenor John McCormack recorded 'Somewhere a Voice Is Calling'.

In December 1981 came the deaths of both Cale's old room-mate and collaborator Terry Jennings and, in a hit-and-run accident, composer Cornelius Cardew, who had helped Cale to organize his 'little festival of new music' at Goldsmiths' College and who had also performed Jennings's work. Cardew had been an active communist and for a while there was talk of foul play being involved in his death.

While Cale spent December and January trying to write new songs in competition with a continuing chaotic lifestyle, he also played the odd gig and jammed with Chris Spedding and James Honeyman-Scott of the Pretenders at the Mudd Club.

A solo set at Syracuse University in January was an amiable performance in front of a receptive audience with, apart from a raging piano break in the middle of 'I'm Waiting for the Man' and the most physical of screams at the end of 'Fear Is a Man's Best Friend', little sign of the soul-tearing mental landscapes that would soon be exposed in the recording studio. 'Chinese Envoy' and 'Thoughtless Kind', which would both be part of the new album, were now fully formed.

Having talked for a while of resurrecting his classical work, Cale had written the music to accompany Jonathan Demme's film adaptation of Kurt Vonnegut Jr's *Who Am I This Time?* and recorded it while watching a print of the film on a monitor and listening to its dialogue on headphones. The film was given a PBS broadcast on 2 February, and his contribution was some sympathetic acoustic guitar and piano refrains, together with more developed solo piano work and a little light orchestration – a nod in a new direction that he would pursue with dedication in the 1990s. Demme had directed *Caged Heat* – which Cale had scored in 1974 – and in January's *New York Rocker* he made *Honi Soit* his number one 'musical choice'. In 1986 Cale would go on to provide music for Demme's *Something Wild*, along with Lou Reed's future girl-friend Laurie Anderson.

In the spring Cale constructed his *Music for a New Society*, a tortured laying-bare of the lives and mental landscapes of the victims of the world's cruelty that he had portrayed in *Sabotage/Live* and *Honi Soit*. While musically as far removed from these two albums as it would be possible to get, it has common cause with them in describing the state of a world that has been led to the brink of nuclear war and that must therefore be destroyed and rebuilt. *Music for a New Society* emphasizes its use of *Honi Soit* as a point of departure by its quotation from 'Wilson Joliet' in 'Sanities' (which uses the same female character), by its continued use of 'found' percussion instruments and in its extension of the sympathy that the previous album had accorded specifically to the victims of war.

What had been originally intended as a simple solo album changed form inside the studio, becoming instead a kind of *Marble Index*: an arranger's album. Chris Spedding had recently suggested to Cale that they improvise an album together, and Cale decided instead to take on the job single-handed, adding other contributions, including Spedding's slide guitar on 'Taking Your Life in Your Hands' after the fact. Spedding's work was done inside a day, with Cale instructing him in what he wanted him to play; the guitarist had wanted the freedom to play what he liked, but Cale had something more specific in mind and refused to let him. Spedding was riled by this and lost his temper with Cale, who shouted back with delight that this anger was what he wanted.

Fragments of songs were recorded over five days, and then many erased. Those that survived to the final cut were re-made with additional instrumentation including bagpipes, viola and harpsichord, plus added sounds such as laughter, hammerings, creakings and hisses, together with 'quotations' from the music of Rimsky-Korsakov, Beethoven and Debussy. Besides Spedding, other guests on the album included Alan Lanier, John Wonderling, Mike McLintock, Tom Fitzgibbon, Robert Elk, Risé Cale, David Young and David Lichtenstein. In the middle of all of this extra life Cale sounds utterly alone.

Music for a New Society was recorded for Michael Zilkha's Ze label, which had taken over Spy Records after it had fallen by the wayside with the end of Cale's partnership with Jane Friedman. Ironically, Ze was distributed by Island Records, and this album saw Cale back underneath the umbrella that he had thrust away back in 1975. Zilkha had intended the album to be a reflection of the largely pre-planned acoustic solo shows that Cale had recently been playing, but Cale, once he was in the studio, had found much more within him than could be expressed by that format. The sessions, mostly unplanned, disorganized and spontaneous, opened up a secret conduit and let it pour forth.

Music for a New Society was recorded at Sky Line Studios in New York, where Cale's friend Mike McLintock worked. The engineer and assistant engineer there, David Lichtenstein and David Young respectively, ended up playing drums and guitar on the album. David Lichtenstein is the son of Pop artist Roy Lichtenstein, whom Cale had met in Bridgehampton in the early 1960s. Roy Lichtenstein lived near by, and Cale had been holidaying there one summer; Lichtenstein asked how Cale was doing socially back in New York, and Cale remembers responding that he was doing fine, considering that it was impossible actually to make any friends there. Young and David Lichtenstein would become members of Cale's next touring band, and Young continued to work with Cale into the 1990s, co-writing songs with him as well as playing guitar and co-producing. Cale was delighted to find out that Young's father had military clout and got him to write him a letter of introduction, which he then successfully used to join the Royal United Services Institute (RUSI), a UK defence and security think-tank of which Miles Copeland Sr was also a member.

Music for a New Society sketches out the terrain of an emotional wasteland, an apocalyptic landscape that has nothing to do with the effects of nuclear war but everything to do with the effects on humanity of a world that is prepared to go far enough to wage one. Many of the people who have survived into this wrecked country have broken lives, but their lives can be rebuilt and their suffering can be overcome. After the First World War the Dadaists decided that art could never be the same because the world had to change, and here Cale creates his own 'anti-art' out of improvisation, found sounds, the piecing together of fragments and the collision of collaboration to put forward the same message. Cale had said in an interview the previous year that the world needed to 'go through the nuclear barrier' and to emerge on the other side. On *Music for a New Society* he effectively dismantles the old world and uses the fractured tapestry that emerges as a blueprint for a new one — an alternative to going through that barrier.

Of the songs used to make up the tracklist of the final album, a reprised 'Close Watch' (retitled in this abbreviated form), together with 'Thoughtless Kind' and 'Chinese Envoy', were an already written core around which the others were arranged. Cale had originally intended to include a piece called 'Mama's Song' — it is listed on the original LP's sleeve and label — but decided at the last moment to delete it. This track featured a recording of a telephone call between Cale and his mother, on which she had sung a traditional Welsh song about love and nature, 'Arlan y Mor' ('On the Sea Shore') to him. When she was suddenly taken ill, shortly before the album was due to be released, he decided it was better removed. On the album's re-release in 1993 the still missing 'Mama's Song' would be replaced by one of the many out-takes from the sessions: 'In the Library of Force'.

The variety of effects and overdubs on *Music for a New Society* help create its fragmented, fractured landscape: 'Taking Your Life in Your Hands' uses the sound of a piano in a far-off room, 'Thoughtless Kind' mad laughter, 'Sanities' deploys a prepared piano and 'found' sounds and 'Close Watch' has hisses, harpsichord and bagpipes; 'Damn Life' quotes from Beethoven's 'Ode to Joy', 'Risé, Sam and Rimsky-Korsakov' from the eponymous Russian composer and 'In the Library of Force' from Debussy. The effects of these additions are various, from the literal emphasizing of separation in 'Taking Your Life in Your Hands' to the irony of using 'Ode to Joy' in a song as desperate as 'Damn Life' — not to mention its equation of Beethoven's misery with Cale's own.

On *Music for a New Society* Cale was also creating music for a new life for himself.

Having, as he himself acknowledged, reached rock bottom, he was searching, on his hands and knees, for ways to start climbing up again. Risé was to be an important part of that process, and she appears on the album, narrating 'Risé, Sam and Rimsky-Korsakov' and co-writing 'Damn Life'. With a new desire to become a father, too, Cale desperately needed the hope of a new world in which his child could grow up, and that hope informs the album as much as anything else.

Throughout these tales of life at the bottom, of despair, mental breakdown, failures of friendship and the disappearance of happiness, there are definite signs of attempted upward movement. There is a longing to physically, even violently, haul a suicide back towards life, and the desperate need to value friendship is emphasized, together with the value of love and the necessity to communicate. On 'Changes Made', the only conventional band number on the album, the message of change is explicitly stated over and over again, and the 'children's caravan' is seen as a sign of hope. Although Cale never wanted 'Changes Made' to appear on the record, it helps to crystallize a part of the album's intent that might otherwise have been overlooked.

Whereas the original version of the album ended with 'Risé, Sam and Rimsky-Korsakov', and its mixture of loneliness, magic and seduction and the voice of Cale's wife as the voice of the future, the re-released version culminates in 'In the Library of Force', a savage restatement of the revolutionary message of the song 'Sabotage' which had closed *Sabotage/Live*. Killing, religion, literature, history and language combine to stamp on humanity to a soundtrack of swooping synthesizer, echoing taps and bangs and jabbings on acoustic guitar. Debussy's serene *Au Clair de la Lune* is played lightly, a four-chord pattern is beaten out and finally the piano lid is heard closing.

The reaction to *Music for a New Society* when it was released in August 1982 was a familiar one, if more polarized than at any other point in Cale's career: critics went into raptures, consumers refused to buy it. For Cale this schizophrenic reaction to his work, telling him how great it was but giving him no reward for it, was hardly a guarantee of a golden future and offered nothing to help him shake off his drinking and drug-taking.

'Changes Made' was seen by the record company as a potential single, and a video was filmed to promote it, but in the end a botched attempt would be made instead finally to score a hit the following year with 'Close Watch' — what could have been a huge success would disappear without trace.

Just before the release of *Music for a New Society* Cale took part in one of his sporadic live collaborations, appearing at the Agent Orange Benefit at New York's Pier 84 with old associates Mick Ronson and Ian Hunter. Also appearing was Todd Rundgren.

On the album Cale had recorded the results of a long-range association with playwright, poet and actor Sam Shepherd. On 'Risé, Sam and Rimsky-Korsakov' he had put music to a poem sent to him by Shepherd, which he had written while on the set of the film *The Right Stuff*. Shepherd had earlier sent Cale the libretto of an operetta, *The Sad Lament of Pecos Bill on the Eve of Killing His Wife*, with the idea that Cale might write the music for it. By now Cale had been working on his own idea, which was to write an opera on the life of Dylan Thomas. Investigating Thomas's biography, however, he had been unable to engage with the boorish character of the poet and felt unable to carry through the project. He decided instead to work on providing music to his poems — an undertaking that would eventually lead to 'The Falklands Suite' on *Words for the Dying*. Cale worked on settings of the poems with a piano and a copy of the collected poems at the studio of Alan Lanier, the Blue Öyster Cult guitarist and ex-lover of Patti Smith, who was now something of an old friend. There was also talk in this period of Cale working with William Burroughs on a video collaboration and a recording project. Although a script would be produced, nothing would come of it, but Cale and Burroughs would later produce joint work for Burroughs's 1990 album *Dead City Radio*.

Another element was added to the mix with Cale also collaborating with Bob Neuwirth, ex-sparring partner from the Warhol/ Dylan era turned ally. This work, too, would eventually lead to an album, *Last Day on Earth*.

On 9 and 10 September Cale and Neuwirth performed at New York's the Kitchen with some saxophone backing. The set was a mixture of originals by each man, with Cale playing some viola as well as piano and improvising at the keyboard along with the saxophone. A Neuwirth narration was accompanied by Cale playing 'Let All Mortal Flesh Keep Silence', and Cale's 'West Watch' piece made a reappearance. What would turn out to be the eclectic mix of *Last Day on Earth* could be heard starting to gel.

After sporadic solo gigs towards the end of 1982 Cale began a lengthy solo European tour at the end of January 1983, playing a set that would form the basis of the one he would perform many times over the next twenty years — a portable and dependable show, cheap, efficient and self-reliant. Later in the year he took this show to Australia and New Zealand. (On the way to Australia a merchant seaman with a shotgun tried unsuccessfully to hijack the aeroplane Cale was travelling on.) By the spring, however, back in New York, Cale was rehearsing a new band and teaching them some of the material he was writing for what would become his next album, *Caribbean Sunset*.

Cale's lifestyle, despite the calming presence of Risé, was still chaotic and explosive. Alcohol and drugs conditioned large parts of his waking life and were responsible for moody behaviour and occasionally psychotic episodes. Conscious and subconscious awareness were sometimes confused, with people surprised to find Cale judging them by fictitious actions and non-existent characteristics. Cale continued to read as widely as ever and still cultivated the friendship of people with specialized knowledge of government, the military and technological advances. In conversation he would find connections within and between these worlds that were sometimes purely speculative – but often prophetic of future events.

While comfortable enough on a day-to-day basis with his lifestyle, he did not have the aura of a happy man.

'If he was unquestionably the apple of his mother's eye, in his father's eye he was still an object of a curiously dispassionate interest.'
(From Dylan Thomas in America by John Malcolm Brinnin)

In 1983 Cale's father died. After the initial shock of the news, which turned him pale, Cale came to terms with it without showing any other signs of great distress. Always very attached to his mother, he had never been as close to his father. The two had never been able to communicate properly, a difficulty born of their early language barrier, and their relationship had always been coloured by the corporal punishment the father had visited upon the son.

On the eve of Cale's departure to London from Wales back in 1960 his father had some words of advice for him. Warning him about women who thought getting pregnant was a good way of winning financial support, the advice was 'don't get caught with a paternity suit'. Cale winced at the prospect.

As an adult Cale would return home to Wales at Christmas and in the summer holidays to find that his mother and father had developed a relationship that did not rely on verbal communication: to Will's increasing deafness Margaret had added a complementary muteness. Visitors, however, reported no problems in communicating with either of them.

Once Cale was ensconced in New York in 1963 he would fire off aggressive missives across the Atlantic to his parents, their tone and content intended to shock – which they did. As their son's career developed in America, Will and Margaret had little in their own experience to help them relate to it and found it bemusing. They made Betsey Johnson welcome when she was taken to visit them after marrying Cale and, although she was impressed with Will's coal miner's sense of humour, there was no disguising the fact that this was a collision of very different worlds.

When Cale flew his parents out to California to meet his second wife, Cindy, and her parents Los Angeles was like an alien planet to them. For Will in particular, who had never thought he would make it across the ocean, it was a remarkable experience, if one tainted by his wife's asthma attack, which led to a brief hospitalization and longer recuperation.

When Cale invited his parents to see him perform his *Fear/Slow Dazzle* material he saw them as 'tiny people with humility built in . . . not like their angry son'. While trying to shock them out of their humility by exposing them to another, more chaotic world, another part of him was nevertheless proud that they were there to hear his songs.

Through the 1970s and into the early 1980s Cale would regularly visit them, and whenever they spoke of him at this time it was always with pride. About a year before Will's death, Gareth Simmonds, son of Cale's cousin Derek – and an international rugby referee – visited Will in Garnant. Will carved a perfect rugby ball for him from a solid lump of coal, which he then mounted on a plinth. After Will's funeral in 1983 Cale was left with little to remember his father by – little knowledge of his father's side of the family and little in the way of mementoes. When he realized this, Gareth Simmonds presented Cale with the rugby ball.

Cale's new band of 1983 was made up of David Young and David Lichtenstein from Sky Line Studios, together with East Villager Andy Heermanns. After several European dates together and a few in the USA, they went into Right Track Recording in New York later in the year to work on Cale's new album. Eno would also put in a brief ghostly appearance to treat the album's closing song, 'Villa Albani'.

In 1913 Marcel Duchamp made his first 'readymade', *Bicycle Wheel.*

Much of the material on *Caribbean Sunset* was co-written with David Young. Typically, Young came up with guitar riffs that Cale would work into finished songs. Young would also find himself with the other traditional duty of being Cale's right-hand men: being woken in the small hours with ideas for the album. One particular idea in this case was that he might like to play some pedal-steel guitar – something he had never attempted before. Cale was undaunted by the difficulties of Young learning a new musical technique, but despite his best efforts Young failed to master the instrument, and the experiment had to be terminated. On one occasion during the sessions Cale turned up at the studio with a bicycle that he had found somewhere. Bringing it into the control room, he put it upside down on its saddle and handle-bars, spun one of the wheels and ordered: 'OK, Dave, get me a sound on that, will you?' Saddened by the news that it would be impossible to get a recording of the bicycle wheel that would survive in a mix with vocals and drums, Cale reluctantly had to agree that they would have to make do without it.

Recording *Caribbean Sunset* was much more predetermined than the same process had been on *Music for a New Society*, particularly as many of the songs this time had already been worked up by the band in live shows. Less spontaneous in its writing than its predecessor, it acquired immediacy in another way: by being 'thrown at' the tape and then left there, with little interference after the fact. Cale this time decided to finish the recording and regard it as complete at an early stage — with many of the songs already part of a set live show they had to stay. Little material was left over from the sessions, although 'Kiddy in the Congo' was one song that never made it on to vinyl.

In interviews Cale would compare *Caribbean Sunset* with *Fear*, and there are certainly similarities. David Young's clean guitar is comparable to Phil Manzanera's, there is another attractive guitar/keyboard meshing and a selection of immediately effective songs — not to mention that this, once more on the Ze label, bore the Island imprint again and that one of *Fear*'s architects, Eno, was back on board, if only for one track.

Mixed in with the distorted love songs and the military and political concerns on *Caribbean Sunset* were a couple of oddities: 'Praetorian Underground', which attacks the then current ransacking of the Velvet Underground's music by new bands, and 'The Hunt', an assault on the practitioners of blood sports. 'Experiment No. 1' is a depiction of desperation that could have come from *Music for a New Society*, a guitar-led piece in a minor key that bleeds misery. Cale shouts the chord changes to the band and issues other instructions to give the emotional bloodletting the immediacy of the moment. One of its lines, 'Christmas comes, just like breakfast, once a year', was one that Cale had come up with in the company of Chris Spedding, as long ago as 1975. 'Model Beirut Recital' is preceded by a piece of Morse code, a snippet of an 'intercepted' Israeli phone call and a Lebanese arms dealer reciting: 'Beirut, you're a whore and you've been raped. I spit on you . . .' Sung with an phoney Arab accent, hammed up towards the end and culminating, like the earlier 'Mercenaries (Ready for War)', in the sound of an explosion, this is nevertheless the nearest Cale has come to a protest song. The carnage inflicted on Beirut, particularly after the Israeli invasion in June 1982, had made a strong impact on Cale, and the massacres of Palestinian civilians in the Sabra and Chatila refugee camps in October 1983 revolted and horrified him.

The album reaches its peak in its final track, 'Villa Albani', a companion piece to *Honi Soit*'s 'Strange Times in Casablanca'. Like that track's eponymous city the title is a translation, this time into Latin, of 'White House', and like its predecessor it is also a documentation of international political intrigue, in this case the Banco Ambrosiano scandal.

'Villa Albani' was written by Cale before the band went into the studio and, particularly with Eno's involvement, is the most worked-on and fully realized song on the album, a detailed description of a foreign policy based on selling death via arms deals in return for oil. Duplicity, greed and desertion spread across its landscape and underneath its surface, permeating every part of its substance. The 'backing vocal' in the first verse has been slowed down so much that it is barely discernible as human.

In Britain at the beginning of 1984 Cale was interviewed by Allan Jones for *Melody Maker*: he talked of threats that had been made on his life, including one by a 'communist-Trotskyist' movement that would not take no for an answer when he declined a request that he play at their May Day celebrations. He also mentioned the stalker who had only been frightened away by a court order and an episode that involved being woken up at three in the morning by policemen because someone had told them that there was an armed man in his apartment. Another topic of conversation was the man with whom Cale had been talking earnestly in the bar where the interview was taking place — it turned out that he worked in the local hospital's morgue and had apparently been letting Cale in to watch the autopsies. Cale was also talking of the possibility of AIDS having started in Brazil and not, following common wisdom of the time, in Haiti. Mesquite Indians in Brazil, he said, were being shot by the Brazilian army and then shipped to Haiti, from where the corpses were sent to American medical schools, the circuitous route accounting for the misunderstanding. Cale also let slip to Allan Jones the information that not only had he met the famously reclusive writer Thomas Pynchon but that Pynchon had asked him to write an opera based on his novel *Gravity's Rainbow*. Apart from this projected collaboration, which went no further, Cale and Pynchon had also discussed aerospace engineering and the development of new weapons systems. Cale remembers the occasion as a 'wild and woolly afternoon', with Pynchon accompanied by a 'cigar-chomping Hollywood producer . . . snorting and fuming' at the *Boys' Own* mentality of the conversation. Cale had recently bumped into Lou Reed — literally in the street — and Cale had noticed that Reed did not look well.

Cale and his new band toured heavily throughout 1984, with extensive dates in Europe both at the beginning and the end of the year and a return in November to some of the US venues least fondly remembered from the tours between 1979 and 1981, as well as visits to the larger cities.

For these tours the band at least had a bus with bunks in it, but some of the American dates were nearly as grim as those played by the 'Sabotage' and 'Honi Soit' outfits. Staying in dirty motels, not getting on stage until after midnight, playing two shows a night and trying to sleep during the day was not a particularly easy existence. Usually the band would spend the evening hours waiting for a show to begin by getting more and more drunk. Often by the time they got to the stage they were totally out of it, and the gigs were consequently often wild and unpredictable. While sometimes this resulted in memorable performances, other shows would sink under the weight of the alcohol. As on the earlier tours it was often a struggle to make the US dates pay, with audiences at the smaller gigs drawing only around 150 people and being subsidized by the larger ones in cities such as Boston and New York.

European touring, of which the band did much more, reversing the pattern of Cale's two previous bands (the 'Sabotage' band never played in Europe at all), was a very different matter. In Europe Cale could rely on attracting audiences of between eight hundred and a thousand; the money and conditions were as a result much better and touring much more of a pleasure.

Cale was usually a congenial travelling companion, interesting and witty, but there were occasions, as on earlier tours, when it was best to stay out of his way. Sometimes this was also advisable when Cale was in a cheerful frame of mind . . .

One night David Young was asleep in his hotel room when Cale crept in. Sneaking up to the bed, Cale leaned over the somnolent guitarist and blew a straw-ful of cocaine up his nose. Exploding suddenly into consciousness, Young screamed at his gleeful attacker. The next day Cale rang Young to say that he owed him ten dollars.

'What for?'

'The line!'

At London's Electric Ballroom in October Cale and the band put on a rampant performance. A new song, 'Autobiography', written from a desperate need for identity and self-confidence (strongly reminiscent of the final part of Apollinaire's 'A La Santé') featured Cale shouting almost random chord changes out to the band. 'Autobiography' led straight into another new song, 'Ooh La La', and its playboy narrator was retained for a version of 'Evidence'. 'Magazines' ('a nonsense song about reading material') was interspersed with repeated shouts of 'Achtung'. As it ended Cale started heaving away at his guitar, dragging desperate, distorted notes from it before being cut off by Young's opening chords to 'Model Beirut Recital'. This featured Cale shouting: 'The PLO is back in Beirut. You are the whore of Babylon, and I spit on you. Not on the PLO and not on Beirut. I spit on music, because it never makes people *pay attention.*'

As soon as 'Model Beirut Recital' ended Cale began hauling at his guitar again, and this time no one could stop him. What followed was a tortured solo version of 'Streets of Laredo', full of feedback, discord and power chords. Cale's hands slid up and down the guitar's neck, as if squeezing the breath from it. His vocal was a measured howl, preserving some of the original melody but also creating a new one, another reinvention, separate from the one he had created for *Honi Soit.* At one point he moved away from the microphone to sing, and his voice almost vanished into the air, nearly drowned by the sound waves from his anguished stabbing at his guitar.

For 'Leaving It Up to You' Cale was 'an admiral in Brazil'; during 'The Hunt' he could not stop himself from laughing and then disappeared off stage, the band continuing without him before the song petered out. Cale returned to ask: 'I can have a laugh once in a while, can't I?' 'Riverbank' was announced as 'the history of the Beatles' and ended over a slow, majestic piano improvisation, with Cale shouting 'Be proud of your heritage', before segueing into a 'Heartbreak Hotel' that was partially played 'blind' by a pair of disembodied hands, with Cale underneath the piano. At one point Cale stopped playing to crawl along the floor. 'I'm Waiting for the Man' ('a little piece of history') ended with Cale on top of the piano shouting to the back of the hall about the need to distrust all governments, the necessity for everyone to rely on themselves, the destructive power of heroin, the political power of the coffee bean and General Pinochet, to whose Augustus he was Claudius. This led straight into a version of 'Mercenaries (Ready for War)' interspersed with 'My rifle is my friend — show us your pass . . . Who do you think I am, Napoleon? You didn't get any secret messages', before descending into musical anarchy and then, finally, a kind of peace.

After encores of 'Fear Is a Man's Best Friend', 'Guts' and 'Pablo Picasso' Cale took issue good-humouredly with elements of the audience before playing a final, slightly disrespectful version of 'Close Watch' to huge applause, closing it with the instruction: 'Applause is not enough. You've gotta think!'

Three days after the Electric Ballroom gig Cale and band were at the Grugahalle in Essen for a performance filmed and later broadcast as part of the German *Rock Palast* television series.

Here, in another dramatic performance, Cale lurched around the stage to uncertain looks from David Young, forgot some words, twitched on occasion like a diseased leviathan, sang like Bela Lugosi and played whole songs fingering the same non-chord on dead strings. Playing a Gibson Flying V and dressed all in black apart from a pair of white trainers, Cale monopolized the attention of the audience, even when leaning against the drum riser for Young's guitar solos. During 'Streets of Laredo' he looked up as he 'saw' the sods of earth falling down on him in his coffin; on 'Magazines' he twirled his black jacket as if he was Dracula and the jacket his cape, while at the keyboard of his electric piano his bare right arm, bathed halfway up in dark orange light, made him look like a surgeon elbow-deep in blood.

'Heartbreak Hotel' was played, once again, mainly from below the piano and was abruptly halted as Cale sank down on all fours, mouthing silently. Slowly reaching out a hand, he pulled at a square of vinyl from the floor and then ripped it up. Carrying it over to the bass player's microphone, he placed it on his head and carried on singing.

In September the *John Cale Comes Alive* album was released. This consisted in the main of part of a live show from London's Lyceum back in February with the addition of two new studio tracks — a version of 'Ooh La La' and a previously unreleased song, 'Never Give Up on You'. The live material was compromised by an anaemic sound and imperfect track selection – particularly strange was the inclusion of 'Evidence' and 'Dr Mudd', both songs that had earlier appeared on *Sabotage/Live*. Cale mixed the album with the help of Stephen Street but found little to interest him in the process, spending a large proportion of the time adjusting the tuning of the tom-toms.

Back in February Cale had been interviewed in Cologne on German radio, the interview interspersed with records and live performances by Cale at the piano. The result was a mixture of long questions, occasionally very short answers and others that changed the subject dramatically, together with improvised piano pieces and mostly straight versions of familiar Cale material. While records were being played Cale managed to snatch the odd nap; when talking to his host, Alan Bangs, he — appropriately — had problems with the pronunciation of the word epistemological.

A near-perfect performance of 'Buffalo Ballet' led into an instrumental passage conjured up on the spot, a delicate, melodic progression that was then used as an alternative tune for a snippet of 'Fear Is a Man's Best Friend'. A long-winded question from Bangs about expressing personality in live shows was turned into a statement about military and political intelligence, and, even more bizarrely, a list of 'Will Powers supporters' was set to improvised music. Cale's interpretation of 'Heartbreak Hotel' here was accompanied in its final verse solely by his banging on the piano, culminating in a long, utterly tormented scream and then more bangs on the wood, between which echoes of the piano's interior swelled gently. After that there was a rare piece of genuine radio silence as the sound was allowed to fade away, uninterrupted, into nothing.

"SAD ALE VICE, JOHN . . ."

On a subject that had recently become pertinent, Cale told his interviewer how he did not believe that there was an insurance company in the world that would give him a policy. He also stated that he was not afraid of death but that he wanted to leave as many 'messages' behind him as possible. Cale had always given the impression that he was indestructible, able to withstand the fiercest onslaughts that drugs and alcohol could mount and surface the next day as if nothing had happened. On this tour, however, the superhuman constitution had finally cracked. Four days before the Cologne interview the band were to play at the Metropol in Berlin, but Cale collapsed in his hotel, the Steigenberger, beforehand. A doctor was called, examined him and told him bluntly that he had to give up what he was doing to himself or he was going to die. Cale was given a large vitamin shot, and he and the band took the stage but performed a show so short that it precipitated a riot when they did not return for an encore. With the situation getting out of control, they agreed to return to the stage for a couple of songs, Cale having almost to be carried back on. In the meantime a GI in the audience had taken it upon himself to cut the cable linking the mixer to the stage, so when the band began to play there was no sound. The band, rather sheepishly, had to walk off again. Fortunately, the fact that they had at least attempted to play again seemed to calm the audience enough to prevent complete chaos. After the gig Cale made enquiries about insurance and received the grim news that his physical state and way of life meant that there was no chance of him being able to get any — he was uninsurable.

Although the band continued with the tour and played all the dates that had been arranged, Cale had now been made fully aware that he needed to take action if he was to restore his health. While taking the news on board, it would still be a while before he began to implement the necessary lifestyle changes.

By the end of 1984, with another Island contract fulfilled thanks to the live album, Cale signed to the British Beggars Banquet label, for whom he would record his *Artificial Intelligence* album and produce Nico's *Camera Obscura*.

There were more live dates in early 1985, but by the time Cale and band played their first date in Spain, for an hour-long concert for live television at the beginning of March, its line-up was substantially different from that on *Caribbean Sunset*. Drummer Kevin Tooley had replaced David Lichtenstein, who had left the previous year, and Ollie Halsall was now playing bass in place of Andy Heermans. Heermans had actually quit the band just as they were about to leave New York's JFK airport the day before. A girl he had fallen for had 'decided to worm her way through the band', as Cale recalls, and Heermans had responded despairingly by, at the crucial moment, refusing to tour with them. On arriving in Madrid Cale had immediately telephoned Ollie Halsall (Halsall and Kevin Ayers had been living in Majorca for several years) and asked him to do the gig that night. Halsall was an Ayers associate whom Cale had known for years and who had played on a 1978 David Kubinec album that Cale had produced, as well as in his band in November and December 1977. In 1982 Cale had appeared on an Ayers live performance broadcast on Spanish television, and Halsall, together with Andy Summers from the Police, had played guitar. As well as playing some manic viola dressed in a blue jumpsuit and mirror shades, Cale had also sung 'Heartbreak Hotel', backed by Ayers's band. Dressed for this song in black, apart from a yellow bow-tie, Cale clutched a letter in one hand, a credit card in another, begun on his haunches and ended by 'dying' live on stage, before jerking into a sitting position and conducting the band in their finale. Halsall, a true professional, now joined the band for an hour's rehearsal, playing bass, which was not his preferred instrument, and they went on to play an amazing, largely improvised hour-long concert.

After the performance Halsall joined the band full-time, playing with them next in Barcelona. This would turn out to be the last time Cale's band ever used real glasses for their on-stage drinks. The glasses were all lined up along the front of the drum riser, as usual, but on this occasion Cale decided to upend it during the show, shattering them all. The rest of the gig was spent with the band wading knee-deep in broken glass, beer and blood.

Two days after the Barcelona gig, on 12 March, Cale was in London to appear on *The Old Grey Whistle Test* on BBC Television. Here he played what was to be the stand-out track from the soon to be recorded *Artificial Intelligence*: 'Dying on the Vine'.

Before this, however, over three weeks in March and April Nico's *Camera Obscura* album was recorded at London's Strongroom Studios. Cale stayed at Nico's flat in Brixton, from which, on moving in, he had evicted punk poet John Cooper Clarke.

Recorded in a rather dazed way, through a haze of alcohol, *Camera Obscura*, surprisingly, turned out rather well. Cale and Nico were on friendly terms on the whole (it had been around two years since they had last seen each other), although Cale insisted on there being no heroin anywhere near him (which was the reason he had got rid of Cooper Clarke). This was difficult to arrange, however, with Nico very much still in the throes of her addiction. Cale was almost evangelical on the subject, drawing a sharp distinction between this particular drug and the cocaine and alcohol in which he was still regularly indulging. He also refused to allow smoking in the studio, which further debilitated and annoyed Nico. Despite the problems, however, she adopted a passive mode for the recording and responded to Cale's occasional urging to 'get on with it' by, in her own way, doing just that.

"CHASE AN OLD JIVE"

Once *Camera Obscura* was in the can attention shifted almost immediately to Cale's *Artificial Intelligence* album, which was also recorded at Strongroom. The lyrics had already been written by Cale back in New York — and for the first time he had collaborated on them, working with *National Lampoon* editor Larry 'Ratso' Sloman, a drinking companion of Cale's and Bob Neuwirth's. While working together the two had made use of William Burroughs's 'cut-up' technique, most apparently on the track 'Everytime the Dogs Bark'. Ironically, considering the lyrical collaboration, *Artificial Intelligence* was to be Cale's most autobiographical work yet: an album that in part found him in contemplative mood about the past and trying to use his memories of it to find routes out of the problems of the present. Another irony that was lost on many critics was that Cale's most lush and listener-friendly production since *Paris, 1919* was the backdrop not only to introspection but also to plenty more of his characteristic abrasiveness.

Work on the music for *Artificial Intelligence* began further into south London at the Balham home of Dids, aka Graham Dowdall, who was Nico's percussionist on

Camera Obscura. In Dowdall's music room at the back of his terraced house Cale, David Young (mainly playing bass) and Nico's keyboard player James Young put together an album that would turn out to be very keyboard-orientated. By the time they returned a week later to Strongroom, Cale was intent on making the most of its new computerized 'midi' technology and experimented enthusiastically with linking up synthesizers to play different sounds at the same time. With David Young concentrating on engineering, there was little scope for guitar-playing from either of them. Typically, much of the pre-production work that had been done was thrown out in the studio, but two and a half weeks later *Artificial Intelligence* was completed, after a last-minute remix for 'Satellite Walk' and a change of title from the original 'Black Rose'.

To a certain extent, the finished album turned out to be the victim of its own technology, its keyboard textures and drum-machine patterns effectively blocking entry to other production ideas and preventing some of the songs from achieving their potential. Artificial intelligence had long been an interest of Cale's, but here the phrase is meant more as an ironical comment on the state of his own mind and emotions. Artificial intelligence, however, also informs the songs ending each side of the album, 'Chinese Takeaway (Hong Kong 1997)' and 'Satellite Walk', both of which have environments and atmospheres that merge cultures to create innovative and potentially dangerous new states, both mental and geopolitical.

On *Artificial Intelligence*, two pieces of image-laden life on the edge, 'Everytime the Dogs Bark' and the dynamic 'Satellite Walk', bookend a familiar mixture of angular approaches to love and political intrigue. There is also, however, further expression given to Cale's longing for an end to the chaos of his life. This is particularly the case in the mournful and beautiful 'Dying on the Vine' and in 'Song of the Valley', and it is a yearning that fights against the rest of the material and signals the fact that the way he was living his life was going to change dramatically soon.

After finishing the album Cale, by his own admission now physically and emotionally exhausted, returned to New York, where on 14 July Risé gave birth to their daughter Eden. Once Eden was born it became obvious to Cale that his current lifestyle was never going to provide her with the care that she needed. Allied to this knowledge was what he already knew about the precarious state of his own health, and the two concerns would soon combine to give the necessity of change a real immediacy.

Although with Eden Cale now had new responsibilities, they could not be discharged unless money kept coming in, and that required his new album to be promoted on already arranged tours, the first a series of solo shows in the USA and Canada.

In Los Angeles in August, in a solo show at the Club Lingerie, Cale was relaxed, reflective and contemplative in between the songs of a largely low-key set. 'Ship of

Cajun Bag & Supply Co.

P. O. Box 330
WEST FIRST ST. AND AVENUE "C"
CROWLEY, LOUISIANA 70526

Multiwall Paper • Burlap Bags • Woven-Poly Bags • Pallet Covers

318/783-8105

Plastic Pails • Plastic Jugs • Construction Film

Wirebound Crates • Baskets • Corrugated Containers

GHOST STORY
SHIP
AMSTERDAM
LEANING
XMAS
BUFFALO
~~RIVERBANK~~ WELL RIVERBANK
WELL DOA
GUIN
HEARTBREAK
~~GAS BOX~~
THOUGHTLESS
CAROLE
CHRISTIE
VIVE WAITING
PARIS
FEAR
CLOSE LATIN

4 · 18 · 86

Fools' prompted memories of his parents, and a slow, world-weary 'Mercenaries (Ready for War)' dispensed completely with its usual climactic countdown to terror, ending instead with a bitter 'War, war'.

In October Cale set out for what would be his last tour with his own band for ten years: another extensive trawl across Europe. He used the same line-up from earlier in the year, with Ollie Halsall now playing guitar, David Young reverting to bass and Kevin Tooley on drums.

Cale was still trying to write new material but without success; nothing he came up with pleased him. In Mannheim in November the band opened the show with one of these songs, 'Something's Gone Wrong', but it had little to recommend it and did not stay in the set. Although the show had a certain amount of power, it failed to gel in the old ways. Some of Cale's vocals sounded tired and his usual tirades forced. He told a joke about a Russian bear and a rabbit that was lost on much of his German audience and found himself unable to play 'Fear Is a Man's Best Friend'. It was only on the newer material and towards the end of the performance that things picked up at all. In contrast, at London's Town and Country Club in December, on the tour's final date, Cale summoned all his old verve and vigour, and the band responded with a tight, fiery set. There was no hint of any health problems here and no sign of burn-out.

Back in New York, having now been told that he had liver damage, he began a course of interferon injections in what would turn out to be a successful attempt to recondition the damaged organ. This treatment necessitated a reduction in live work but also allowed him to spend time with his daughter and to begin working, on keyboards and computer, on the orchestral projects that he had long intended to pursue.

Cale would keep the cash flowing through 1986 with a series of solo shows, although spending nothing like as much time abroad as in earlier years; brief trips to England and Wales and then to Australia and New Zealand were the only occasions he was away from his wife and daughter for any significant length of time in the year.

By now Cale had narrowed his suite of vocal and piano settings of Dylan Thomas poems from nine pieces down to only four. Although he had discussed the project with several people, there was as yet no concrete sign of the chance to perform them with an orchestra and choir, which was what he felt they — and he — needed. In the meantime there was more film work from Jonathan Demme, for whose highly successful *Something Wild*, released in 1986, Cale composed part of the soundtrack.

From now on Cale would undertake a variety of one-off commissions to supplement his major projects. One of these, from 1986, was a piece with actress Ann Magnuson that was included on *Caged Uncaged*, a tribute to Cale's early inspiration, John Cage.

By May Cale had begun a new regime of physical fitness that involved daily trips to the local gym — where other regulars included Lou Reed, Laurie Anderson and Suzanne Vega (who would later record with Cale) — plus regular games of squash. His new regimen was already starting to pay off, with a return to a slimmer figure and a greater sense of well-being. Gone now were the bags under his eyes and the air of defeat that had sometimes surrounded him. His diet changed as well — dairy products were out and menus in restaurants would be analysed and rewritten. Cale was well into the process of kicking his cocaine and alcohol addictions, although getting through daily life without them was a nail-bitingly slow grind and would sometimes result in behaviour that would leave people with the impression that nothing had really changed. Cale, however, wore his new-found asceticism without the artificial trimmings of sentimentality or the self-aggrandising bravado of other 'newly clean' media personalities.

In October Cale renewed his working relationship with Chris Spedding when Spedding joined him for a series of dates in the USA and Canada that would continue sporadically well into the new year and on into 1988. A few of these would feature drums and bass as well, but this was an experiment that did not last long. With the two of them alone on stage Spedding had hoped that they would be able to improvise and take the songs in new directions, but Cale now saw such dates as professional engagements to be completed efficiently and without unnecessary embellishment and was unwilling to do much in this direction. Despite this, Spedding brought plenty of passion and invention to these shows, and they were very well received.

Back in Britain in December Cale had been called in to produce the first Happy Mondays album, at an early stage in the band's development when they had yet to show much sign of being anything out of the ordinary. The band were stoned throughout the sessions, with Cale newly straight and sober, and it was left to David Young to 'translate' between the two parties. Cale spent much of the time chewing mints and reading the *Guardian* newspaper, while Young got on with business. Cale would OK a take with a muttered 'Hmm', occasionally suggest the band do such-and-such a song and generally keep things moving by telling them to 'Just get on with it!'

In February 1987 Cale opened the *New York Times* and was stunned to read that Andy Warhol had died from complications after a routine gall-bladder operation. Cale had not seen Warhol for nearly two years but had never felt less than close to him, and to hear of his unexpected death, particularly in this impersonal way, was shocking. He attended the memorial service on 1 April and at a gathering afterwards a meeting with artist Julian Schnabel led to him suggesting that Cale write a requiem for Warhol. Lou Reed was present, too, and he and Cale found themselves getting along together better than at any time since the days of the Velvet Underground. This set in motion a chain of events that would before long lead to Cale's and Reed's joint memorial to Warhol, *Songs for Drella* – their first recorded work together since *White Light/White Heat* – and eventually to the Velvet Underground's reunion.

With the intention of eventually composing a symphony still pushing him forward, Cale was now working on smaller-scale classical pieces at home, writing mainly for local ballet productions. One of these pieces, *Four Sketches for a String Quartet*, was performed at the Massachusetts School of Art after the end of the tour with Chris Spedding. With the intended instrumental work in memory of Warhol in the pipeline as well, his live performances may still have been strictly rock 'n' roll but his writing was very much classical.

By October Cale had been commissioned to write the music for a ballet, *Sanctus*, to be performed by an orchestra for the Randy Warshaw Dance Company in November. Cale would later release his own version of the work, played completely by himself, using the 'electronic orchestra' of his home studio.

Also in 1987 came renewed contact with Tony Conrad. La Monte Young's record label of the time, Gramavision, wanted to release archival recordings of his that featured Conrad and Cale, but the two decided to make it abundantly clear that any such release that did not credit them with co-compositional credits would result in them going to court. Gramavision, unwilling to release anything that might result in costly legal action, dropped their plans.

'While Dylan did for a time seem genuinely intrigued by the possibilities of a professional acting début, nothing came of his talks with Anita Loos.'
(From *Dylan Thomas in America* by John Malcolm Brinnin)

Cale was now constructing a variegated jigsaw of projects. This was to act as a replacement for the album/tour schedule that had sustained him for so many years but which was embedded too deeply in the way of life that he was in the process of jettisoning. Another element in this jigsaw was a tentative sideline in acting. Cale had earlier taken lessons with theatre and film actor F. Murray Abraham and had recently made his movie début in Franz Harland's thirty-minute black-and-white film *The Houseguest*. Harland describes this as a 'low-budget spoof of a Bergmanesque summer resort love triangle that ends with a surreal twist', while Cale calls it 'a modular skip through history'. Now Cale was in discussion with horror director George A. Romero's production company about the possibility of him playing roles in the tradition of the British Hammer films. Nothing was to come of this particular proposal, but acting would continue to intrigue him for a few years.

In November, as well as seeing *Sanctus* performed, Cale finally achieved the completion of his long-cherished attempt to set Dylan Thomas's poems to music; his

Falklands Suite was premièred at the Paradiso in Amsterdam. The Paradiso had commissioned a performance for an orchestra, and this had forced Cale to develop the piano arrangements that he had already written on the large scale — which is what he had always intended anyway. The performance featured the Metropole Orchestra in suits, white shirts and bow-ties; above and to the left of them was a children's choir in red and grey. Stage right was Cale behind a piano, black-suited with stiff collar, bow-tie and neatly combed hair, while in the middle at the front was the orchestra's conductor. This was at last an expression of the part of Cale that had always been destined to become a classical composer. It was a confirmation that he could not only write a sizeable work for orchestra but that it could successfully be transferred to the concert hall. Even here, however, as Cale fought for a new kind of respect he could not settle for a completely straight reproduction of the past worlds of classical music and the poetry of Dylan Thomas. The orchestra was accompanied by a pedal-steel guitarist and accordion player, and the words of one of Thomas's poems had been altered to include a reference to the Falklands War that provided a framework for the piece as a whole.

In March of 1988 *The Falklands Suite* would be performed at St Ann's Church in New York, where Lou Reed would be in the audience — he and Cale would shortly begin work on *Songs for Drella*.

In February, after completing his long series of dates with Chris Spedding, Cale made his first trip to Japan for joint shows with Nico. For these he utilized James Young and Graham Dowdall; the Japanese promoters had been under the impression that he was bringing a backing band, but in the end he had come without one. Having recently swapped heroin for methadone, Nico's lifestyle was for Cale still rooted in a past that he was trying to forget, while she in her turn could find little to recommend the new, clean Cale. Cale was fascinated by the shops selling the designer clothing that had recently become an interest and, by being on the technological edge of the world, living briefly in the future.

After *The Falklands Suite* was performed in New York Cale flew to Europe for a handful of dates, including another one with Nico at the Palais des Beaux Arts in Brussels. Here he accompanied her on a version of *Paris, 1919*'s 'A Child's Christmas in Wales', helping her through the lyrics when she forgot them. A friendly goodbye at the end of the performance was given added poignancy because Nico died that July, making this the last time they met — the final note of a fitful, magical duet.

Part 7
Caledonite
(a copper and lead sulphate,
often in the form of blue/green prisms)

On 9 March 1942 Bobby Fischer, arguably the world's greatest chess player, was born. In 1967 Marcel Duchamp and his wife Teeny, who had followed Fischer's career with interest, having met him when he was twelve, chaperoned him through a Monte Carlo tournament.

By May 1988 Cale had written an instrumental piece, consisting of four minute-long segments, which he intended to use as the basis of his requiem for Andy Warhol. Harvey Lichtenstein of the Brooklyn Academy of Music agreed to stage the piece once it was completed, and Cale visited Lou Reed at his 81st Street home, where the two discussed the requiem's development as an orchestral work. Soon afterwards Reed took Cale to dinner at Da Sylvano in Greenwich Village where, with Reed's wife and manager Sylvia hovering, Cale was told, as if on cue, how highly Reed thought of him. He and Reed then, after a musical 'try-out' session — with Sylvia again in the background — rented a small studio for three weeks, playing together for fun and enjoying refound musical and personal channels of communication. It was decided that the orchestral requiem would be put aside, with Reed and Cale agreeing to work together again on a full-time project for the first time in twenty years. Using Warhol's Factory nickname, the project would be called *Songs for Drella*. Lichtenstein was more than happy to take on the altered proposal, and Cale and Reed decided that, as in the early days of the Velvet Underground, everything, including copyright, would be shared equally.

Over the summer and autumn of 1988 Reed recorded his *New York* album and Cale played some solo dates in the USA and in Canada. There was talk of Cale appearing on *New York*, but, having worked again with Reed as an equal partner, he did not want to return to the role of side man that had for him characterized the final days of his time in the Velvet Underground. By the time they returned to work together in December Cale had negotiated a joint deal with St Ann's Church and the Brooklyn Academy of Music to stage *Songs for Drella* at both venues. The first 'workshop' performances would be at St Ann's on 7 and 8 January 1989, and this gave Cale and Reed three weeks in which to come up with enough finished songs to constitute a proper show. In this short time they came up with fourteen, which together made up a chronological portrayal of Warhol's life from his 'escape' from his birthplace of Pittsburgh to his death in New York.

By the time they began working together again Reed and Cale had been fencing around each other for almost exactly twenty years, their meetings occasional and sometimes cordial, sometimes caustic. Inhabiting the same milieu, it would have been

174

hard to avoid each other completely, and there was always a mutual suspicion about the past when they met that vied with their remembered intimacy. Rivalries over each other's subsequent achievements made for a continuing competitiveness that threatened any renewal of their friendship. Strange parallels had developed between their careers and personal lives, and the movements of one had always seemed to relate to those of the other. Neither had been able to banish the presence of his former partner from his life, and there had always been a sense that neither really wanted to, that their joint history had a pull on their presents and futures. The album that Reed had recently finished, *New York*, would be a creative rebirth for him. One song on it in particular, 'Dime Store Mystery', had found him starting to crystallize some of the feelings he had for Andy Warhol; the musical setting of this track, too, came closest to the sound of the Velvet Underground than anything in his solo career had since 'Street Hassle'. Warhol's death had led him to question his relationship with the artist and to regret that they had not been able to re-establish a friendship that had faded away as a result of mutual mistrust and resentment. Warhol's death had also provoked a spate of disrespectful biographies of him, and Reed felt that these books' combined portrait of an untalented, shallow celebrity-chaser who had somehow struck it lucky needed refuting. By collaborating on *Songs for Drella*, Reed could do his best to right past wrongs in his association with Warhol by restoring his public reputation, and he could also repair the other significant relationship from that time that had been broken — that with Cale. By reuniting with his old Velvet Underground partner, he would help to rebuild Warhol's world and would ensure that this other relationship did not go the same way, leaving another open wound. However, it was also hard to escape the feeling that Reed was being urged on by his wife Sylvia. On a business level, the time was right, finally, to tap into the rich legacy of the Velvet Underground.

By beginning to work together again Cale and Reed were effectively returning to Ludlow Street in 1965, and they recognized this by ruling out the idea of bringing any other musicians into the project — the backing of a rock 'n' roll rhythm section and a full orchestra were considered and rejected. For the most part, the freedoms and pressures that they had encountered in their original song-writing no longer existed. Instead there were new combinations that would produce a similar creative environment: the freedom brought by lack of responsibilities was replaced by the freedom of financial security; the pressure of struggling for survival and trying to get their music heard replaced by the responsibility of doing justice to their joint reputations and that of Warhol.

As they had done twenty years earlier Cale did most of the arranging, and Reed wrote most of the lyrics — and with tape-recorders rolling all the time everything was recorded, each man keeping a copy of the result. Cale, however, with the experience of twenty years of writing his own words, contributed more of these now than he had before. Reed, worryingly, soon began to ignore them. However, the sound of twenty years earlier reappeared immediately, the unique combination of Reed and Cale providing something that neither could produce on his own – and that no other combination of individuals could produce either. Twenty years of separate development, of growing older and of a technical development that saw Reed now with a battery of sound effects and electronically perfected guitars and Cale working on computerized keyboards, were unable to restrain the resurgence of that sound. The constant discussions that punctuated these rehearsals and collaborations, re-creations of the world of Warhol, the Factory and the New York of the 1960s, the era when the lives of Reed and Cale had been woven together so tightly, redrew that landscape and reassembled that atmosphere, enabling that same music to flow again.

Cale and Reed built up the songs by taping their improvisations, isolating riffs and using them as bases. Reed stored all the lyrical ideas that he wanted to use, took them away to his word processor and returned with them as finished pieces; the music they had come up with was moulded by Cale to the lyrical structures, and the suite became a solid construction. As they worked, Cale and Reed identified songs that each particularly wanted to sing; others would naturally fall to one or other when a musical accompaniment proved too difficult to play at the same time.

The first two performances of *Songs for Drella* at St Ann's billed it as a 'work in progress' and 'A Tribute to Andy Warhol'; it would later become 'a fiction'. By the time of the Brooklyn Academy of Music shows in November and December of 1989 some of the arrangements would be changed and one new song added. Two more that Cale and Reed would write would not be included. For the St Ann's performances a visual element was added by the projection of a series of slides of Warhol's artworks; when the production moved to the Brooklyn Academy of Music this element would become much more refined with an integrated sequence of images, manipulated and colourized by Jerome Sirlin.

After playing at St Ann's Cale departed temporarily, travelling to Moscow in April to record the orchestral parts of *The Falklands Suite* for inclusion on his *Words for the Dying*. Although the absence had been agreed, Cale found on his return that his commitment to the project was being questioned and his publishing rights threatened. A less than flattering photograph of him, sanctioned by Sylvia, had also been used for a magazine centre-spread. In the face of these problems Cale gritted his teeth and concentrated on the fact that the music he and Reed were producing was satisfying enough to compensate for them.

When they reconvened in New York in December, having also made a joint television appearance on the *David Letterman Show* on 17 November, it was to perform *Songs for Drella* to heightened anticipation. This had been stirred up in the wake of the January dates and also by a media publicity campaign tied in to the recording of a video immediately after the live show and then an album. If the St Ann's shows were modest and low-key, befitting their surroundings in a small church and their status as a work in progress, those at the Brooklyn Academy of Music nearly eleven months later, as part of its 'Next Wave' festival, were well trailed in the media, fully rounded as finished work and presented as integrated mixed-media experiences. Only one song had been added to the set played earlier in the year, but it was one that added an extra dimension. 'A Dream' not only expanded the biographical format of the rest of the piece by moving into Warhol's unconscious and exploring it but also extended the area of Cale's and Reed's previous experimentation into the realms of synthetic sound. Far from compromising their original sound, it built on and developed it. When getting back together to work on their existing songs and also to come up with some more, Cale and Reed had discussed writing a short story for Cale to narrate, as they had done with 'The Gift' on *White Light/White Heat*, and from there the idea had grown to construct a dream narrative. For Cale in particular, this would be a pivotal element in his development; from now on narration would become a bigger and bigger interest, a way to fight against what he describes as the 'dictatorial' sound of his singing voice.

The Brooklyn Academy of Music provided a large rehearsal studio for Cale and Reed. Cale's piano was connected to a sampler to provide electronic effects and to make up for the strings they had decided not to use. Here 'A Dream' took shape and would become the highlight of the new performances of *Drella*. Changes would also be made to some of the existing songs: 'Small Town' would be shorn of its line specifically linking Warhol's childhood to that of Cale ('My father is a coal miner'), 'Faces and Names' would have its original burlesque feel toned down, and 'Slip Away' would be slowed down dramatically.

Jerome Sirlin had previously designed stage sets for a collaboration with Philip Glass, *1000 Airplanes on the Roof*, and had also worked with the New York City Opera. He was engaged to create a backdrop of Warhol artworks and photographs of both the artist and various Factory people; on top of these he superimposed coloured moving images. On the screen Leonardo da Vinci's *Mona Lisa* was transformed into Warhol's as it changed colour again and again in a version of Warhol's own screen-printing process. A gun moved across the Factory's elevator gates as Warhol's shooting was described, and the phrase 'Images worth repeating' was flashed behind the musicians as Reed sang the same words to a hypnotic musical backing. A black-and-white photograph of Warhol acquired makeup and lipstick, and one of Cale looked out over its real-life counterpart. The musical assault at the beginning of

'Images' — Cale's sawing viola and Reed's heavily distorted guitar — was met on the screen by Warhol's monolithic red 'Electric Chair'.

During the performances Cale often looked across at Reed, an expression of concentration on his face. Reed looked back less often, only to signal Cale to begin the background vocals or to draw a song to its end.

There were four performances of *Songs for Drella*, from 29 November to 3 December, and on the final night Maureen Tucker emerged from the wings to sing a version of 'Pale Blue Eyes' backed by Reed and Cale: the closest thing to a Velvet Underground reunion since Cale's departure from the band. Despite Lou Reed's continued denials, his standard line having been for many years that it would never happen, momentum seemed to be building for a reunion. It was an issue that the massive media coverage of the performances and subsequent recordings certainly did not ignore. Cale, for his part, professed himself happy with *Songs for Drella* and stated his willingness to take his renewed partnership with Lou Reed further, despite the resurgence of some of its old tensions.

After the final performance at the Brooklyn Academy of Music Reed and Cale played *Drella* again to an empty house to create a video version and then paused briefly before going into the studio to record it for an album. Recording, and particularly the post-production, turned out to be fraught. Cale would come in to the studio in the morning after Reed had stayed late the evening before to find that his computerized keyboard settings had been altered. Later on in the day smoke would be blown at his face in the control room. The final mixes were negotiated on a strict quid pro quo basis, over which Cale recalls that he 'yielded nothing'. The two parties emerged, somehow, just about talking.

The album was well received, filled as it was with evidence of new creative life in the old partnership. Lyrically direct, precise and honest, but also imaginative in its integration of Warhol's art into its lines, the music found new forms of life in two- and three-chord structures. Cale's hypnotic patterns once again found the path into Reed's subconscious, from where they drew the kind of guitar work that no one else could find — certainly not Reed alone.

Cale was already talking about live work with Reed being more of an option than another recorded venture, but Reed, as it turned out, did not want even to perform *Songs for Drella* again. It would happen once in Tokyo, and they would play part of it together in France, but this was a project that would basically go no further, its commercial potential largely untapped. For Cale, keen to capitalize as much as he could on his work, it was a big disappointment. It seemed to him that the project possessed a parallel significance for Reed as part of a hidden agenda.

In between the sets at St Ann's and the Brooklyn Academy of Music Cale had recorded his *Words for the Dying* album. Two instrumentals, 'Songs Without Words I and II', were recorded in New York, as was the electronic soundtrack to a fifteen-minute film, *Dick*, by Jo Menell released later in the year. A new collaboration with Brian Eno, however, 'The Soul of Carmen Miranda', was recorded at Wilderness, Eno's home studio in Woodbridge, England. Also at Wilderness, and at London's Strongroom Studios where *Artificial Intelligence* had been made, Cale put down the vocal and piano tracks for his orchestral *Falklands Suite* which was finally to appear on record. Choral parts were to be taped in Cardiff, featuring the choir of Llandaff Cathedral Choir School, but Cale had decided to record the orchestral sections in Moscow. He had written pieces that needed a large string section and had been faced with the choice of either using two college orchestras or finding a single larger one that was not prohibitively expensive. The first option was impractical, and for the second he turned to Russia.

Words for the Dying was to appear on Eno's Land Records label. Cale had played him a tape of *The Falklands Suite* recorded at the Paradiso in Amsterdam, and Eno had decided that he wanted to take on the project. Through the agency of Eno's wife Anthea it was arranged to use Moscow's Orchestra of Symphonic and Popular Music of Gosteleradio. At the end of April 1989 Cale and Eno travelled to Moscow for the recording sessions, accompanied by film-maker Rob Nilsson who was to record the week-long trip and its aftermath for his own documentary, also to be called *Words for the Dying*. This film is not only a memento of the recording of an album in an unusual environment; it also looks at the relationships between Cale and Eno and, surprisingly, Cale and his mother over a short set period of time. Both of these were put into relief by events that overtook the film. Eno refused to cooperate once it was under way, dodging the camera and being filmed only in secret, providing some unexpected comic moments in the process, while in an episode close to tragedy Cale's mother is filmed allowing the house where she has lived all of her life to be sold after it has been vandalized and she is deemed unable to look after herself there on her own any more. In between these episodes Cale sleeps at the airport, observes in a detached manner a couple of Russian rock bands, watches in awe a performance by double-bass player Rodion Azarkhin and narrates a prose piece, 'Year of the Patriot', at the piano while Azarkhin plays. Back in Britain Cale travels with sleeping daughter Eden and records his vocal tracks at Strongroom in London, while Eno cajoles and encourages him. Cale describes his homeland as 'like a blind side' — he has no understanding of it — and he revisits the site of his father's mine, with his primary school a hundred yards behind it. Cale feels that he has not pushed Eno far enough in the recordings they have made, while Eno defines their relationship as a combination of Cale's unusual ideas and his own attention to detail. Cale informs the camera that he has no interest in providing 'gargoylish' entertainment to audiences any more and exits the film by running off down the hillside.

The resulting documentary is a bewildering succession of snapshots of Cale's life — and a plausible picture of it as a result.

Work was finished on *Words for the Dying* in July, after which Cale performed in Germany and then returned to New York to work on *Songs for Drella*. In the meantime his acting sideline had moved forward with the broadcast on 11 June of an episode of Edward Woodward's *The Equalizer* series, 'Race Traitors', with Cale as 'Aryan Leader'. While working on *Songs for Drella*, Cale was approached by film-maker Zoe Beloff to appear in a short feature she was making entitled *Wonderland USA*. Managing to fit in two days' filming within the *Drella* schedule, Cale — in a relocation of *Alice in Wonderland* to New York — played a lonely writer who lures Alice into 'a wonderland of decadence and despair'. Cale went through the script with Beloff beforehand and was driven to and from the studio: quiet, reserved and professional on set, he would spend the time when he was not being filmed by reading. *Wonderland USA* has no dialogue but instead uses a voice-over by Cale, which he returned to the studio to record afterwards. As a soundtrack it employs a solo Cale version of 'Heartbreak Hotel'. The film is shot in black and white, with Alice falling into Times Square and being chased through the Coney Island fair-grounds, and is part of what Beloff describes as her 'ongoing investigation into the relationship between imagination and moving image technology'. Cale's brief per-formance is moving and his narration beautifully judged — another step in one of the directions in which he saw his words and music starting to move. He enjoyed the result and asked Beloff to work with him again in 1994 when he was putting together his *Life Underwater* project.

Words for the Dying was released on 2 October, and Cale returned to Europe to promote it. While in England he bought a copy of the newly published *Andy Warhol Diaries* from Harrods department store in London, and his and Lou Reed's reading of these would provide the inspiration for 'A Dream'.

Words for the Dying — and particularly its centrepiece *The Falklands Suite* with its search for the new in the forms of the past — was received with a kind of awe-struck bemusement. While Dylan Thomas's poems already dealt with death, Cale specifically tied them to the Falklands War that had coincided with his first work on them by inserting a reference to the 'drownèd of Falklands' into 'Lie Still, Sleep Becalmed'. When the HMS *Sheffield* went down as he was working on these poems, the force of this particular piece, with its desperate images of death at sea flying in from the past and crashing into the present, must have leaped from the page. There were more personal echoes of death in the words of a son to a father in 'Do Not Go Gentle Into That Good Night'. Cale's orchestral work was lyrical and melancholy, grand and sombre, highly accomplished in its movements and expositions.

The Falklands Suite was a way of coming to terms with the past: Cale's education in classical music, his relationship with Wales and his father and the role in Cale's life of the poetry of Dylan Thomas. The defiantly modern electronic sounds of the album's three final pieces, however, subvert these legacies once more. The 'Songs Without Words' are stark in contrast with the complexity and power of the suite's orchestrations, and 'The Soul of Carmen Miranda', as melancholy in its way as the central work, is also ornate and otherworldly in ways outside the parameters of the mainstream classical orbit.

A major result of the album's appearance was to show that Cale's ability as a composer of orchestral music that was constructed and developed to a substantial length was now proven, and this would be important for attracting future film soundtrack projects. While instrumental work of this and other sorts would soon begin to take up more and more of Cale's time and become a source of steady income, its often limited opportunities for experimentation would also stoke up the pressure for further trips into the unknown.

Although *Songs for Drella* had not managed to prolong its life much beyond its performances at the Brooklyn Academy of Music and its recorded releases, Cale continued to collaborate with other artists as a way of attacking his dissatisfaction with the songs he had been writing on his own. In 1990 he worked with Brian Eno and William Burroughs, as well as performing live with Bob Neuwirth, Richard Thompson and, for the first time in more than twenty years, the Velvet Underground.

On 18 February Cale appeared with Richard Thompson on NBC Televisions's *Night Music*, playing a version of 'Heartbreak Hotel', and at St Ann's Church on 10 March he and Bob Neuwirth gave the first 'work in progress' performance of their mixed-media piece *Last Days on Earth*, which had been in the mix for as long as *The Falklands Suite*. The performance consisted of fourteen songs, four spoken interludes, an overture and an epilogue. Part of the advertising read: 'The meek, if they so want, can inherit the earth, and it's time the road maps were rewritten.'

'[Dylan Thomas and Igor Stravinsky] would do a 're-creation of the whole world' — an opera about the only man and woman left alive on earth.'
(From *Dylan Thomas in America* by John Malcolm Brinnin)

After his appearance with Neuwirth Cale headed over to Britain and to Woodbridge, Suffolk, where Eno had his home studio. Apart from 'The Soul of Carmen Miranda', Cale and Eno had recorded two other pieces together at the time of *Words for the Dying* and were now to collaborate on a full album, *Wrong Way Up*, with Cale staying at Eno's house while they worked.

In the film *Words for the Dying* Eno had commented on the contrast between the ways in which he and Cale worked but also on how the different techniques complemented each other. For Cale a successful combination of the two approaches depended on the mixture being given a good stir.

Work would begin in the morning at Woodbridge and then proceed until the end of 'office hours' when Cale would disappear to the squash court. After dinner Cale would retire for a perusal of the papers and television, and Eno would return to the laboratory on his own.

When Cale arrived at Woodbridge Eno had already written one complete song and had also recorded basic drum tracks for the rest. An initial concept revolving around a deck of cards was shelved, and the two set about writing songs together, based on Eno's existing rhythms, by exchanging chords and melodies as well as lyrical ideas. Cale had wanted Eno to have a strong vocal presence and encouraged him to voice the lyrics with energy. Each had wanted to produce an album of songs that were full of vitality, and the result was a collection characterized by melody and rhythm, as well as by the sunshine and tranquil surroundings in which it had been recorded.

The album's airiness did not tell the whole story of its making, however. The largely joint aims of its collaborators were often subverted by their different approaches. Eno's methodical and patient working techniques could only accommodate Cale's chaotic surges at the material for so long, and halfway through the project David Young had been brought in to do the latter's engineering. This was a job that Eno had been doing, but the two had become too much in each other's pockets. With a substantial part of the album completed, remaining work was effectively split into two halves with Cale and Young on one side and Eno on the other — although Young would end up playing guitar with both men.

By the time the album was finished there had been more disputes about the mixing and about Eno's erasing of certain parts. There were more problems, as there had been with *Songs for Drella*, when it came to promoting the album — Eno did not want to perform it live, despite having earlier agreed to do so. Not for nothing did the cover of *Wrong Way Up* feature photographs of Cale and Eno separated by a line of daggers.

Wrong Way Up had a warm reception, and much of the acclaim on its release came from the reaction by the music critics to two experienced conceptualists working together to produce an album of pop songs underpinned by funk and R&B rhythms. Commercial potential, of which there was even more than on *Songs for Drella*, was again to be largely unfulfilled, however, thanks to Eno's embargo on live promotion.

Cale produced complete lyrics for three songs on *Wrong Way Up*: murky tales of duplicity and subterfuge set against a variety of landscapes. Of the lyrical collaborations with Eno, 'Cordoba' inhabits the same ground, with phrases that the latter found in sequence in the Hugo *Spanish in Three Months* guide being used to reveal a portrait of two terrorists about to bomb a bus.

The impact of *Songs for Drella* had not died away by the time *Wrong Way Up* was recorded. In the middle of the sessions Cale travelled to Jouy-en-Josas outside Paris for the opening of an Andy Warhol retrospective to be held in the grounds of the château home of the Fondation Cartier pour l'Art Contemporain. Cale and Lou Reed had agreed to play a selection from *Songs for Drella* at the opening, and Sterling Morrison and Maureen Tucker were also to attend. Within the exhibition there would be a section dedicated to the Velvet Underground for which Sterling Morrison had contributed posters, equipment and memorabilia, much of which had lain unseen since he had left the band. All this made Cale uneasy, commenting: 'We're not ready for museums yet.'

Shortly before Cale and Reed were to perform on a canopied stage above one of the château's lawns, an announcement was made that the Velvet Underground would briefly be re-forming for the first time in twenty-two years.

Cale and Reed played five numbers from *Songs for Drella* and then, at the end of the short set Reed ushered Sterling Morrison and Maureen Tucker on-stage, and with the minimum of fuss they locked together in a version of 'Heroin' that seemed to tap straight back into the time and the place that had conspired to create it. At the song's peak Cale darted forward and crouched in front of his amplifier, presenting his viola to it like a priest offering a sacrifice on an altar, the result a series of terrified screeches and screams. Nihilism in the midst of tranquillity seemed briefly like a perfectly reasonable combination.

On 9 March 1989 the Soviet Union came voluntarily under the rule of the World Court.

At the end of the performance, the band put their arms around each other. Asked afterwards, as the band drove off to their hotel what the experience had been like, Cale replied, 'Emotional.'

Sterling Morrison told Billy Name: 'Billy, now I know why I haven't played for years, 'cause *these* are the people I play with.' At dinner that night (they dined together at different restaurants on each night of their stay in Paris) the band discussed old times and what it was like to be together in one room again, without any lawyers present, for the first time in twenty-two years. Much of the bonhomie had to do with the presence of Billy Name, who was able to sense Lou Reed's state of mind at any given time and pre-empt any problems. This skill almost reached the level of mind-reading, and he was able to explain Reed's thought processes as he was having them, something that had, as Cale remembers, 'an enormous calming effect on Lou'.

With the band left to ponder on the ramifications of those ten minutes in the French countryside, they went their separate ways again for the moment, and Cale returned to the various projects that were being stitched together into his new tapestry of work patterns.

Of Cale's other 1990 collaborations, *Dead City Radio* allowed him to work with William Burroughs, a seemingly ever-present figure in the New York avant-garde and one of the patron saints of the Velvet Underground. Cale added some restrained harpsichord, piano and pizzicato strings to Burroughs's mordant delivery of three short prose pieces.

Cale also worked on *Les Nouvelles Polyphonies Corses* by the Corsican Choir. David Young had gone to Corsica to record the native singing group and then sent the tapes to Cale, who added synthesizers to them.

In November Cale and Bob Neuwirth were given three weeks in a rehearsal loft space at the Brooklyn Academy of Music – much as Cale and Reed had been for *Songs for Drella* – to put in more work on *Last Day on Earth* and make it into a presentable theatrical piece. In March 1991 they took the show to Germany for several 'try-out' dates.

Back in New York Cale appeared at 'Ten Years of Arts at St Ann's', a benefit for the Brooklyn church, along with Aaron Neville and Dr John. In June he performed *Sanctus*, his four-movement work for 'electronic orchestra' that had started life as a ballet piece, on the same bill as David Byrne and Glenn Branca at New York's Town Hall. A studio version of *Sanctus* formed part of a new album, *Paris S'Eveille*, which also contained the soundtrack to the eponymous French film, written by Cale and performed by the Soldier String Quartet, which would go on to work with him again several times. There was a disparate collection of other mainly instrumental works, as well as, jarringly, a previously unreleased live Velvet Underground performance from 1968 of 'Booker T': the backing music from 'The Gift'. The wide range of this collection is testament to Cale's search for new directions for his music and new territories to permeate, the insertion of the Velvet Underground track almost a subversion of his own current work but also, given the band's recent reunion, a dragging of the past into the present.

In October an album of cover versions of Leonard Cohen's songs, *I'm Your Fan*, was released. The stand-out track was Cale's version of 'Hallelujah', an amalgam of sex, religion, inspiration, love and despair refined to a point of absolute purity. Cale had contacted Cohen beforehand for the lyrics, and Cohen responded with reams of unrecorded verses. On 1 November, Cale went to see Jeff Buckley perform, and Buckley would later use Cale's arrangement of 'Hallelujah' on his début album *Grace*.

As well as working on *Last Day on Earth* and *Sanctus* Cale had also been involved with his first full-scale ballet piece, *Iphigenia in Tauris*, which was presented between 16 and 19 January at the Merce Cunningham Studio in New York.

This multi-stranded activity continued through 1992, with film scores, more ballet work, a live album and video and another new mixed-media piece, *Life Underwater*. Towards the end of the year the Velvet Underground reunion, on the cards since *Songs for Drella*, would come closer to reality. None of this mattered, however, in the face of the year's most significant event: the death of Cale's mother.

For Cale his mother had been a constant presence, even when they were physically separated by the Atlantic Ocean. In childhood she had been part of his achievements and in adult life had proudly overseen them. Once she was gone his childhood, first home and family would seem remoter and more unfathomable than ever – and his father, of whom he still knew so little, would take a step further back into obscurity.

In Europe in the spring Cale played several solo dates, tapes of which would be used later in the year to make up a live album, *Fragments of a Rainy Season*. An accompanying video was filmed at Brussels' Palais des Beaux Arts in April. By now Cale's solo show was a well-honed whole, an immaculate showcase for some of the highlights from his recording career. Several interviews were conducted for the release of the album and video, entailing plenty of looking back on his past working life, just as the death of his mother pushed him back into the roots of his personal life.

Cale's contribution to Hector Zazou's *Sahara Blue* album, a collection of interpretations of Rimbaud's poetry, saw him experimenting further with combinations of music and narration, and in September he presented a new sixteen-minute work in progress, *Life Underwater*, at the Munich Philharmonic Art Project.

The piece's story was very loosely based on the legend of Orpheus, with fraternal and sexual jealousy tied in to a modern tale of a bank robbery gone wrong. A segmented experiment with narration and music, *Life Underwater* employed Cale's solo piano, the Soldier String Quartet and a barbershop quartet as well as various sound effects. The piece was presented in a concert that also featured songs from *Last Day on Earth*, for which Bob Neuwirth joined Cale on stage, and a selection of material from Cale's back catalogue. Back in New York *Life Underwater* would take on new life as a mixed-media presentation in collaboration with film-maker Zoe Beloff.

Towards the end of the European tour Cale, backed by a string quartet, performed 'Dying on the Vine' and 'Hallelujah' for BBC Television's *Later* programme and, once home again, played a handful of US dates. One of these, at New York University, turned into what, alongside the 1989 *Songs for Drella* appearance with Moe Tucker, was the closest thing to a Velvet Underground reunion the USA would ever see, as Sterling Morrison and Lou Reed briefly joined him on stage. The four members of the

Velvet Underground had all recently reconvened in New York to discuss the upcoming release of a boxed set of the band's work, and Lou Reed, as a joke, suggested that they play Madison Square Gardens for a million dollars. The fact that Reed had even mentioned the idea was so unexpected that it immediately gained a kind of life. Reed seemed to be at a loose end after his recent *Magic and Loss* project and, with the boxed set, the recent memory of *Songs for Drella* and the events at Jouy-en-Josas, not to mention the constant supply of new bands successfully mining the rich seam of the Velvet Underground's music, the time seemed to be ripe. Reed suggested the idea of a Christmas carol concert, and he and Cale discussed singing 'White Christmas' as well, in an arrangement where the modulations would get lower and lower until it became impossible to sing. In the event, over lunch together in the lobby of the Paramount Hotel a date in February was set for an informal jam session to see if the old fire could be reignited. Although Cale was wary of working with Reed again, knowing that his 'recidivist' mentality was likely to bring more problems similar to the ones that had surfaced during *Songs for Drella*, there was the tantalizing possibility of creating new work that would carry on from where the band had left off in 1968. There was also the strong feeling that Sterling Morrison and Moe Tucker were due some rewards for their part in the unique music that had been created.

In February Cale also began preparing a full-scale version of *Life Underwater* for eventual presentation at St Ann's. Zoe Beloff had already been involved in discussions about the piece and its future extension into film and slides, as a way of dramatizing the story. The idea had first been mentioned when they had previously worked together in 1990, but fund-raising had taken nearly four years. Beloff had begun visiting Cale's house the previous August, taking notes on what he had already written and on ideas for the development of the piece — his ideas were often abstract and part of her role was to ground them in such a way that they could be expressed on film. As these meetings progressed into the winter of 1992/3, so did the development of its story and *mise-en-scène*, and Beloff went off to shoot black-and-white sixteen-millimetre film and stereo slides for use on stage. Cale had wanted to incorporate three abstract concepts in visual terms — 'Savagery', 'Conscience' and 'Fear'. To do this Beloff carved the words into rocks to be positioned on the beach where filming took place. On this wintry windswept seashore and in the forest and abandoned house behind it Cale as Orpheus looked back on his childhood with his brother and his sister, Eurydice, with flashback scenes played by child actors. With no other signs of human life around the players, the atmosphere of the filmed segments, inspired by the minimalism of early film with its stationary camera, became dreamy and fairytale-like, a return to a forgotten time and place.

In April, after a week's rehearsal to coordinate the projections, narration and music, *Life Underwater* was performed over two nights at St Ann's with actress Ann

Magnuson sharing narration duties with Cale. On a stage with no ornamentation Cale, the Soldier String Quartet and Magnuson performed what was now an hour-long piece, dominated by narration, to the accompaniment of Beloff's slides and film.

By now the Velvet Underground reunion had, after what had been a successful jam session at Big Mike Productions in New York, become a firm undertaking. Work began on scouting out European venues for a summer tour, Lou Reed's record company started talking about a live album and a video, a documentary was commissioned, and Big Mike's was rebooked for three solid weeks of rehearsal in May.

Even at this early stage the reunion was already more than just fun — which had been the stated reason for it. It was a large commercial enterprise involving many people in two continents. There were other pressures, too: the constant worry of whether old arguments and rivalries might still be revived and the question of whether the band would be able to do justice to their reputation. There was also the fact that Sylvia Reed was placing herself more and more in between her husband and the rest of the band, with his business interests assuming greater and greater importance. Despite these pressures, the old songs came back to life as completely as anyone could have hoped, and there was immediately a genuine air of excitement about the whole enterprise. As in the early days the presence of Moe Tucker looked like holding the band together both on and off stage.

The band flew to England in July, rehearsing again briefly in West London before flying up to Scotland for the start of the tour in Edinburgh. Although generally acknowledged to be only warming up, they were well received. By the time they were back in London again, the shows were tight and acclaimed, with the sound accurately surviving the passage of the years and Reed visibly enjoying himself, seemingly happy to share centre-stage with Cale. However, it soon began to look ominously as if the sets were to be pretty much the same every night, with improvisation largely to be limited to the guitar and viola firefights of 'Hey Mr Rain'. It was almost as though Reed was saying 'This far but no further', an attitude that was never going to satisfy Cale. Once they reached mainland Europe nothing much had changed, and three Paris gigs were concerned mainly with getting enough good versions of the existing songs to make a successful live album and video. Tensions within the band were growing, with Reed and Sylvia on one side squeezing Cale, Morrison and Tucker on the other. Reed seemed to need to dominate now, making what should have been collective decisions on his own, the others becoming victims of his undemocratic stance. At the end of the tour there were dates supporting U2 in the kind of big stadia that were alien to everything the band had ever been about. The members of U2 themselves were more than happy to be playing with a group that had been a formative influence on them and enjoyed the company of all of its members. Reed, feeling that he was being marginalized, hired an expensive limousine in Lausanne to transport himself, his bodyguard and his baggage to the next stop in Basle, in order to avoid having to travel with his band-mates. After the Swiss dates Reed insisted that a projected MTV *Unplugged* album could only happen if he produced it. That was effectively the end of the comeback, although the dispute was protracted by a series of faxes between Reed and Cale and press statements issued by all parties.

For Cale the reunion had been fun for a while, but crucially it had been a lost opportunity — and events would soon dictate that another would not occur. Having recaptured the old magic it had been allowed, through Reed's insistence, to evaporate again. One presence that might have changed things was that of Billy Name, Cale reckons. 'I see now how smart I could have been if I had brought him into the fold after the U2 tour when we were into the fax wars. One meeting with him attending and I bet we could have had an agreement on the way ahead . . . he was the only antidote I knew of for Lou's malignant obsessivenesses.'

As it was, Cale effectively shrugged his shoulders and returned to his briefly interrupted solo career. The frustration of going through the motions with the Velvet Underground would soon be blown away in a renewal of avant-garde activity. Meanwhile another soundtrack album was released in September, *23 Solo Pieces for La Naissance de l'Amour*, a collection of short solo piano sketches for a film by Philippe Garrel, the French director with whom Nico had worked extensively. Another John Cage tribute album, *A Chance Operation — The John Cage Tribute*, featuring another new Cale track, had been put together after Cage's death in August 1992 and was released in October.

On 25 October the Velvet Underground's live album, *Live MCMXCIII*, was released, attracting largely respectable reviews. The same week, Cale returned to the Forum in London's Kentish Town, where the Velvet Underground had played five months previously, for a show accompanied in part by B.J. Cole on pedal-steel guitar. In a set full of interest the most striking piece that the two produced was a menacing reinvention of 'The Jeweller' that took the story 180 degrees away from Eno's original disorientation of it.

In February 1994, after *Songs for Drella* and *Wrong Way Up*, Cale's third collaborative album in five years, *Last Day on Earth*, was completed in the studio with Bob Neuwirth several years after beginning life during an improvisation at the Kitchen in New York. In the intervening period this collaboration about travellers meeting had been added to and refined each time their paths had crossed. Rewritten and edited by its co-authors for its transfer from theatrical presentation to recorded album, the piece is set in the Café Shabu, a staging-post on the edge of the new millennium. Here the patrons provide a travelogue to the journey into a new era against an eclectic musical backing of instruments and styles from across the spectra of time and culture. A rewarding piece to listen to but difficult to promote, excerpts would be performed in Europe later in the year. The project, however, would suffer in the wake of Cale's more media-friendly Reed and Eno collaborations.

In February London's Institute of Contemporary Arts played host to a celebration marking William Burroughs's eightieth birthday, and Cale sent faxed his congratulations through as the proceedings took place. Cale had himself started to use Burroughs's prose techniques as points of departure, and textual experiments in narrative pieces would now become a large part of his art. Cutting and assembling pieces of foreign texts, along with the use of actual narrative voices derived from tapes of authors reading from their own work, as well as his own live narrations, would be used by Cale to create montages in the same way as the Dadaists. By breaking down existing works and recombining elements of them a new work would be created.

In May Cale set off for an extensive European tour. On this he was accompanied by a similar backing group to that of 1992, with the Soldier String Quartet, Bob Neuwirth, B.J.Cole on pedal-steel guitar and blues singers Tiyé Giraud and Sam Butler. Entitled the '99 *Greenwich Delusion*, the tour also took in a date in Amsterdam that featured Cale presenting a series of prose readings from *Life Underwater*, as well as from *The Collected Works of Billy the Kid* by Michael Ondaatje and a biography of Marilyn Monroe. Cale ended the reading with Lou Reed's poem 'Forewarned Is Forearmed', which Reed had sent to him in 1967.

This is Memory Broadcast Network – please enjoy the reading.

Back in New York on 15 June Cale gave a performance at the Thread Waxing Space. Entitled *Memory Broadcast Network*, it had originally been a way of using public access television to allow Michael McLintock, who had worked on *Music for a New Society*, to perform live the text of a spy novel that he had written. Sadly, McLintock died before he and Cale could complete it. Cale decided to continue with the project but to use projections as a visual element and to choose new texts. This was a spoken-word piece along the lines of the Amsterdam performance but with the added dimension of slides projected by Jerome Sirlin, who had designed the *Songs for Drella* productions in New York, on to shifting screens. The texts used covered the history of Iranian torture, madness and rape and featured the work of Dylan Thomas, Michael Ondaatje, Tennessee Williams and Lynne Tillman in a stream-of-consciousness presentation of 'memory as a presumption of misleading facts'.

This has been a programme from the Memory Broadcast Network – thank you for reading your television.

Cale's accommodation of other people's writing into his music – as distinct from collaborating with other songwriters and musicians – which had begun with the setting of Dylan Thomas's poems to music, was based on a love of literature that he had indulged since childhood. Always a voracious and eclectic reader, he now gets through around five hundred books in a year, reading three or four at a time, but does not collect them. At the end of each year the New School for Social Research – specializing in social research, political science and international affairs – gratefully picks them up from him.

In April Cale had recorded three tracks with Chris Spedding and ex-New York Doll David Johansen for Marc Almond's album *Fantastic Star*, and Spedding joined Cale once more for the soundtrack to Manuel Huerga's film *Antártida*, which was shot in July. Huerga had developed the film from an idea given to him by Cale's song 'Antarctica Starts Here', and Cale was to appear in the film in a nightclub scene, singing this and two other songs. Huerga commissioned him to come up with a whole score for the film and, together with the instrumental work, this included a new version of 'Antarctica Starts Here' featuring Spedding on classical guitar, as well as a version of Jim Carroll's 'People Who Died'. The latter featured a kind of 'alternative' Velvet Underground: Cale, Moe Tucker, Sterling Morrison and Chris Spedding.

Although Lou Reed had removed himself from the equation, Cale, Morrison and Tucker were only too happy to continue working together, and after a week's rehearsal they were also to perform live in November at the Andy Warhol Museum in Pittsburgh, providing music to accompany showings of Warhol's silent films *Kiss* and *Eat*.

In August Cale was commissioned to write an opera, *Mata Hari*, and also took part in the televised *Elvis Presley Tribute*, playing his iconoclastic version of 'Heartbreak Hotel'. By now he had also finished production work on a new Siouxsie and the Banshees album, *The Rapture*, and this project led to Cale touring the USA with Siouxsie Sioux's 'other' band, the Creatures, in 1998.

As mentioned in his 1984 song 'Autobiography', Cale and his namesake J.J. Cale (first name also John) had, over the years, often been confused. On 18 September they met for what was – strangely enough, considering their shared longevity on the music scene – the first time, at the studio of New York's WXRK Radio, an encounter that was broadcast on the station's *Idiot's Delight* programme. After years of 'avoiding' each other, both were due to play at the Bottom Line club during the same week. Here they got the chance to discuss years of misfiled albums, mislabelled photographs and the possibility of misplaced royalties. These identity problems would continue into the future – at a show at Ronnie Scott's, in Birmingham, UK, in the year 2000, a party of businessmen would be most upset to sit through a whole Cale set without hearing either 'Cocaine' or 'After Midnight', not realizing that they had bought their corporate tickets for the 'wrong' one.

In Paris in 1924 Ezra Pound's *Antheil and the Treatise on Harmony* was published.

In October, Cale continued his experiments with texts and music combined with visual elements by making several performances of an accompaniment to Todd Browning's film *The Unknown* at screenings in Europe. Whereas the improvised Warhol films had allowed him plenty of space to fill, *The Unknown*, with its violent circus-set plot and twisted emotions, was already filled with its own dramatic elements. Cale decided to throw even more into the mix, however, rather than merely accompany the action on the screen, and he employed sound effects as well as the voices and words of T.S. Eliot, Ezra Pound (whose *Cantos* he still has ambitions to set to music) and Winston Churchill in order to create new artistic shocks to jar with those of the film itself.

A mooted new collaboration with Terry Riley in November had been cancelled, but Cale recorded a piece with Suzanne Vega, based on a poem by Oscar Wilde, for another Hector Zazou album, *Songs from the Cold Seas*. He continued to develop his burgeoning film work in the new year with soundtracks for Xavier Beauvois's *N'Oublie Pas Que Tu Vas Mourir*, Mary Harron's *I Shot Andy Warhol* and old friend Julian Schnabel's *Basquiat*. Alongside these projects he also took on production work in 1995 for Goya Dress and played two series of live shows with the Soldier String Quartet and B.J. Cole. These live shows, undertaken in the spring and summer and then again in December, now encompassed some new songs under the collective title 'Songs from the Shimmer'. These, however, would be put aside when Cale, having recently been signed by old associate Joe Boyd's Hannibal label, recorded a new solo album in the new year.

Three of the 'Songs from the Shimmer' — 'This Is Then, That Was Now', 'Salman Rushdie' and 'René Descartes in Berlin' — were performed on 22 July in New York's Central Park. These were songs that would never see the light of day but which would have made the basis of a very different album to the one that would appear on Hannibal the following year. Death, acerbic political commentary, prophecy and philosophy, morality, literature and war were the subjects here, and their contexts were eclectic: strings (both sweet and sour); piano that was ethereal on the right hand, earthly on the left; panting, breathing vocals; pace shifts and gear changes. Although Hannibal obviously wanted something different, these were songs that deserved to be heard.

As well as putting aside these pieces for his new album, Cale was to be forced also to suspend the kind of textual and narrative experiments that he had been pursuing, which would have been even less appropriate on what was to be a commercially attuned pop/rock collection. Cale regarded these experiments, however, as the way in which his art should be developed and was to return to them as soon as circumstances allowed.

Cale had been due to work with Sterling Morrison and Maureen Tucker, possibly in a touring band but most likely in a recorded version of the performance they had given as accompaniments to the two Andy Warhol films *Eat* and *Kiss*. Tragically, Morrison, who had looked noticeably ill in Pittsburgh, was fighting a losing battle with cancer, and he died in his home town of Poughkeepsie on 30 August. Cale went to visit him in his last days and was able to maintain their friendship until the end, but this was a devastating loss, especially as they had rekindled the old collaboration so recently. An album of music based on what Morrison, Tucker and Cale had played in Pittsburgh was recorded in Lille, France, in October, with Tucker among the musicians. It was eventually released in 1997 as *Eat/Kiss Music for the Films of Andy Warhol*, with due homage to Morrison's part in it.

Also in October a performance of Cale's opera *Mata Hari* was filmed in Vienna. Cale wrote the music for the production and shared the rest of the writing and staging with director Franz Harland, who had directed Cale's first screen role in *The Houseguest*. *Mata Hari* consisted of 'the story of the famous dancer-spy retold by historical and fictional witnesses in a high-tech multimedia musical production'.

As a sad irony, the Velvet Underground were inducted into the Rock and roll Hall of Fame in January 1996 at the New York Waldorf-Astoria six months after the death of Sterling Morrison. Morrison's widow, Martha, represented him at the ceremony and Cale, Lou Reed and Maureen Tucker all attended. Cale remembers all of them being 'very aware of our missing comrade. Very aware.' The introductory speech was made by Patti Smith, and the three surviving members of the Velvet Underground even got together beforehand to write a song in memoriam, 'Last Night I Said Goodbye to My Friend', which they performed on-stage. In his own speech Cale spoke of Morrison, Andy Warhol and Nico and of how the band had been an inspiration to 'musical failures' with low sales the world over.

There had been talk of Patti Smith staying in New York to record with Cale on his new album, but she was out of town when recording was completed. She was back in New York in February, however, at Carnegie Hall, and playing on the same bill as Cale at Philip Glass's annual Tibet House Benefit. Here, Glass, Cale and Billy Corgan of the Smashing Pumpkins backed Allen Ginsberg — who had appeared with the Velvet Underground at the Dom back in 1966 — as he recited his poem 'Ballad of the Skeletons'.

Cale's new album, *Walking on Locusts*, begun the previous year, was finished in the early months of 1996 but was not to be released until September. He flew over to Tokyo in mid-April to perform at a club, Milk, and the next day in the open-air courtyard of the new Museum of Contemporary Art, whose first exhibition was to be 'Andy Warhol 1956-86: Mirror of His Time'.

Back in New York a few days later Cale made an appearance on the same bill as John Giorno and Lydia Lunch for 'Decay, Poetry and Hope' at the Bathurst Street Theater. Two weeks later he was at the Artists' Space for a celebration of the Squat Theater.

In the summer Cale composed a soundtrack for a film set in Wales, *House of America*, a story of the pull of the USA on his homeland, while a few months earlier *I Shot Andy Warhol* had been released. Set together, they were twin reminders of the two most formative periods in his past.

Part 8
Calendula
(a marigold that flowers for most of the year)

The birthdays of Taras Shevchenko, Modest P. Mussorgsky, Mickey Spillane and Raul Julia fall on 9 March.

Walking on Locusts was a conscious attempt by Cale — with encouragement from Joe Boyd and Hannibal records — to bring himself back into the arena of writing and performing rock music, trying to get him back on the album/tour merry-go-round that he had leaped off after *Artificial Intelligence*. Cale's reluctance to get on it once again can be seen by the gap of more than ten years between these two albums, but it was something that he had been working towards for a while, even while pursuing other projects in a variety of other directions.

The Cale revealed here is a more Epicurean figure than before, one pausing to savour a few pleasing environments before resuming his journey into more unpredictable lands. Warm and easy-paced, suffused with Cajun, Latin and African rhythms but with enough trademark Cale touches to make it distinctly his, *Walking on Locusts* is distinctly less twitchy than any other album he had yet released.

Promoting *Locusts* in September, Cale appeared on television on the *Jay Leno Show*, playing one of its catchiest songs, 'Dancing Undercover', and also on KCRW Radio, where he performed 'Some Friends', a tribute to Sterling Morrison. He started to tour the USA in October — David Byrne, who had guested on the album, joined Cale on stage at New York's Supper Club for an encore of 'Pablo Picasso' — coming over to Europe in November and December, before resuming the tour in the USA in February and March. Distinct from his recent work with the Soldier String Quartet and B.J. Cole, these shows were largely a return to the sounds of the rock bands he had worked with in the 1980s, garnished with some sampling and extra keyboards. Songs such as 'Evidence' and 'Mercenaries (Ready for War)' were restored to the set. Shorn of some of their production gloss, the new songs from *Walking on Locusts* settled well into the canon.

At the end of the dates Cale returned again to Wales to be filmed by director James Marsh who was putting together a BBC Television documentary on him to be broadcast in 1998.

Cale continued his film work in 1997, recording the soundtrack for 'noir screwball comedy' *Somewhere in the City*, and also pursued his narrative experiments with a version of 'The Moon' for the Jack Kerouac tribute album *Kicks, Joy, Darkness*. Much of this kind of recording work would be done with his own equipment at home, but he would also rent commercial studios when he needed something more specialized. There was also talk of a contribution to a collection of erotic poems read to musical backings, *Man in Moon: The Loving Tongue*, and of another tribute album for the Bonzo Dog Band; neither project was to get the green light. Cale also made some one-off live appearances. One of these was at the opening of 'Flaming Creature: Jack Smith, His Amazing Life and Times' – a retrospective exhibition at New York's Institute for Contemporary Art that paid tribute to his old collaborator – and another with John Giorno during the 'Next Stage Series' at the University of Kentucky Student Activities Board.

Cale was continuing to work on his opera *Mata Hari* and also on a new ballet based on the life of Nico, his most long-standing of collaborators. *Nico, the Ballet* was premièred on 4 October in Rotterdam, and performances were recorded for release following year as a Cale CD, *Dance Music*. He used a variety of textures for the ballet, including some electric guitar reminiscent of the Velvet Underground, a solo piano piece and Nico's own speech, taken from the flexidisc that had accompanied *Andy Warhol's Index (Book)* back in 1967.

By the end of 1997 Cale had split up with Risé after a period during which their relationship had been increasingly strained. Cale felt guilty about the failure of the marriage and anxious about what would befall his daughter and his relationship with her. It was decided that Eden would live with her mother, and Cale was worried that as a result it would be difficult to keep the channels of communication open with her. He was worried, too, about the financial implications of running two homes in central New York. As it happened, while the financial issues would continue to weigh heavily on him he and Risé had no problems over the maintenance of his contact with Eden. His relationship with his daughter continues to flourish, and he is at his happiest when spending time with her.

Once he and Risé had separated Cale was forced to find a new apartment quickly and was shown one in Greenwich Village's Christopher Street. Arriving there he remarked, 'I think Lou lives in this building', and he was not mistaken. Cale took the apartment, and sometimes he and Reed, who had also recently split up with his own wife, would meet in the lift. Claudia Gould, Cale's later partner, remembers hearing that, on these occasions, while Reed was generally friendly Cale was distant.

In February 1998 Cale performed with Siouxsie Sioux's band the Creatures at a benefit at the Paradiso in Amsterdam called 'With a Little Help From My Friends'. They played Cale's 'Gun', which the Banshees had previously covered, and a joint Cale/Sioux song, 'Murdering Mouth'. This show was the precursor to a US tour by Cale and the Creatures that would spread across June, July and August.

On 9 March he made another appearance, again on a bill with Philip Glass and Patti Smith, at Carnegie Hall's Tibet House Benefit. A feature of the performance this time was a performance of 'Pablo Picasso' with ex-Modern Lovers Jerry Harrison and Ernie Brooks.

Cale had now assembled the John Cale Trio, a pared-down touring band featuring the multi-instrumental versatility of Mark Deffenbaugh and Lance Doss. Allied to Cale's own talents, the wide-ranging abilities of these two musicians allowed for a huge range of possibilities in terms of arrangements for such a small group. Doss had been a part of Cale's *Walking On Locusts* live band, and Deffenbaugh had played on the album as well as contributing to Cale's score for *House of America* and the music for *Nico, the Ballet*. This band now played a few European gigs and would be used again once Cale's shows with the Creatures were over.

Cale's tour with the Creatures, on which they had equal billing, saw him play a set consisting mainly of previous stage favourites to audiences consisting in large part of Goth fans of the Banshees. Cale and Siouxsie Sioux's band took turns to play selections of their own material and came together on songs such as 'Gun', 'Pablo Picasso' and even 'Venus in Furs', on which Cale accompanied Sioux on viola. It was a useful way for Cale to play to good-sized audiences and to tap into a potential new fan base, but it was not a wholly satisfactory enterprise, emphasizing, as it did, the past rather than the future.

By September *Mata Hari* was finished, with Cale looking for somewhere to stage it while also playing solo dates in Europe. After performing in Scandinavia in October he returned to New York, appearing at St Ann's Church on Hallowe'en with another new collaborator, Adam Dorn. As Cale recited poetry by Edgar Allan Poe, Dorn provided samples and electronic rhythms; he would soon collaborate with Cale again, assisting him in further sorties into the new territory thrown up by the collision of music and texts.

By now Cale had moved out of his Christopher Street apartment to a new loft not far from the World Trade Center. Here he was living alone in a certain amount of chaos, surrounded by racks of clothes, plastic bags shoved into corners, books and magazines. Soon the racks of clothing in the apartment started to disappear. Designer quality, but from the 'extreme' end of the line, some of these were donated to the Philadelphia Museum of Art, home of the world's foremost collection of works by Marcel Duchamp.

A typical day for Cale now might begin around six thirty or seven in the morning, hooked up to the internet and phoning Europe. Acquiring and exchanging information electronically had become a passion now, with his interests ranging far and wide — including, for example, ways in which certain diseases were developing and the movement of Chinese politics. Cale was more than happy with a combination of work and computer and, apart from dining regularly in restaurants, would not often venture out for entertainment in the evenings. Much of his free time was now spent with his new partner, Claudia Gould, who was shortly to become director of the Institute of Contemporary Art at the University of Pennsylvania. As the two shared artistic interests, Cale's preferences including a strong admiration for the work of Gerhard Richter, Claudia would 'drag' him out occasionally to an art gallery, a play or a film — not the kind of art films he scored but more likely a thriller or sports movie. Once in company, Cale would be talkative and full of life, his voracious reading and curiosity allowing him to communicate with almost anyone on almost any subject.

BBC Television's documentary on Cale was shown in December, at a time when evidence of his influence on a new generation of bands was becoming apparent. The Manic Street Preachers played album tracks of his during the interval of their show in Cardiff on 22 December and they would alsogo on to play a Cale 'soundbite' before their 'Millennium' concert on New Year's Eve 2000. Wales had now become fertile ground for rock bands. Not only the Manic Street Preachers but also Gorky's Zygotic Mynci and Super Furry Animals were keen to credit Cale's part in their development, and he was to go on to record with them all.

Cale's autobiography, *What's Welsh For Zen*, co-authored with Victor Bockris, was published in January 1999. The process of writing it had required some concerted digging into the past, with Cale emerging from the experience with the feeling that certain issues had been dealt with but that mysteries still remained. After splitting up with Risé Cale had begun to look hard at himself and his life in an attempt to deal with the failure of the marriage and the guilt that he had felt as a result. Delving into the past would inevitably focus attention on his childhood and relationships with his parents. Here he would find the roots of his feelings of guilt: a desire, in the face of talents which had been developed in partnership with his mother, not to succeed where he perceived his father to have failed. This desire may account for the many occasions in his career on which he has turned away from success or the promise of it. Although his father's background and psychological make-up were still largely hidden from him, Cale would soon, with the discovery and rediscovery of members of that side of his family, at least see some of it revealed.

On 7 February Cale took his narrative interests in a new direction by reading to children — 'Zen for toddlers', as he describes it — on a sunny Sunday afternoon at the Drawing Center in New York, with young children 'crawling everywhere'. In April he took up residence for four days at London's Institute of Contemporary Arts, where he put on a mixed-media presentation, *Dead Agents*. This consisted of films of live work with the John Cale Trio, an exhibition of Eve Vermandel's black-and-white photos of him and readings by Cale from *What's Welsh for Zen*, followed by musical performances. Accompanying Cale on-stage on the opening night were Adam Dorn and Astrid Williamson — Cale had recently produced an album for Williamson's band Goya Dress.

In the opening musical performances Cale, with Dorn's help, mounted an assault on his own back catalogue, submitting it to the rigorous mauling he had already dealt out to the works of other writers. Staple parts of his regular set, such as 'Cable Hogue', 'Gun' and *Vintage Violence*'s 'Ghost Story', had their vocal melodies leached from them and in their place were whispered recitals of the lyrics, which emphasized the new rhythms that he had given to the lines and gave them new layers of menace. Cale also performed 'Hallelujah', cutting into it references to Tennessee Williams's *A Streetcar Named Desire*, together with an extract from the soundtrack of Elia Kazan's film of the play — Marlon Brando's voice screaming 'Stellaaaaa!' — that became unnerving in a whole new way in its icy new setting.

He also introduced a new piece, 'Dead Agents', based on poems from *Between Silk and Cyanide* by Leo Marks. For these Astrid Williamson joined him and Dorn. Marks had written the poems while working for British Intelligence during the Second World War as a way of concealing secret messages. By combining them with Dorn's rhythms and Williamson's vocals, together with his own narration and that on tape of Kate St John, Cale created secrets of his own. *Dead Agents* rolled along like a ghost train.

After this piece Cale and Dorn created another reinterpretation of 'The Jeweller', ending on a series of deep bass reverberations against which the tones of an electric piano soared off into space.

On 10 May, Cale returned to Goldsmiths' College, which had been his springboard to America and a new life back in 1963, for a question-and-answer session with students and staff. Cale had been made an Honorary Fellow of Goldsmiths' in September 1997 and was keen to repay some of the help he felt that the college had given him — even if it had seemed more like a restriction at the time. Two days later Cale was at the Subterania club in west London, where he recorded a programme in the BBC Television series *Songwriters' Circle*, together with Chrissie Hynde of the Pretenders and Nick Cave. The three played together on Cale's 'Ship of Fools', as well as on a version of 'I'm Waiting for the Man' that would not be broadcast when the programme went out in July. Two days after the recording Cale was back on BBC Television, again appearing on *Later*, and on 26 May was in Cardiff performing as part of the celebrations for the new Welsh Assembly.

Back in Britain again in August Cale appeared on consecutive nights at the Queen's Hall in Edinburgh as part of the Flux Festival. Here there were strong signs of his continued interest in the combination of text and music, with the performance of his settings and narrations of three Dylan Thomas poems. 'In My Craft or Sullen Art' was given a backing of bass poundings and slowed-down surges of scratching, 'If I Were Tickled by the Rub of Love' by the low and high registers of strong, dark synthesizer and 'Lament' by the conjuring up of a well of bleak sound from the depths of the soul of a dying man.

By early December, Cale had completed his most prestigious film score yet, for Mary Harron's *American Psycho*. He had also written the soundtrack for her feature *I Shot Andy Warhol*, and Harron had known him for some time through her previous career as a journalist. For *American Psycho* he produced a classical score of controlled menace that was geared to the dramatic action of the film, while making a cool counterpart to the hot 1980s pop and rock songs which also featured. Cale had been producing an album for the Mediaeval Baebes and began trying to accommodate their vocal style into his soundtrack but was dissatisfied with the results. Jokingly, he suggested instead attempting to get hold of some of the tapes that the FBI had played as noise-torture to the members of the Branch Davidian Sect at the siege of their compound in Waco; he was surprised to find himself being taken seriously by the disconcerted record company. At one point Cale's whole score was due to be released as a soundtrack album, but this was pared down to a collection of three instrumental sections accompanying monologues: an unsatisfactory compromise. These three monologues were credited to John Cale and 'Patrick Bateman', Bateman being the name of the central character, the American Psycho of the title, rather than to Christian Bale the actor who was speaking his lines.

American Psycho was Cale's first solo big-budget Hollywood soundtrack and while the writing and recording of the music had come easily to him the convoluted negotiations and false promises had been harder to deal with. Unwilling to surrender ground he saw to be his, Cale may as a result have gained himself a feisty reputation in the film world, deferring possible future offers of work. Certainly the rest of Hollywood did not rush to his door, despite the obvious success of his score.

At the turn of the year *The Wire* magazine asked Cale to comment on 1999, and he responded with a short piece on opportunism, revenge and 'Murder most popular', ending it with: 'Most of us had better things to do . . . roll on./forward slash/forward slash/.'

The following year would bring new revisions of his old work and new reassessments of the past, with a continuing stream of film soundtracks, one-off collaborations and live projects — and the prose writing that had once taken the form of short stories now encompassing some journalism as well.

In January Cale spent ten days back in Wales, filming sequences at the Point and the Coal Exchange in Cardiff for *Beautiful Mistake*, a film by Marc Evans who had made *House of America*. This new project, for which Cale had also previously recorded a soundtrack back in New York, was 'a snapshot of Cardiff in the year 2000' and featured Cale as a 'musical janitor' in the studio building, moving into different rooms to collaborate with some of the new Welsh bands that had recently sprung up. The 'Beautiful Mistake' of the title was the synchronicity of the different confrontations. Silent sequences shot in Cardiff were intercut with the musical performances.

Beautiful Mistake was Cale's most substantial contact with the culture of his home-land since his youth and significantly concerned itself with new life and creativity.

The film's opening interior shows photographs of Cale and his parents and is followed by a sequence tracking across a studio, in which a microphone and an electric piano can be seen. Over these shots is a narration by Cale, in Welsh, which continues over cityscapes of a factory, sluice gates opening, a shopping mall, kids playing on waste ground by Cardiff Bay, streaming cars at night, a tattooist and a stripper in a pub. This footage is cut to link the musical sequences that follow, in which Cale performs with James Dean Bradfield of the Manic Street Preachers, as well as with Gorky's Zygotic Mynci, Julie Murphy, Big Leaves, Catatonia, Super Furry Animals and with Tystion on a droning electric viola. It had been planned originally to end the film with Super Furry Animals accompanying Cale on a version of a new song, 'Things', which he had written in his hotel room two days earlier, but this was rejected in favour of a jam featuring all the performers.

Back in the USA, Cale appeared on 15 and 16 March at the annual South by Southwest Music Conference in Austin, Texas. Here he performed a tribute to Sterling Morrison with Alejandro Escovedo, who had played in Judy Nylon's band at the end of the 1970s. This included 'Some Friends', Escovedo's 'Tugboat' and 'I'm Waiting for the Man'. Cale also appeared as part of a panel the next day, answering questions on Sterling Morrison and the Velvet Underground. On the night of 16 March he appeared in his own right, accompanied by Mark Deffenbaugh, Lance Doss and Adam Dorn, playing 'Things', another new song, 'Sold Motel', and further pursuing the campaign of assault and reconstruction on his back catalogue.

In April the campaign advanced still further with some low-key provincial dates in England with Adam Dorn. At the Stables in Milton Keynes the two concocted a new setting for *Songs for Drella's* 'A Dream', with a soundtrack of industrial crashes, choral phrases, jazz chords and Latin beats against the bass pulses of a rhythm machine. 'Gun', perversely, was given a tiny melodious lilt for its opening couplet, but this was succeeded by a menacing narration and a backing track of looped saxophone and clanging metal, occasional machine-gun rattles and small-arms fire, over which Cale played sinister patterns of bass notes on his piano. 'Fear Is a Man's Best Friend' was partially whispered and laced, too, with hissed fragments of lyrics.

Cale returned to New York to perform at a party to celebrate the release of *American Psycho* on 12 April. The production work for the Mediaeval Baebes, with which the film had coincided, resulted in their *Undrentide* album, which was released at the end of April. Brought in to update their sound, he had taken tapes of what they had recorded themselves back to New York, where he had removed reverb from the vocals and added drum loops, saxophones and electric guitars — although some of this was later taken away again by their record company BMG. A difficult exercise in market shifting from BMG's point of view but another opportunity to break down and reconstruct for Cale, the production was warmly received by those for whom the concept was not total anathema.

"DOC. ELIJAH EVANS?"

By now Cale was working with director Uwe Mengel on a theatre piece based on *What's Welsh for Zen*, but it was later abandoned when Mengel wanted too large a share of the credit for it. On 26 May Cale took another step up the academic ladder when he was awarded an honorary doctorate by the University of Antwerp.

In June two more film soundtrack albums were available, for *Love Me* and *St Cyr*, and another score completed, for *Abschied*, a film about the last day in the life of Bertholt Brecht. Many of Cale's soundtracks for European art movies were completed very quickly. The work came easily to him and often would be completed in two or three days. Sometimes by the end of the first day he would be able to say that all that was left to do on a score was a little fine-tuning.

A row that had simmered for twenty-seven years finally came to the surface in July with the release of *Day of Niagara*. This CD was a recording of a Theater of Eternal Music performance from 25 April 1965 that had escaped the clutches of La Monte Young, who had tenaciously hung on to all the tapes on which Cale and Tony Conrad had collaborated with him. Its release would become almost a test case for the ownership of the material, with letters going to and fro between Young, Conrad and Arnold Dreyblatt, Young's archivist, who had passed on the tape to Table of the Elements, the record company that had released it. Cale and Conrad passionately believed that their input into the work qualified them as co-composers and that it should be allowed into the public domain, whereas Young wanted to confirm his status as its sole progenitor and to keep it in his archive until it could be issued in a way that he thought appropriate. Despite legal threats from Young the CD was released and made widely available.

In September British Sunday newspaper the *Observer* published an article by Cale on the history of New York's Chelsea Hotel. An elegiac piece, overflowing with colour and connections, it paid apt personal testimony to a place that had been a backdrop to a substantial part of his New York life and for a while his own home. Cale would later provide a similarly fascinating, hitherto unpublished piece on Bob Dylan for the same paper.

On 18 November Cale made an appearance on an Andy Warhol panel convened as part of a day-long tribute to Warhol's work with the homeless and three days later was in London for a press screening of *Beautiful Mistake*. From 24 November until 1 December he was in Gijón, Spain, as one of the judges for its 38th International Film Festival.

Cale began a European tour at the end of January, which continued into March and took in Italy, Spain, England, Ireland and Belgium, where he played two shows supported by Jools Holland's Big Band and Belgian star An Pierlé. He accompanied Pierlé as she sang 'Buffalo Ballet' and one of her own songs, 'Helium Sunset'. As well as 'Sold Motel' and 'Things', Cale had another new song, 'Over Her Head',: a beautiful, melancholy piece accompanied by sombre, stately piano, radio interference — ghostly voices and hisses — and by low bass pumping from a rhythm machine.

After the death of former CBGB compadre Joey Ramone in April there was more sad news the next month when Fred Hughes, Andy Warhol's business manager, died. Cale was invited to attend the memorial service but was in two minds about whether to go, setting off from home, turning back and then setting off again — this time, as he says, 'full steam ahead'. Once there he was rewarded by the presence of friends such as Julian Schnabel and Victor Bockris and a collection of funny stories about Hughes and the 'English muffins', the aristocratic girls who had come to play at working at the Factory in the 1970s.

By now, with so many reminders of the past and chances to fill in some of the detail of what had happened there, both in Wales and in his subsequent career, Cale was beginning to feel that he was acquiring a more fully rounded sense of himself. A week earlier Eden had celebrated her landmark sixteenth birthday, and a few days later he received an e-mail, in return to one of his own, from Gareth Simmonds, whose late father, Derek, was Cale's first cousin. Simmonds's message, as well as reintroducing a part of the family that Cale had once known well, also brought the astonishing news that Cale had an uncle on his father's side of whose existence he had never known. This uncle, too, had fathered children — Cale's cousins. Simmonds also told Cale that two weeks before receiving Cale's e-mail (the two had not seen or spoken to each other since 1975) he had been walking in the hills near Taff Wells, a small village near Cardiff. He had known relatives of his were buried there and had come across a small chapel where he had immediately discovered the grave of Cale's grandmother and grandfather.

Ever since his childhood Cale had felt that his father's side of the family had been consciously obscured by his mother and her mother. Now, as he began to inch his way towards a better understanding of the paternal branch of the family, he still felt the pull of the maternal side, urging him not to explore there, an urge that he resisted but only with difficulty. With a parallel understanding developing — thanks to events such as Fred Hughes's memorial service, *Songs For Drella* and the Velvet Underground reunions — of the role of the Factory and its associated crowd in his life discernible patterns were starting to fall into place.

With the release of *Sun Blindness Music* in May more evidence from this era came out into the open. This was the first of a collection of three CDs documenting the side projects that Cale had pursued with a variety of collaborators while he was still in the Velvet Underground. Tony Conrad had put the collection together the previous year, selecting the material following conversations with Cale. The discs were compiled from material contained in a box of tapes that Cale had given Conrad and also from some tapes that the latter had recorded himself. In all, about forty source tapes were accessed for the compilation, all reel-to-reel — some with only half an hour of music, but others, with four tracks recorded at slow speed, containing more like three or four hours' worth.

Cale returned to Europe in June, visiting Ireland, Holland, Italy and Germany in another extensive trip that did not conclude until the end of July, with him returning home in August.

2001—

On 11 September 2001 Cale is on line to his old guitarist, Sturgis Nikides, discussing possible tutors for Eden, when the first and then second aeroplanes hit the Twin Towers of the World Trade Center two blocks away. Outside his window the existing world order is falling . . .

```
From: Sturgis
  Date: Tuesday, September 11, 2001 09:11
  To: John Cale
  Subject: Re: Looking For tutors
  2 diFFerent jets have crashed into the 2 buildings
  oF the World Trade Center. An obvious terrorist
  attack. Thousands have probably died already. At
  least 30 or 40 Floors are completely destroyed.
  No doubt a day that will live in inFamy, to
  paraphrase.
```

From: John Cale
  Date: Tuesday, September 11, 2001 09:17
  To: Sturgis
  Subject: Re: Looking For tutors
   The calmest reporting is on NY1 . . . I Felt the
  second one they were running screaming past my
  place . . .? . . . they're going to be busy . . .
  I was getting the paper . . . there was a stream
  oF Floating debris coming down . . . one guy saw
  a wheel drop out of the sky and bounce on the
  street next to him . . . I'm staying in . . .
  call me when it's over . . . bre'r rabbit

From: John Cale
   Date: Tuesday, September 11, 2001 9:46
   To: Sturgis
   Subject: Re: Looking for tutors

   The Pentagon is also hit . . . BBC.

From: Sturgis
   Date: Tuesday, September 11, 2001 09:52
   To: John Cale
   Subject: Re: Looking for tutors

   Yup . . . they're even evacuating the White

   House. So who does Dubya declare war on?

From: John Cale
   Date: Tuesday, September 11, 2001 10:01
   To: Sturgis
   Subject: Re: Looking for tutors
    That one was a long low rumble . . . people
    screaming . . . running down to the seaport . . .
    the warning that Japan should be careful last
    weekend was misdirected . . .

From: John Cale
   Date: Tuesday, September 11, 2001 10:03
   To: Sturgis
   Subject: The smoke is filling gold street
    Can't see a thing . . . out of the window . . .
    smell is strong . . .

From: Sturgis
   Date: Tuesday, September 11, 2001 10:04
   To: John Cale
   Subject: Re: The smoke is filling gold street

   John - get the hell outta there

From: John Cale
Date: Tuesday, September
11, 2001 10:05
To: Sturgis
Subject: Re: The smoke is
Filling gold street
It's ash . . . every-
body and everything is
covered with ash
the air is closing off
the sun . . . weird
. . . I hope they don't
collapse this way . . .

From: John Cale
Date: Tuesday, September 11, 2001 10:08
To: Sturgis
Subject: Re: The smoke is Filling gold street
Phone service is shot . . .

From: John Cale
  Date: Tuesday, September 11, 2001 10:21
  To: Sturgis
  Subject: Out my window . . .

    [photo]

From: John Cale
  Date: Tuesday, September 11, 2001 10:31
  To: Sturgis
  Subject: The cloud just got here

The sun just went out

From: Sturgis
  Date: Tuesday, September 11, 2001 10:51
  To: John Cale
  Subject: Oh no
    You still there??? Report just announced that the

collapse of the second tower fell on a bldg 2
blocks away, maybe an elementary school . . .
I hope you're safe, pal

From: John Cale
Date: Tuesday, September 11, 2001 11:01
To: Sturgis
Subject: Re: Oh no
Yep . . .

Armed with a digital camera, Cale had walked down the street and taken several photographs of what was happening, some of which he had e-mailed immediately to Nikides. By mid-afternoon, however, since he was considered to be in the danger area, he had been evacuated from his apartment, moving in temporarily with Claudia Gould. She noted that, despite seeming in his e-mails to have taken the events with equanimity, he was actually deeply shocked.

Back online a couple of days later he transmitted some of his digital images across the internet. The events of 11 September and their aftermath would soon inspire a new song, 'Chums of Dumpty'.

In the wake of the terrorist attacks Cale cancelled a planned performance in Chicago but, while others were hesitating, soon returned to taking his place on transatlantic flights at regular intervals. In Berlin at the beginning of December he reported: 'Today is noisy with choppers in Berlin. The neos are parading with counter-demos from left-wing and Jewish groups.'

In the UK on 11 and 12 December Cale recorded an appearance to be broadcast on Jools Holland's New Year *Later*. He sang an ebullient version of 'I Wanna Be Around', an old Johnny Mercer song from the 1950s, which he had recently recorded with Holland for his album *Small World Big Band*. The song, while certainly a departure for him, both in its style and in his involvement purely as a vocalist, is off-centre enough to be more than interesting. On the album Cale rolls it around his voice box and flings it out again with plenty of gusto.

By the end of the month Cale had recorded demos of four new songs and was progressing steadily now towards a new album. Once recorded the songs were sent for technological additions from a variety of sources and then on to Chicago to be mixed.

"JOVIAL EDEN. CASH"

Once the working year was complete, Cale and Claudia took Eden to Midnight Mass, an experience that bored Cale although he sang the hymns vigorously. The two then went on holiday together to Anguilla. On vacation Cale was relaxed, sunbathing on the beach and reading. Uninterested in sightseeing he preferred to seek out good food and exotic clothes.

Still affected by the privations he suffered in his childhood, Cale makes up for them in part by indulging selective expensive tastes. These indulgences include electronic gadgets, which fascinate him, and computers which, as well as being of interest technologically, have opened up new realms of information-gathering. Having given up drinking and drug-taking, these are the activities that now satisfy the strong obsessive-compulsive part of his personality.

The Wire magazine interviewed Cale for its January 2002 edition and asked him how he would like to spend his last day on earth. Allowed to choose three visitors, he went for 'My daughter Eden, her dog Lucky and a banjo player'. His last meal was to be *'Rote grütze'* (red fruit jelly) and his final message to the world 'Thanks for stopping by!'

As well as working on recording a new album, which he described as 'very present', Cale put together two more film soundtracks in 2002: for *Paris* by Ramin Niami and *Otherworld*, an animated version of the *Mabinogi*, the Welsh traditional tales said to date back to pre-Christian times. While the latter drew Cale back once more to his Welsh heritage, the Warhol years called upon his attention again, too, when the Tate Modern in London asked him to play at a celebration of the opening of its Warhol retrospective on 2 February.

Marianne Faithfull had been asked to sing her 'Song for Nico', and Cale decided to invite Eno to accompany him on a five-song set, consisting of 'Over Her Head', 'Heartbreak Hotel', Nico's 'Frozen Warnings', 'Style It Takes' and 'A Dream'.

At the old Billingsgate Fish Market overlooking the river Thames, on a stormy night that saw lightning flying above London Bridge, silver balloons floated in packs around the old warehouse shell and cameramen and photographers hunted alone in the floor area between the bar and food tables. The stage on which Cale, Eno and Faithfull were to perform was simple, set at one end of a large dining area, the tables of which had silver cloths and silver chairs. Behind the stage oilscapes were projected on to a white wall. Marianne Faithfull played 'Song for Nico', backed by acoustic guitar, and then introduced Cale and Eno. The former sat behind a Steinway wearing white shirt and black leather trousers, while Eno, in black, stood behind the synthesizer that would occupy most of his attention during the performance. Little was said during the short set, with Eno motionless and Cale moving only to to recite 'A Dream' from a centre-stage microphone. Eno's contributions consisted mainly of sound effects over drum-machine rhythms, but he also added harmony vocals for their version of 'Frozen Warnings'. The interpretation of 'Heartbreak Hotel' conjured up on this night came from that establishment's jazz lounge and was stylishly suicidal. At the end of the performance the two men climbed down from the stage to be embraced by Marianne Faithfull. In front of them the party rumbled on.

In March, just before he turned sixty, Cale looked in the mirror and said, 'I look more and more like my father.'

In London, in July, he opened a show at the Royal Festival Hall with a fierce droning and sawing viola, filling its space with raw sound.

DISCOGRAPHY

UK, USA, etc. = place of first release

Solo albums

Vintage Violence, Columbia, CS 1037, 25 March 1970 (USA)
Church of Anthrax (with Terry Riley), Columbia, C 30131, 10 February 1971 (USA)
Academy in Peril, Reprise, MS 2079, 19 July 1972 (USA)
Paris, 1919, Reprise, MS 2131, 25 February 1973 (USA)
Fear, Island, ILPS 9301, 10 January 1974 (UK)
June 1st 1974 (with Kevin Ayres/Brian Eno/Nico), Island, ILPS 9291, July 1974 (UK)
Slow Dazzle, Island, ILPS 9317, 25 March 1975 (UK)
Helen of Troy, Island, ILPS 9350, 14 November 1975 (UK)
Sabotage/Live, SPY, SP 004, 4 December 1979 (USA)
Honi Soit, A&M, AMLH 64948, 10 March 1981 (USA)
Music for a New Society, ZE/Island, ILPS 7019, September 1982 (UK)
Caribbean Sunset, Ze/Island, ILPS 7024, 14 January 1984 (UK)
John Cale Comes Alive, Ze/Island, ILPS 7026, 3 September 1984 (UK)
Artificial Intelligence, Beggars Banquet, BEGA 68, 16 September 1985 (UK)
Even Cowgirls Get the Blues, Special Stock, R 1267 (mail order), 1986 (USA); cassette version
    ROIR A196, May 1991 (USA); CD version Danceteria, DANCD 113, 15 December 1992 (France)
Words for the Dying, LAND 09, 22 September 1989 (UK)
Songs for Drella (with Lou Reed), Sire/Warner Brothers, 7599-26140-2, 20 April 1990 (USA)
Wrong Way Up (with Eno), LAND CD 12, 12 October 1990 (UK)
Paris S'Eveille, Crepuscule, DE 030924, October 1992 (France)
Fragments of a Rainy Season, Rykodisc, HNCD 1372, 28 September 1992 (USA/UK)
23 Solo Pieces for La Naissance de l'Amour, Crepuscule, TWI 954-2, 11 September 1993
    (France)
Last Day on Earth (with Bob Neuwirth), MCA, MCAD 11037, 26 April 1994 (USA)
Antártida, Crepuscule, TWI 1008, 7 August 1995 (France)
N'Oublie Pas Que Tu Vas Mourir, Crepuscule, TWI 1028, 22 January 1996 (France)
Walking on Locusts, Rykodisc, HNCD 1395, 23 September 1996 (UK)
Eat/Kiss, Rykodisc, HNCD 1407, 10 June 1997 (UK)
Dance Music, Detour, 3984-22122-2, March 1998 (France)
Le Vent de la Nuit, Crepuscule, TWI 1083, February 1999 (France)
The Unknown, Crepuscule, TWI 1023, 17 May 1999 (France)
Saint Cyr, Virgin, 8-49545-2, 15 May 2000 (France)

Day of Niagara (with Tony Conrad/Angus MacLise/La Monte Young/Marian Zazeela), Table of
the Elements, TOE CD 74, 9 May 2000 (USA)
Sun Blindness Music, Table of the Elements, TOE CD 75, 4 June 2001 (USA)
Dream Interpretation, Table of the Elements, TOE CD 79, 19 November 2001 (USA)
Stainless Steel Gamelan, Table of the Elements, TOE CD 80, 19 November 2001 (USA)

Singles (promotional singles listed only if they include exclusive tracks)

'Loop', seven-inch flexidisc (credited to Velvet Underground) given away with *Aspen* magazine,
Vol. 1, No. 3, December 1966 (USA)
'Big White Cloud'/'Gideon's Bible', Columbia, 4-45266, seven-inch, March 1970 (USA)
''The Man Who Couldn't Afford to Orgy'/'Sylvia Said', Island, WIP 6202, seven-inch, October
1974 (UK)
'Animal Justice', EP, Illegal, IL 003, seven-inch and limited twelve-inch, September 1977 (UK)
'Mercenaries'/'Rosegarden Funeral of Sores', SPY, IR 9008, seven-inch, 14 March 1980 (USA)
'Dead or Alive'/'Honi Soit', A&M, AMS 8130, seven-inch, May 1981 (UK)
'I Keep a Close Watch'/'Close Watch', Ze, IS 113, seven-inch, April 1983 (UK)
'Close Watch'/'Changes Made', Island, 104876, seven-inch, April 1983 (Germany)
'Hungry for Love'/'Caribbean Sunset', Island, 106 302, seven-inch, February 1984 (Germany)
'Villa Albani (Remix)'/'Villa Albani (Instrumental)'/'Hungry for Love', Island, 601 267-213,
twelve-inch, June 1984 (Germany)
'Ooh La La'/'Magazines', Ze, IS 197, seven-inch, August 1984 (UK)
'Dying on the Vine'/'Everytime the Dogs Bark', Beggars Banquet, BEG 145 and 145T, seven-inch
and twelve-inch, 9 August 1985 (UK)
'Satellite Walk (Remix)'/'Dying on the Vine'/'Crash Course in Harmonics', Beggars Banquet,
BEG 153T, twelve-inch, November 1985 (UK)
'Nobody But You'/'Style It Takes' (with Lou Reed), Sire 5439 19808-7, seven-inch, April 1990
(Germany)
'Ring of Fire' (Eno)/'Shuffle Down to Woodbridge' (Cale)/'Merry Christmas' (House of Freaks)
(with Eno), Warner Brothers, PRO-S-4573-A, promo CD, August 1990 (USA)
'One Word'/'Grandfather's House'/'Palanquin' (with Eno), LAND H04, CD, and LAND T04,
twelve-inch, September 1990 (UK)
'One Word (Edit)'/'Empty Frame'/'You Don't Miss Your Water' (Eno)/'One Word (the Woodbridge
Mix)'/'Grandfather's House' (with Eno), Opal, 9 40001-2, CD, October 1990 (USA)
'Spinning Away (Edit)'/'Grandfather's House' (with Eno), Warner Brothers, 5439-19475-7,
seven-inch, 1990 (Germany)
'Hallelujah'/'Hallelujah (Leonard Cohen version)'/'The Queen and Me', Columbia, COL 657644 2,
CD, 1991 (Holland)

'Paris S'Eveille'/'L'Heritage du Dragon' (unknown singer)/'Booker T' (Velvet Underground), Crepuscule, DE 035080, CD, 1992 (Belgium)

'More Fragments', live CD EP, free with *Les Inrockuptibles* magazine (out-takes from official *Fragments* CD), 1992 (France)

'The Long Voyage' (with Suzanne Vega/Hector Zazou), Columbia, COL 661201 1, CD, June 1995 (France)

Cale as guest musician (album or single listed rather than specific track or tracks; album unless indicated otherwise)

Marc Almond, *Fantastic Star*, 1996

Vince Bell, *Phoenix*, 1996

Art Bergmann, *Crawl with Me*, 1988

Big Vern, *Lullabies for Lager Louts*, 1989

William Burroughs, *Dead City Radio*, 1990

Chelsea, *Chelsea*, 1969

Julie Covington, seven-inch single, 'Only Women Bleed', 1977

Julie Covington, *Julie Covington*, 1978

Nick Drake, *Bryter Layter*, 1970

Earth Opera, *The Great American Eagle Tragedy*, 1969

Element of Crime, *Try to Be Mensch*, 1987

Brian Eno, *Another Green World*, 1975

Brian Eno, *Music for Films*, 1978

Gordon Gano, *Hitting the Ground*, 2002

Garageland, 'Feel Alright', seven-inch single B-side, 1997

Glass Harp, *Glass Harp*, 1970

Goya Dress, *Rooms*, 1996

Mike Heron, *Smiling Men With Bad Reputations*, 1971

Jools Holland, *Small World Big Band*, 2001

Ian Hunter, *You're Never Alone With a Schizophrenic*, 1978

Ivan Kral, *Nostalgia*, 1995

David Kubinec, *Some Things Never Change*, 1978

Les Nouvelles Polyphonies Corses, *Les Nouvelles Polyphonies Corses*, 1991

Lio, *Pop Model*, 1986

Angus MacLise, *The Cloud Doctrine*, 2003

Made for TV, 'Spies Everywhere', twelve-inch EP, 1983

Ann Magnuson, *Caged Uncaged* (various artists compilation, three tracks with Ann Magnuson), 1993

Maids of Gravity, *The First Second*, 1996
Marie et les Garçons, 'Attitudes', seven-inch single, 1978
Modern Lovers, *The Modern Lovers*, 1973
Modern Guy, *Une Nouvelle Vie*, 1980
Geoff Muldaur, *Geoff Muldaur Is Having a Wonderful Time*, 1975
Nico, *Chelsea Girl*, 1967
Nico, *The Marble Index*, 1969
Nico, *Desertshore*, 1970
Nico, *The End*, 1974
Nico, *Camera Obscura*, 1985
The Replacements, *All Shook Down*, 1990
Sister Double Happiness, *Heart and Mind*, 1991
Jack Smith, *Silent Shadows on Cinemaroc Island*, 1997
Jack Smith, *Les Evening Gowns Damnées*, 1997
Patti Smith, 'My Generation', seven-inch single (appears on B-side of 'Gloria'), 1976
Patti Smith, *Gone Again*, 1996
Alan Stivell, *1 Dour*, 1998
The Stooges, *The Stooges*, 1969
Super Furry Animals, *Rings Around the World*, 2001
Tax Free, *Tax Free*, 1970
Maureen Tucker, *I Spent a Week There the Other Day*, 1992
Jennifer Warnes, *Jennifer*, 1972
Hector Zazou, *Sahara Blue*, 1992
Hector Zazou, *Songs from the Cold Seas*, 1995

With the Velvet Underground

Albums
The Velvet Underground, Verve, V-5008 (Mono), V6-5008 (Stereo), March 1967 (USA)
White Light/White Heat, Verve, V-5046 (Mono), V6-5046 (Stereo), 30 January 1968 (USA)
VU, Verve/Polydor, 823721-1, February 1985 (USA)
Another View, Verve/Polydor, 829405-1, 25 September 1985 (USA); originally part of a five-LP
     box set, Polydor, VUBOX 1, 829 404-1, July 1986 (UK)
MCMXCIII, Sire/Warner Brothers, 9 454 64-2, 26 October 1993 (USA)

Singles
'All Tomorrow's Parties'/'I'll Be Your Mirror', Verve, VK 10427 (Mono), July 1966 (USA)
'Sunday Morning'/'Femme Fatale', Verve, VK 10466 (Mono), December 1966 (USA)

Untitled flexidisc in *Andy Warhol's Index Book*, February 1967 (USA)
'White Light/White Heat'/'Here She Comes Now', Verve, VK 10560 (Mono), February 1968 (USA)
'Venus in Furs (Edit)'/'Sweet Jane'/'Heroin'/'I'm Waiting for the Man' (Live), Sire/Warner
    Brothers, WO224CD, 1994 (UK)

John Cale compilations

Guts, Island, ILPS 9459, 11 September 1977 (UK)
Seducing Down the Door, Rhino, R2 71685, 19 July 1994 (USA)
The Island Years, Island, 314 524 235-2, 1996 (USA)
Close Watch: An Introduction, Island, IMCD 259/524642-2, 22 February 1999 (USA)

Various artists compilations with exclusive Cale tracks

'*Love Kills'*, *From the Motion Picture Soundtrack Sid & Nancy* ('She Never Took No for an
    Answer'), MCA, 1986 (UK)
I'm Your Fan ('Hallelujah'), Columbia, 1991 (USA)
A Chance Operation ('In Memoriam John Cage – Call Waiting'), Koch, 1993 (USA)
Your Pain Shall Be Your Music ('Your Pain Shall Be a Music'), Consipio, 1994 (Japan)
Kills Joy Darkness ('The Moon'), Rykodisc, 1997 (USA)
De Granada a la Luna ('Daybreak'), Sombra, 1998 (Spain)
Bleecker Street ('So Long, Marianne), Astor Place Records, 1999 (USA)
More Fans, CD EP ('The Queen and Me'), Columbia, 1991 (France)
An Anthology of Noise and Electronic Music: First A – Chronology Vol. 1 1921–2001, (with
    Angus MacLise and Tony Conrad), Sub Rosa, 2002 (France)
Positions, Trash Palace ('The Insult'), Discograph, 15 October 2002 (France)

Official video/DVD with soundtracks by Cale (dates of original release)

Heat (features 'Days of Steam' over credits), 1972
Caged Heat, 1974
Who Am I This Time?, 1981
Something Wild (co-composer), 1986
Dick, 1987
I Shot Andy Warhol, 1996
Basquiat, 1996

Somewhere in the City, 1997
American Psycho, 2000

Official Cale videos

Words for the Dying, 1989
Songs for Drella (with Lou Reed), 1990
Fragments of a Rainy Season, 1992
Velvet Redux Live MCMXCII (with the Velvet Underground), 1993

Cale as producer/co-producer/arranger (producer only, except where indicated)

Lester Bangs, seven-inch single, 'Let It Blurt/Live' (arranger), 1979
Art Bergmann, LP, *Crawl with Me*, 1988
Big Vern, LP, *Lullabies for Lager Louts*, 1989
Chunky Novie and Ernie, LP, *Chunky Novie and Ernie* (co-producer), 1973
Julie Covington, seven-inch single, 'Only Women Bleed/Easy to Slip' (arranger), 1977
Cristina, twelve-inch single, 'Disco Clone' (co-producer), 1978
Modern Guy, LP, *Une Nouvelle Vie*, 1980
Element of Crime, LP, *Try to Be Mensch*, 1987
Louise Feron, CD, *Louise Feron*, 1991
Garageland, seven-inch single, B-side, 'Feel Alright', 1997
Goya Dress, CD, *Rooms*, 1996
Happy Mondays, LP, *24-Hour Party People . . .* , 1987
Jesus Lizard, EP, 'Jesus Lizard' (producer of one track), 1998
David Kubinec, LP, *Some Things Never Change*, 1978
Larry and Tommy, seven-inch single, 'Yo-Yo/You've Gotta Bend a Little' (co-producer of A-side), 1968
Les Nouvelles Polyphonies Corses, CD, *In Paradisu*, 1996
Lio, LP, *Pop Model*, 1986
Los Ronaldos, CD, *Sabor Salado*, 1992
Made for TV, seven-inch EP, 'Spies Everywhere', 1983
Ann Magnuson, CD, *Caged Uncaged* (co-producer of three tracks), 1993
Maids of Gravity, CD, *The First Second*, 1996
Marie et les Garçons, seven-inch single, 'Attitudes/Re-bop', 1978
Mediaeval Baebes, CD, *Undrentide*, 2000

Menace, seven-inch single, 'I Need Nothing/Electrocutioner', 1977
Model Citizens, seven-inch EP, 1979
Modern Lovers, LP, *The Modern Lovers*, 1976
Necessaries, seven-inch single, 'You Can Borrow My Car/Runaway Child', 1979
Nico, LP, *Marble Index* (arranger), 1968
Nico, LP, *Desertshore*, 1970
Nico, LP, *The End*, 1974
Nico, LP, *Camera Obscura*, 1985
Sham 69, seven-inch single, 'I Don't Wanna'/'Ulster'/'Red London', 1977
Siouxsie and the Banshees, CD, *The Rapture*, 1995
Patti Smith, LP, *Horses*, 1975
Snatch, twelve-inch single, 'Shopping for Clothes'/'Joey'/'Red Army', 1980
Squeeze, seven-inch EP, 'Packet of Three', 1977
Squeeze, LP, *Squeeze*, 1978
Alan Stivell, CD, *1 Dour* (producer of one track), 1998
The Stooges, LP, *The Stooges*, 1969
Harry Toledo and the Rockets, seven-inch EP, 'Harry Toledo and the Rockets', 1977
Jennifer Warnes, LP, *Jennifer*, 1972

INDEX